John Eastwood   Ronald Mackin

A Basic English Grammar with Exercises

self-study edition

Oxford University Press

Oxford University Press
Walton Street, Oxford OX2 6DP

Oxford   New York   Toronto
Delhi   Bombay   Calcutta   Madras   Karachi
Petaling Jaya   Singapore   Hong Kong   Tokyo
Nairobi   Dar es Salaam   Cape Town
Melbourne   Auckland

and associated companies in
Berlin   Ibadan

Oxford, Oxford English and the *Oxford English* logo
are trade marks of Oxford University Press.

ISBN 0 19 432938 0

© Oxford University Press 1982, 1984, 1988

First published 1988
Second impression 1989

A Basic English Grammar with Exercises is
a combined edition of *A Basic English Grammar*
and *A Basic English Grammar: Exercises*.

A Basic English Grammar is an adaptation
of *A Grammar of Spoken English* by
Ronald Mackin and John Eastwood, first
published in Germany by Cornelsen &
Oxford University Press GmbH, Berlin, in 1980.

The publishers thank Barnaby's Picture Library for
permission to reproduce photographs. The location
photographs are by Rob Judges and Rosie Potter.

Illustrations are by Alex Brychta, Roy Ingram, Peter
Joyce, Mike Ogden, Barrie Rowe, and Alan Suttie.

Typeset in Linotron 202 Helvetica by
Promenade Graphics Limited, Cheltenham, England.

Printed in Hong Kong.

Contents

Introduction

A Basic English Grammar with Exercises is a combined edition of *A Basic English Grammar* (1982) and *A Basic English Grammar: Exercises* (1984). The material from both books has been fully integrated and presented in a larger format.

Each exercise is as close as possible to the corresponding grammar section, which makes it easier for students to look up a grammar point when doing an exercise. Almost all grammar exercises are on right-hand pages.

The book contains all the material from *A Basic English Grammar,* including the sections on communication, numbers, word-building etc (29–40), which do not have exercises. There have been slight changes to a number of exercises from *A Basic English Grammar: Exercises,* and there are some completely new exercises.

The grammar

The grammar sections cover the structures and functions that are generally taught in the first three or four years of learning English. The language described is contemporary standard British English although some British-American differences are included. The examples are mostly of everyday spoken English with a small number which are typical of formal or written style. Where necessary, usages are marked as informal/formal or as spoken/written. Examples are printed in colour and notes giving basic information on form and use are printed in black. The examples and notes are numbered whenever the notes refer to individual examples: note 1 refers to example 1 and so on. Throughout the book technical terms have been kept to a minimum, and there is a glossary of those used. There is also a full index.

The exercises

The exercises practise the main grammatical structures covered in the book, and at the head of each exercise there is a reference to the section or sections in the grammar. The exercises consist of a controlled practice followed by a more open-ended Activity. The controlled practice is the main part of the exercise. It is always set in an overall context and can be done orally and/or in writing. This part of the exercise is particularly suitable for self-study students but can also be done in class or for homework.

The Activity is optional and would usually be done in class. It may involve pair or group work, discussion, a game or problem-solving etc, and is designed to encourage a more communicative use of the grammar being practised.

Some exercises deal with a single grammatical point, while others cover wider topics, such as 'Talking about the past'. The exercises also provide opportunities to compare and contrast grammatical forms as well as to practise some points individually.

Two editions are available, one with a key and one without a key.

Key to phonetic symbols

iː see	ʊ good	aɪ by
ɪ big	uː soon	aʊ how
e get	ʌ bus	ɔɪ boy
æ man	ɜː third	ɪə near
ɑː bath	ə away	eə fair
ɒ top	eɪ day	ʊə sure
ɔː saw	əʊ go	

p pen	f fine	h help
b book	v very	m mine
t time	θ think	n new
d dog	ð that	ŋ long
k can	s say	l last
g game	z zoo	r room
tʃ cheap	ʃ shop	j yes
dʒ job	ʒ measure	w water

(r) The sound [r] is used before a following vowel.
ˈ   The next syllable is stressed, e.g. *away* [əˈweɪ].
↘ The next word has a falling intonation.
↗ The next word has a rising intonation.

Glossary

This glossary gives the meaning of the grammatical terms used in this book.

active ▷ **passive**
adjective In the sentence *It's a big house*, the word *big* is an adjective. An adjective is used to describe a noun. ▷ 23.1
adverb In the sentence *She was speaking quietly*, the word *quietly* is an adverb. ▷ 24
adverb phrase a phrase which we use like an adverb, e.g. *I found it **with some difficulty**. They came **yesterday morning**.*
agent the person or thing that does the action ▷ 10.2
alternative question a question with the word *or*, e.g. *Do you want a large one or a small one?*
apostrophe In the phrase *my sister's book*, there is an apostrophe between *sister* and *s*. ▷ 39.5
apposition In the sentence *Do you know Don Burgess, the actor?* the noun phrases *Don Burgess* and *the actor* are in apposition. ▷ 18.16
article *a/an* and *the* ▷ 19
auxiliary verb helping verb: *be, have* and *do* ▷ 5.1. See also **modal verb**.

base form the simple form of the verb without -ing, -ed or -s, e.g. *go, play*

cardinal numbers *one, two, three* etc. are cardinal numbers. *first, second, third* etc. are ordinal numbers.
clause In the sentence *We can go in the car if it rains*, there are two clauses – *We can go in the car* and *if it rains*. ▷ **main clause, sub clause**
collective noun a noun used to refer to a group, e.g. *family, crowd* ▷ 18.14
comparative *smaller* and *more interesting* are the comparative forms of the adjectives *small* and *interesting*.
comparison the comparing of two or more things with forms like *longer, most exciting, as quickly as*
complement In the sentence *She's a doctor*, the phrase *a doctor* is the complement. The complement is used to describe the subject. Sometimes an object has a complement; in the sentence *They made him captain*, the word *captain* is the complement.
compound a word formed from two or more other words, e.g. *milkman* (milk + man), *somewhere* (some + where), *ten-year-old*

conjunction a word used to join two clauses, e.g. *and, but, or, when, if, because*
consonant ▷ **vowel**
continuous a verb form with *be* and the -ing form, e.g. *He **was working**.*
countable noun a noun which can have a plural form. *book, coat* and *plate* are countable nouns. ▷ **uncountable**

defining relative clause e.g. *That's the man **who won the prize**.* ▷ 22.12
definite *ten minutes* is a definite time; we know how many minutes. *a few minutes* is an indefinite time; we do not know exactly how many minutes.
degree *very, rather* and *almost* are adverbs of degree. ▷ 24.8
demonstrative adjective/pronoun *this, that, these* and *those* ▷ 20.12
direct object In the sentence *The boy gave his father a book*, the noun phrase *a book* is the direct object, and the noun phrase *his father* is the indirect object.
direct speech ▷ **reported speech**

-ed form ▷ **past participle**
emphasis greater stress or importance given to a word or phrase ▷ 28. (Adjective: **emphatic**)
emphatic pronoun e.g. *He built the house **himself**.* ▷ 20.9
ending In the noun *rooms*, *-s* is the plural ending.
end position In the sentence *We go out sometimes*, the word *sometimes* is in end position. ▷ 24.4
exclamation words spoken suddenly and with feeling, e.g. *Stop! How beautiful!* ▷ 34.1

falling intonation the voice going down ▷ **intonation**
formal Friendly, everyday conversations and personal letters to friends are informal. Business letters and polite conversations with strangers are more formal.
frequency how often something happens. *sometimes* and *often* are adverbs of frequency. ▷ 24.7
front position In the sentence *Sometimes we go out*, the word *sometimes* is in front position. ▷ 24.4
future the time that has not yet come, the time after now

imperative the base form of a verb used to give orders etc., e.g. ***Wait** a minute. **Come** here.* ▷ 6.1
indefinite ▷ **definite**
indirect object ▷ **direct object**
infinitive the base form of a verb, e.g. *wait, come*. The infinitive often has *to* in front of it, e.g. *to wait, to come*. ▷ 14
informal ▷ **formal**
-ing form form of a verb with -ing, e.g. *opening, walking* ▷ **present participle, verbal noun**
intonation the speaker's voice going up and down. We normally use a falling intonation in a statement (e.g. *It's half past five*) and a rising intonation in a yes/no question (e.g. *Is it half past five?*).
irregular ▷ **regular**

linking word a conjunction (e.g. *and, when*) or a word or phrase which makes a link between two sentences, e.g. *therefore, on the other hand* ▷ 27

main clause In the sentence *I was there when it happened*, *I was there* is the main clause and *when it happened* is a sub clause. Every sentence has a main clause, and sometimes a sentence is a main clause only. A main clause usually has a subject and verb.
main verb the verb in the main clause. In the sentence *I stopped because I was tired*, *stopped* is the main verb.
manner *nicely, angrily* and *strangely* are adverbs of manner. ▷ 24.5
mid position In the sentence *We sometimes go out*, the word *sometimes* is in mid position. ▷ 24.4
modal verb (or **modal auxiliary verb**) The modal verbs are *can, could, may, might, will, would, shall, should, ought to, must, need* and *dare*.

negative A sentence with *n't* or *not* or with *no, neither* etc. is negative, e.g. *I haven't got a watch. Are there no eggs?* Other sentences are positive, e.g. *I've got a watch.*
non-defining relative clause e.g. *Alex, **who came first**, won the prize.* ▷ 22.12
normal verb an ordinary verb (e.g. *look, come*), not an auxiliary or modal verb
noun In the sentence *The chair is in the garden*, the words *chair* and *garden* are nouns.
noun phrase a phrase which can be the subject or object of a sentence, e.g. *my bag, these old clothes*

object ▷ **direct object**

ordinal numbers ▷ **cardinal numbers**

pair noun a noun which is always plural in form and can be used with *pair of*, e.g. *trousers, scissors* ▷ 18.12

participle ▷ **present participle, past participle**

passive *The police arrested the man* is an active sentence. *The man was arrested* is a passive sentence. ▷ 10.1

past the time that is already over, the time before now

past continuous a tense with *was/were* and the -ing form, e.g. *I was washing my hair.* ▷ 3.7

past participle the -ed form of a verb, e.g. *opened, walked*; some forms are irregular, e.g. *seen, come*

past perfect a tense with *had* and the -ed form, e.g. *The concert had already started.* ▷ 3.6

past perfect continuous a tense with *had been* and the -ing form, e.g. *He was hot because he had been running.* ▷ 3.10

perception *see, hear* and *smell* are verbs of perception.

perfect a verb form with *have* and the -ed form, e.g. *They had already arrived.*

person 1st person = *I, we*; 2nd person = *you*; 3rd person = *he, she, it, they*

personal pronoun e.g. *I, me, you, he, him* ▷ 20.1

phrasal-prepositional verb a verb + adverb + preposition, e.g. *Keep away from the edge of the cliff.*

phrasal verb a verb + adverb, e.g. *Let's wash up. Take your coat off.* ▷ 26.1

phrase a group of words but not a full clause or sentence, e.g. *the small box* (a noun phrase), *is going* (a verb phrase), *very often* (an adverb phrase)

plural a form used to talk about more than one thing. *dogs* is the plural of *dog*. ▷ **singular**

positive ▷ **negative**

possessive a form used to show that something belongs to somebody, e.g. *Peter's, ours*

possessive adjective e.g. *my, your, his, her* ▷ 20.5

possessive pronoun e.g. *mine, yours, his, hers* ▷ 20.5

prefix something added to the beginning of a word to change the meaning, e.g. *unfair, re-open*

preposition e.g. *in, on, under, at, to* ▷ 25

prepositional adverb an adverb which is like a preposition but has no noun phrase after it, e.g. *A man went past.*

prepositional verb a verb + preposition, e.g. *Let's listen to the news. We laughed at the joke.* ▷ 26.3

present the time now, at this moment

present continuous a tense with *am/are/is* and the -ing form, e.g. *I'm making the dinner.* ▷ 2.3

present participle the -ing form of a verb when used as an adjective or adverb or in a continuous tense form. The -ing forms in these sentences are present participles; *He jumped from the moving train. They ate standing up. The girl was sleeping.*

present perfect a tense with *has/have* and the -ed form, e.g. *We've finished.* ▷ 3.4

present perfect continuous a tense with *has been/have been* and the -ing form, e.g. *I've been waiting for ages.* ▷ 3.8

pronoun e.g. *you, it, mine* ▷ 20

pronounce say words correctly (Noun: **pronunciation**)

punctuation A comma (,) and a full stop (.) are punctuation marks.

quantifier a word that tells us about quantity (how many or how much), e.g. *some, every, enough*

question tag e.g. *It's Monday today, isn't it?* ▷ 8.5

question word *what, who, where, when, why, how* and *whose* are question words ▷ 21

reflexive pronoun e.g. *I've hurt myself.* ▷ 20.8

regular the same as most others. *boys* and *girls* are nouns with regular plural endings in *-s. children* is an irregular plural form.

relative clause e.g. *That's the girl who lost her money.* ▷ 22

relative pronoun In the sentence *The man who spoke to you is a detective*, the word *who* is a relative pronoun. We can use *who, which, that, whose, whom* and *what* as relative pronouns. ▷ 22

reported speech The sentence *'I can come'* is direct speech. In the sentence *He says he can come*, the clause *he can come* is reported speech. ▷ 12.1

reporting verb a verb used to report speech or thoughts, e.g. *say, tell, ask, think, mention* ▷ 12.1

rising intonation the voice going up ▷ **intonation**

sentence A sentence is one or more clauses. It can be a statement, a question, an order or an exclamation. A written sentence begins with a capital letter and ends with a full stop (.), question mark (?) or exclamation mark (!).

sentence adverb an adverb that refers to a whole sentence, e.g. *Luckily, no one was hurt.* ▷ 24.9

short answer e.g. *Yes, he was. No, I'm not. Yes, you can.*

short form e.g. *you're, they'll, isn't* ▷ 39.6

simple past a verb tense, e.g. *I washed the floor yesterday.* ▷ 3.3

simple present a verb tense, e.g. *I see him every day.* ▷ 2.4

singular a form used to talk about one thing only. *cup* is singular; *cups* is plural.

spelling how words are written

statement a sentence which gives information, e.g. *It's raining. The meat is very good*; not a question or an order.

stress the speaking of a word (or part of a word) more loudly than other words. In the word *remember*, the stress is on the second syllable – *re'member*.

sub clause e.g. *I'll give it you when I see you. If she comes, I can meet her. Is that the man who you spoke to? Someone said that it was ready.* A sub clause (= subordinate clause) usually begins with a conjunction, e.g. *when, if, that*, or with a relative pronoun. It cannot stand alone as a sentence like the main clause. It usually has a subject and verb, but it can be an -ing form or infinitive without a subject, e.g. *Coming out of the shop, I suddenly felt ill. You need a hammer to do that.*

subject In the sentence *The man opened the door*, the noun phrase *the man* is the subject.

superlative *smallest* and *most interesting* are the superlative forms of the adjectives *small* and *interesting*.

syllable The word *information* has four syllables (*in for ma tion*).

tag ▷ **question tag**

tense a form of the verb which tells us when something happens, e.g. in the present, the past or the future

uncountable noun a noun which cannot have a plural form. *butter, coffee* and *oil* are uncountable nouns.

verb In the sentence *I go to work by bus*, the word *go* is a verb.

verbal noun the -ing form of a verb when used as a noun, e.g. *I like reading.*

verb of perception e.g. *see, hear, smell*

verb phrase either a verb on its own (e.g. *I was hungry. We played cards.*) or a verb with an auxiliary and/or modal verb (e.g. *They were singing. She must have gone home.*)

voiced/voiceless Voiced sounds are all the vowel sounds (e.g. [iː], [e], [aʊ]) and the consonant sounds [b], [d], [g], [z], [ʒ], [dʒ], [v], [ð], [l], [r], [m], [n], and [ŋ]. **Voiceless** sounds are the consonant sounds [p], [t], [k], [s], [ʃ], [tʃ], [f] and [θ].

vowel The letters *a, e, i, o* and *u* are vowels. The other letters are consonants.

wh- question a question that begins with a question word, e.g. *What/Who/Whose . . .?*

yes/no question a question that we can answer with yes or no

A Basic English Grammar with Exercises

1 Word order

1.1 Positive statements

1   *Subject*   *Verb phrase*
    Two girls   were talking.
    My foot   hurts.

2   *Subject*   *Verb phrase*   *Object*
    We   had   a marvellous holiday
    I   .   can see   something.

3   *Subject*   *Verb phrase*   *Complement*
    Margaret   is   very nice.
    She   seems   a nice person.

4   *Subject*   *Verb phrase*   *Adverb phrase*
    Your friend   is   over there.
    The money   was   on the table.

The word order in a statement is

1   subject + verb phrase
2   subject + verb phrase + object ▷ 1.4
3   subject + verb phrase + complement ▷ 1.5
4   subject + verb phrase + adverb phrase

1.2 Adverbs and adverb phrases

Two girls were talking **loudly**.
Last year we had a marvellous holiday **in Italy**.
Margaret is **always** very nice.
The money was **certainly** on the table **this morning**.

We can add one or more adverbs or adverb phrases to the four sentence types in 1.1.
Adverbs and adverb phrases can come at the beginning, in the middle or at the end of a sentence. There are different rules for the different types of adverbs. ▷ 24.4

1.3 Other kinds of sentence

1   *Negative statements*
    This apple isn't very nice.
    The letter has not arrived.
    I don't like that colour.
    It must not happen again.

2   *Questions*
    Where are my keys?
    What have you got there?
    Did the game start on time?
    Will Helen be at the meeting?

3   *The imperative*
    Wait here.
    Don't touch anything.

4   *Exclamations*
    What a beautiful day!
    How stupid!

1   In a negative statement we put *n't/not* after *be, have, do* or a modal verb. ▷ 8.1
2   In a question we put *be, have, do* or a modal verb before the subject. ▷ 8.2
    Questions can be with or without a question word, e.g. *where, what.* ▷ 21.1
3   For the imperative ▷ 6.1
4   For exclamations ▷ 34.1

1.4   Direct and indirect objects

	Subject	Verb	Indirect object	Direct object
1	Aunt Jane	gave	Sarah	a record.
	She	sent	Peter	a book.

	Subject	Verb	Direct object	Indirect object
2	Aunt Jane	gave	the record	**to** Sarah.
	She	sent	the book	**to** Peter.

1 The indirect object without *to* comes before the direct object.
2 The indirect object with *to* comes after the direct object.

The direct object is the thing or person to which something happens. The indirect object is the person who receives something. ▷ 18.3 direct and indirect objects

1.5   Types of complement

	Subject	Verb phrase	Complement
1	I	was	ill.
	That man	is	Mac.

	Subject	Verb phrase	Object	Complement
2	The food	made	me	ill.
	Everyone	calls	him	Mac.

1 The subject complement is used to describe the subject.
2 The object complement is used to describe the object.

1.6   Sub clauses with **when, if, because** etc.

	(*Sub clause*)	Main clause	(*Sub clause*)
1	When I've finished,	I'll make a cup of coffee.	
	If it's nice,	we can go out.	
2		We can go out	if it's nice.
		I bought the coat	because it was cheap.

A sentence can have one or more clauses. A sub clause can come either

1 before the main clause or
2 after the main clause.

A sub clause begins with a conjunction, e.g. *when, if, because, after*. The word order after the conjunction is the same as in a main clause, e.g. *I've finished, it's nice.*

For reported clauses and relative clauses ▷ 27.1
For that-clauses ▷ 27.3

1 (1.1–1.6)

Four men have kidnapped the son of a very rich family. The men are going to send a letter to the family, and they have cut these words out of a newspaper. Put the words in the correct order.

Example

| son | we've got | your |

We've got your son.

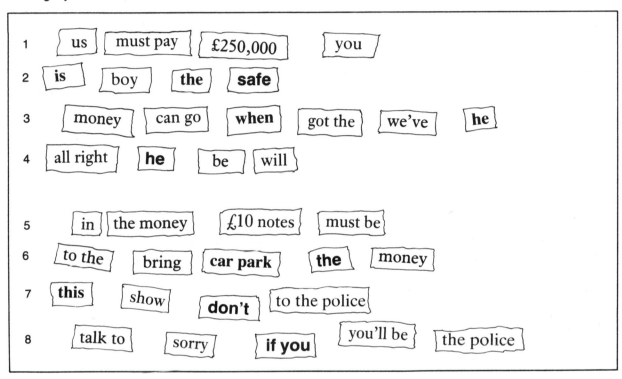

1 | us | must pay | £250,000 | you |

2 | is | boy | the | safe |

3 | money | can go | when | got the | we've | he |

4 | all right | he | be | will |

5 | in | the money | £10 notes | must be |

6 | to the | bring | car park | the | money |

7 | this | show | don't | to the police |

8 | talk to | sorry | if you | you'll be | the police |

Activity

Cut a sentence out of an English newspaper or magazine. Then cut the sentence into separate words or phrases and ask a partner to put them in the correct order.

If you haven't got an English newspaper, write a sentence on a piece of paper and then cut it up. You can copy the sentence from an English book.

2 Verbs: Talking about the present

2.1 The present tense of be

I**'m** tired. I**'m not** very fit.
Am I fat? ~ Yes, you **are**.

You**'re** in good time. You **aren't** late.
Are you ready? ~ No, I**'m not**.

Peter **is** at home, but Judy **isn't** here today.
Is he in bed? ~ No, he**'s** in the bath.
Is she out? ~ Yes, she **is**.

It**'s** July, but it **isn't** very hot.
When **is** the concert? ~ On Tuesday.

We**'re** on holiday. We **aren't** here for long.
Are we in this photo? ~ No, we **aren't**.

Those people **are** students. They **aren't** doctors.
Are they French? ~ Yes, I think they **are**.

Form

I **am**	we **are**
you **are**	you **are**
he **is**	they **are**
she **is**	
it **is**	

Short forms

'm = am
're = are   **aren't** = are not
's = is   **isn't** = is not
For the use of short forms ▷ 39.6

Short answers

Yes, I **am**.	No, I**'m not**.
Yes, you **are**.	No, you **aren't**.
Yes, he/she/it **is**.	No, he/she/it **isn't**.
Yes, we/you/they **are**.	No, we/you/they **aren't**.

▷   20.1 personal pronouns

2.2 The present tense of have (got)

1 **have got**

I**'ve got** an envelope, but I **haven't got** a stamp.
Have you **got** a pen? ~ Yes, I **have**.

Andrew **has got** a car, but his sister **hasn't**.
What**'s** the baby **got** in his mouth?
Has Susan **got** a ticket? ~ Yes, she **has**.
Has the car **got** a radio? ~ No, it **hasn't**.

The Joneses **have got** a television. We **haven't got** one.
Have they **got** a video recorder? ~
No, they **haven't**.

Form

1

I **have got**	we **have got**
you **have got**	you **have got**
he **has got**	they **have got**
she **has got**	
it **has got**	

2 **have**

I **have** two sisters. I **haven't** any brothers.
Have you any money? ~ No, I **haven't**.

Mr Hill **has** a beard.
Has Sarah many friends? ~ Yes, I think she **has**.
The house **has** four bedrooms.

We**'ve** a lot to do, and we **haven't** much time.
Have the others any ideas?

Use

We normally use *have got*, especially in speech.
have is sometimes more formal than *have got*.

▷   5.5 other uses of *have*; 5.6 USA

2

I **have**	we **have**
you **have**	you **have**
he **has**	they **have**
she **has**	
it **has**	

Short forms

've = have   **haven't** = have not
's = has   **hasn't** = has not

Short answers

Yes, I/you **have**.	No, I/you **haven't**.
Yes, he/she/it **has**.	No, he/she/it **hasn't**.
Yes, we/you/they **have**.	No, we/you/they **haven't**.

2 (2.1)

It's the Drama Club tonight, but not everyone has arrived yet. Complete the dialogue using present tense forms of *be*. Some forms are positive (e.g. *is*) and some negative (e.g. *isn't*); some are full forms (e.g. *are*) and some short forms (e.g. *'re*).

Jane ... we all here now?
Mark Where ... Tom? He ... here.
Helen Oh, he ... very well. He ... in bed.
Lynn Oh, dear. Poor Tom. And Sarah ... here.
Sarah Oh, yes, I ... .
Jane Oh, there you ... , over in the corner. Sorry, Sarah.
Mark Angela ... late. Or ... she ill, too?
Helen No, she ... ill.
Lynn Peter and Sue ... here.
Jane Yes, they ... . They ... in the kitchen.
Angela Hello, everybody. ... I late?
Jane Yes, you ... .
Angela Oh, I ... sorry.
Jane Tell Peter and Sue to come, Mark.
Peter It ... all right. Here we ... .
Jane Good. Now we ... ready to start.

Activity

One student thinks of a famous living person or a group of people such as a pop group. Ask questions to find out who the person is, e.g. *Is it one person? Is it a man? Is he European? Are they a sports team? Is she Queen Elizabeth?*

3 (2.1, 2.2)

Mr and Mrs Johnson want to sell their house. Say things about the house using a form of *be* or *have*.

Examples

house – 200 years old.
The house is 200 years old.

all rooms – central heating.
All the rooms have central heating.

1 garden – lovely
2 views to the north and east – beautiful
3 house – six bedrooms
4 rooms – large
5 downstairs rooms – carpets
6 sitting room – lovely old fireplace
7 kitchen – plenty of cupboards
8 garage – big enough for three cars

Activity

Write a short description of the house or flat you live in.

4 (2.2)

It's the first week of January. There are sales at the big department stores, and you can buy some things very cheaply. What have these people got?

Examples

He's got a shirt.

They've got some chairs.

Activity

Find some more pictures. Look through a magazine or a textbook and talk to a partner about the things people have got. If you don't know the word in English, ask your teacher.

2.3   The present continuous tense

1   Jane **is talking** to a friend at the moment.
The boys **are sitting** in the garden.
2   It **isn't raining** now, look.
3   What **are** you **doing** now? **Are** you **writing** a letter?
4   **Is** Richard **working** today? ~ No, he **isn't**.

Form

I **am** talk**ing**	we **are** talk**ing**
you **are** talk**ing**	you **are** talk**ing**
he/she/it **is** talk**ing**	they **are** talk**ing**

1   The present continuous tense is the present tense of *be* + the -ing form of a verb. ▷ 2.1 *be*; 38.3,5,6 spelling of the -ing form
2   In the negative *n't/not* comes after a form of *be*.
3   In questions a form of *be* comes before the subject. But ▷ 21.2
4   Short answers are with a form of *be*.

Use

We use the present continuous tense to talk about things that are happening now, at the moment.

▷   2.5; 4.5 with a future meaning

5 (2.3)

These people are playing a game. They are miming things. You have to say what they are doing. These phrases will help you: *brush his/her teeth, carry something, climb a ladder, comb his/her hair, eat an apple, play cards, read the newspaper, take a photo, wash his/her hands.*

Example

She's taking a photo.

Activity A

Play the miming game. One student mimes an action, and the others ask *Are you sweeping the floor? Are you writing something?* etc.

Activity B

Talk about these photos and say what the people in them are doing.

2.4   The simple present tense

Positive statements

1a   We **sit** here every evening. I sometimes **read** a book.

b   Emma **reads** the newspaper or **watches** television.

Form

I **sit**	we **sit**
you **sit**	you **sit**
he/she/it **sits**	they **sit**

1a   With *I, you, we* and *they*, we use the base form of the verb, e.g. *sit, read.*

b   In the third person singular (e.g. with *he, she* or *it*), the verb ends in *-s* or *-es*, e.g. *reads, watches.*
▷ 38.1–3,6 pronunciation and spelling

A very few verbs have an irregular pronunciation in the third person singular, e.g. *does* [dʌz], *says* [sez]. ▷40

Negative statements

2a   I **don't live** in England; I live in Scotland.

b   My friend **doesn't come** from France; he comes from Germany.

I **don't** live	we **don't** live
you **don't** live	you **don't** live
he/she/it **doesn't** live	they **don't** live

2a   With *I, you, we* and *they*, we form the negative with *don't/do not* and the base form of the verb.

b   In the third person singular we form the negative with *doesn't/does not* and the base form of the verb (without *-s*), e.g. *live.*

Questions

3a   **Do** you **like** this music? ~ Yes, it's nice.
Which record **do** you **want**? ~ This one here.

b   **Does** Jane **want** a drink? ~ No, she's got one.
How **does** she **feel** now? ~ Better, she says.

Do I like . . .?	**Do** we like . . .?
Do you like . . .?	**Do** you like . . .?
Does he/she/it like . . .?	**Do** they like . . .?

3a   In questions with *I, you, we* and *they*, we put *do* before the subject.

b   In questions in the third person singular we put *does* before the subject. We use the base form of the verb (without *-s*), e.g. *like.*

For questions with *who* and *what* asking about the subject (e.g. *Who likes this music?*) ▷ 21.2

Short answers

4   Do you think it's a good idea? ~ Yes, I **do**.
Does Ann know the address? ~ No, she **doesn't**.

Yes, I/you/we/they **do**.	No, I/you/we/they **don't**.
Yes, he/she/it **does**.	No, he/she/it **doesn't**.

Uses of the simple present tense

We use the simple present to talk about

1   things that happen again and again, e.g. *We sit here every evening*

2   facts, things that stay the same for a long time, e.g. *I live in Scotland*

3   feelings, e.g. *I like, I want*

4   thoughts, e.g. *I think, I know*

▷   2.8 dramatic use; 4.6 with a future meaning;
11 if-clauses; 13.2 in a sub clause of future time

6 (2.4)

Complete this newspaper story about Lord Stonebury.
Put in the correct simple present form of these verbs:
go (× 4), *have* (× 3), *live* (× 2), *get, meet, own, play,
read, spend, talk.*

LORD STONEBURY TELLS ALL!

from an interview by our reporter Tim Bennett, and
only in the Daily Talk

Lord Stonebury is twenty-eight years old. He … in
Belgravia in London's West End. He's very rich, and
he … the company Office Blocks International. Every
morning the young Lord … breakfast in bed and …
the newspapers. He … up at ten o'clock and usually
… for a walk in Hyde Park. He … lunch at his club. He
sometimes … the Directors of OBI, and they … about
the company's plans.

In the afternoon Lord Stonebury and his friends
sometimes … golf. Then they … a few drinks. Or
sometimes he and a girl-friend … for a drive in his
sports car. After dinner Lord Stonebury … to a night
club or a casino with one of his girl-friends. They …
home at about two o'clock.

Activity

Write the story of a typical day in *your* life.

7 (2.4)

Amanda hasn't got a boy-friend. The Find-a-Friend
Club wants to help her. Look at Amanda's answers to
the club's questionnaire and write sentences about
her.

Examples

Amanda reads books.
She doesn't watch a lot of television.

Put a tick in the box.

Do you …	Yes	No
read books?	✓	
watch a lot of television?		✓
play computer games?		✓
like music?	✓	
often visit people?	✓	
like sport?		✓
go swimming?		✓

Activity

You are writing a letter to the Find-a-Friend Club.
Write a paragraph saying what you like and what you
do in your spare time.

8 (2.4)

Tim Bennett is interviewing Brenda Bagg. Brenda
writes love stories, and millions of people read her
books. Complete Tim's questions by putting in the
missing words.

Tim Brenda, where … your ideas for all your stories?
Brenda Where do I get my ideas? That's hard to say.
They just come to me.
Tim … a long time to write a book?
Brenda No, it doesn't take long. I write one in about
two weeks.
Tim Really? That's very quick. … every day?
Brenda Yes, I write every day.
Tim And … ?
Brenda Oh, I work here in the sitting-room.
Tim … your stories?
Brenda No, I don't — my secretary types them.
Tim … your husband … your stories?
Brenda No, he doesn't. He hates them.
Tim … your husband … , Brenda?
Brenda Oh, he doesn't work. He hasn't got a job. My
stories bring us lots of money, you know.
Tim … so many people … your books, Brenda?
Brenda I think they read them because I tell a good
story. Everyone likes a good story, you know.

Activity

Take the role of a famous person who you know
something about. Your partner interviews you and
asks about your daily life.

9 (2.1, 2.2, 2.4)

This paragraph is from a book about British towns. It's
about a town called Milchester. Complete the
paragraph by putting in present tense forms of *be* and
have and the simple present tense of *bring, live*
and *work.*

Milchester … a lovely old town on the River Swenley.
The famous castle … lots of tourists to the town. The
old streets near the castle … many interesting little
shops, and there … a very good museum. The town
also … a theatre and a cinema. 27,000 people … in
Milchester, and quite a few of them … at the new
computer factory. Other industries … paper-making
and chocolate.

Activity

Write a short description of a town that you know well.

2.5 Present continuous or simple present? [A]

The present continuous and the simple present tenses do not have the same uses. Study carefully the differences between them.

Present continuous

1   Kate**'s listening** to the radio at the moment.
     Mr Brown **isn't working** today.

Simple present

2   She **listens** to the music programme every day.
     He **doesn't work** on Saturdays.

3a   I **think** you're right.
 b   Mike **wants** a sandwich.
 c   He **says** he's hungry.
 d   I **have** two children.
 e   The camera **costs** £55.

Present continuous

1   things that are happening *at the moment*

Simple present

2   things that happen *again and again*. But ▷ 2.6–8

3   Verbs which describe actions can have a continuous or a simple form. But some verbs are normally only used in simple tenses. These are

 a   verbs of thinking, e.g. *think* (= believe), *believe, agree, understand, know, remember, forget*
 b   verbs of feeling, e.g. *want, wish, like, love, hate*
 c   reporting verbs, e.g. *say, ask, tell, answer*
 d   verbs of possession, e.g. *have, own, belong*
 e   some other verbs, e.g. *cost, weigh, seem, appear, need*

Note We use *can* instead of a present tense with *see, hear* and other verbs of perception, e.g. *I can see a café over there.*

▷   28.6 after *here* and *there*

2.6 Present continuous or simple present? [B]

Present continuous

1   **I'm learning** English at evening classes this year.
     Don't take that book, please. Judy**'s reading** it.

Simple present

2   My children **learn** English at school.
     She often **reads** detective stories.

1   We can use the present continuous to talk about something that is happening for a limited period of time (e.g. *this year*) but is not happening just at the moment.

2   We use the simple present for something that happens over a longer period of time.

2.7 The present continuous tense with **always**

Jennifer**'s always losing** her key.
I'm always paying for your coffee. Why can't you pay for a change?

Form

▷   2.3. *always* comes between *be* and the -ing form.

Use

We use the present continuous tense with *always* to talk about something that happens too often.

▷   24.7 adverbs of frequency

2.8 The simple present tense: dramatic use

1   The car **stops** outside the National Bank. Three men **get** out and the driver **stays** in the car. The three men **walk** into the bank and **take** out their guns . . .

2   Ellis **throws** the ball in to Snow, but he **loses** it. Watson **gives** the ball to Tanner. Tanner **goes** past two men, he **shoots**, but the ball **hits** a Liverpool player . . .

Form ▷ 2.4

Use

We sometimes use the simple present tense

1   to tell a story, to describe the dramatic action of a play or film

2   to describe actions (e.g. in sport) while they are happening

10 (2.5)

It's a holiday today. The people below aren't working. Say what they do in their jobs and what they're doing at the moment. Use these verbs in the present continuous: *eat, jog, listen, play, read, ride, swim, wash, watch.*

RAY, WINDOW CLEANER

Example

Ray cleans windows.
He's listening to the radio
at the moment.

BRIAN, HOUSE BUILDER

ALICE, MUSIC TEACHER

MAUREEN AND JACKIE, DRESSMAKERS

ALAN, LORRY DRIVER

STEPHEN, GOLFER

JESSICA, NEWSREADER

TONY AND ROGER, CAR SALESMEN

MIRANDA, PHOTOGRAPHER

Activity

Make sentences about the people in these photos. Use both the present continuous and simple present tenses.

11 (2.5, 2.6)

Complete this postcard using the correct form of the verbs on the right.

Greetings from Wales! Ben and I ...   *do*
something different this year. We're at the
North Wales Activity Centre. People ...   *come*
here every summer to learn more about
their hobbies and interests. I ...   *do*
photography and tennis this week and
Ben ... about computers. We ... up at half   *learn, get*
past eight every morning and ... lessons   *do*
from ten to half past twelve. We ... lunch   *have*
at one, and then there are more lessons.
So it's hard work. But I ... it here. We ... a *like, have*

super time. It's half past seven in the
evening now, and we ... out on the grass   *sit*
in front of the Centre. The weather is
good. See you soon.

Love,

Kate

Activity

Write a postcard to an English friend from the place where you last went on holiday. Say what you do every day on holiday and what you are doing at the moment.

3 Verbs: Talking about the past

3.1 The past tense of be

I **was** in London last week. I **wasn't** here.
Was I asleep? ~ Yes, you **were**.
You **were** rude to that woman just now. You **weren't** very polite.
Were you at the meeting yesterday? ~ Yes, I **was**.
Philip **was** at the club last night, but Ann **wasn't** with him.
Was he with Julia? ~ Yes, he **was**.
Was she at home? ~ No, she **was** at a party.
It **was** fine yesterday, but it **wasn't** very warm.
How **was** the meal? ~ Very good.
We **were** at the back. We **weren't** near the front.
Were we in France two years ago? ~ Yes, we **were**.
The early Britons **were** hunters. They **were** not farmers.
Were the Romans here? ~ Yes, they **were**.

Form

I **was**	we **were**
you **were**	you **were**
he/she/it **was**	they **were**

Short forms
wasn't = was not
weren't = were not

Short answers
Yes, I/he/she/it/ **was**.   No, I/he/she/it **wasn't**.
Yes, you/we/they **were**.   No, you/we/they **weren't**.

3.2 The past tense of have (got)

have got
I **had got**/I**'d got** a little money, but I **hadn't got** enough for a taxi.
Had you **got** an umbrella with you? ~ Yes, I **had**.

have
I **had**/I**'d** a little money, but I **didn't have**/I **hadn't** enough for a taxi.
Did you **have**/**Had** you an umbrella with you? ~ Yes, I **did/had**.

Form

had got or **had** in all persons

Short forms
'd = had   **hadn't** = had not

Short answers
Yes, I/you/he/we/they **had**.
No, I/you/he/we/they **hadn't**.
Yes, I **did** etc.

We can form negatives and questions with *had got*, with *had* or with *did*. ▷ 3.3
had is more usual than *had got*, and we normally use *did* in negatives and questions.

12 (3.1)

Helen and David are talking about a barbecue. (At a barbecue people cook meat over a fire. They cook and eat the meal outside.) Complete the dialogue. Use *was, wasn't, were* or *weren't*.

Helen I hear there … a barbecue at the college last Saturday. … you there?
David Yes, I … . Where … you?
Helen Oh, I … here on Saturday. I … in London.
David That's a pity. It … a very good barbecue. The food … great.
Helen What … the weather like here?
David Oh, we … very lucky with the weather. It … nice and warm.
Helen … there a lot of people there?
David Yes, lots. Lynn … there, though. She … very well.
Helen What about Mark and Jane?
David Oh, they … still on holiday last Saturday, so they … at the barbecue. But all the others … there.

Activity

One student imagines that he/she was in a certain place yesterday evening, e.g. at a concert, in a plane. Ask questions to find out where the person was, e.g. *Were you in hospital? Were you at a disco?*

13 (3.1, 3.2)

A number of people saw a monster in the sea on the south coast of England. One of them was Henry. He's talking to reporters about it. Put in *was, wasn't, were, weren't, had* or *didn't have*.

Reporter What happened? Where … you? And where … the monster?
Henry I … here on the beach. I saw the monster in the water. Then it swam out to sea. It … a great shock. It … very nice, I can tell you.
Reporter What … the monster like?
Henry Big. It … a very large animal. It … a large body, but it … a small head. Its eyes … blue and round. It … teeth, but they … very big. It … any ears.
Reporter Did you take a photo of it?
Henry I … my camera with me, I'm afraid. And it … very quick. It all happened in a moment.

Activity

Imagine that you were out in the country one evening and you saw a spaceship land and two Martians get out. Your partner is a reporter interviewing you about it.

3.3   The simple past tense

Positive statements

1   We **enjoyed** the show last night.
I once **worked** in a restaurant.
The plane **landed** safely in a field.

2   I **went** to Finland about five years ago.
She **sang** all her favourite songs.

Negative statements

Andrew **didn't stay** very long yesterday.
We **didn't get** home until midnight.

Questions

Did you **enjoy** the show? ~ Yes, we **did**.
Did she **sing** her new hit? ~ No, she **didn't**.
What time **did** you **arrive** home? ~
About midnight.

Form

1   We form the simple past tense of most verbs with
-*ed* or -*d*, e.g. *enjoyed, worked, liked*.
▷ 38.3–6 pronunciation and spelling

2   Some verbs have an irregular past form, e.g. *went,
sang*. ▷ 40
Regular and irregular past forms are the same in
all persons (but not *be* ▷ 3.1).

We form the negative with *didn't/did not* and the
base form of the verb (without -*ed*), e.g. *stay*.

We form questions with *did* and the base form of
the verb (without -*ed*), e.g. *enjoy*. For questions
with *who* and *what* asking about the subject (e.g.
Who enjoyed the show?) ▷ 21.2

Short answers
Yes, I/you/he/we/they **did**.
No, I/you/he/we/they **didn't**.

Use of the simple past

We use the simple past tense to talk about things
that happened at a time that is now finished, e.g.
last night, five years ago, yesterday.
We often use the simple past tense to tell a story.

▷   3.5 present perfect or simple past?

14 **(3.3)**

Find the correct action for each person.

Examples

Copernicus studied the planets.
Shakespeare wrote plays.

People	Actions
Copernicus	going to the moon
Shakespeare	inventing the electric light
Picasso	making clothes
Billie-Jean King	painting pictures
Neil Armstrong	playing tennis
Marco Polo	sailing to America
Martin Luther King	studying the planets
Christian Dior	travelling to China
Columbus	working for Black people's rights
Edison	writing plays

Activity

Say what these people did.

Elvis Presley
Agatha Christie
Henry Ford
Alfred Hitchcock
Marconi

15 **(3.3)**

Melinda Burns is a famous film star. Two weeks ago she suddenly disappeared, and no one knew where she was. The police looked everywhere for her. Yesterday she arrived home, and now she is speaking to reporters for the first time. Read what the reporters are thinking and ask their questions.

Examples

(She went somewhere. Where?)
Where did you go?

(Perhaps someone kidnapped her.)
Did someone kidnap you?

1 (She disappeared. Why?)
2 (Perhaps she left the country.)
3 (She travelled. How?)
4 (Perhaps her friends hid her.)
5 (She did something in all that time. What?)
6 (Perhaps she read the stories about her in the newspapers.)
7 (She came home. Why?)
8 (Perhaps her husband found her.)

Activity

You work for a magazine called 'Holiday'. You are interviewing people. Ask your partner about his/her last holiday. Find out all the details.

16 **(3.3)**

Bob had a lot of jobs to do last weekend. He didn't have time to do all of them. Which ones did he do?

Examples

He washed the car.
He didn't buy a new battery for the car.

Weekend

wash car ✓
buy new battery for car
repair broken window
book holiday
write to bank ✓
phone sports club
pay electricity bill ✓
tidy garage ✓
paint gate
clean windows

Activity

Write down five things you did last weekend. (They needn't just be jobs.) Compare your list with your partner's. Say if you did the same things or not.

3.4   The present perfect tense

1   I**'ve cleaned** my shoes. (So they're clean now.)

2   Mr Green **has bought** a new car. (So it's his car now.)

3   Joanna **hasn't eaten** any toast. (The toast is still on the table.)

4a   **Have** you **finished** the housework? ~
b   No, I **haven't**. I'm still doing it.

5   I**'ve just written** that letter.

6a   You **haven't posted** the letter **yet**.
b   **Have** you **found** those stamps **yet**? ~ No, not **yet**.

7a   **Have** you **seen** Sarah **today**? ~
b   No, I **haven't**. I **haven't seen** her **this week**.

8a   **How long has** Ann **lived** here? ~
b   Oh, only **for six months**. She**'s been** here **since April**.

9a   **Have** you **ever eaten** rabbit? ~ Yes, lots of times. ~
b   Well, I**'ve never had** it.

Form

I/you **have** cleaned
he/she/it **has** cleaned
we/you/they **have** cleaned

1   The present perfect tense is the present tense of *have* + the -ed form (past participle). ▷ 2.2. *have*; 38.3–6 pronunciation and spelling of the -ed form.

2   Some verbs have an irregular past participle, e.g. *bought*. ▷40

3   In the negative, *n't/not* comes after *have* or *has*.

4a   In questions, *have* or *has* comes before the subject. But ▷ 21.2
b   We form short answers with *have/has*.

Note the irregular past participles of *be* and *have*:

8b   *be   →   have been*
9b   *have →   have had*

Use

We use the present perfect to talk about

1–4   the present result of a past action

5   something that happened only a short time ago (. . . *just* . . .)

6   an action that we are expecting (. . . *yet*)

7   something that happened during a period of time that is not yet finished (. . . *today*, . . . *this week*)

8   something that began in the past and has stayed the same up to the present (. . . *for six months*, . . . *since April*)

9   something that happened during a period of time which began in the past and has gone on up to the present (. . . *ever* . . . , . . . *never* . . .)

Note In British English we sometimes use the present perfect tense where Americans use the simple past, e.g. *Did you find those stamps yet?*

▷   5.4 *been to* and *gone to*

17 **(3.4)**

A month ago the members of the Parkway Sports and Social Club decided to clean and decorate their club. The club hasn't got much money, so the members have done the work in their spare time. They've just finished now. Say what they have done.

Examples

(The windows needed painting.)
Sue and Peter have painted the windows.

(The members decided to plant a tree.)
Jane has planted a tree.

1   (The fence needed repairing.)
2   (The club room needed decorating.)
3   (They decided to buy some new curtains.)
4   (The cups needed polishing.)
5   (The minibus needed servicing.)
6   (They decided to lay a new carpet in the bar.)
7   (The kitchen needed cleaning out.)
8   (They decided to put up some more shelves.)

Activity

Four students leave the room and the rest of you decide to change four things in the room, e.g. to open a window, to take down a poster, to put some books on top of the cupboard or to move the waste bin. The four students come back and have a good look round. They ask e.g. *Have your turned that desk round?* *Have you rubbed out the sentence on the board?* and you answer *Yes, we have* or *No, we haven't.*

3.5   Present perfect or simple past?

Present perfect

1   They**'ve opened** the new road. (So it's open now.)
2   I**'ve just got** up.
3   I **haven't seen** the exhibition **yet**.
4   It **hasn't rained today**.
5   **How long has** Mrs Peters **had** that car?
6   **Have** you **ever travelled** by plane?

Simple past

1   Yes, they **opened** it **last week**.
2   Peter **got** up **at half past six**.
3   Tom **saw** it in town **on Saturday**.
4   And it **didn't rain yesterday**.
5   Let me see. **When did** she **buy** it?
6   Yes, we **travelled** to London by plane **six months ago**.

The present perfect and simple past tenses do not have the same uses. Study carefully the differences between them:

Present perfect

1   the present result of a past action
2   a short time ago
3   something that we are expecting
4   an unfinished time
5   something that has stayed the same
6   a time up to the present

Simple past

1   a past action
2   a longer time ago
3   something that is already over
4   a finished time
5   an action that changed something
6   a time in the past

We use the simple past (not the present perfect) with a phrase of past time which says (or asks) when something happened, e.g.

1   *last week*   4   *yesterday*
2   *at half past six*   5   *When . . .?*
3   *on Saturday*   6   *six months ago*

18 (3.5)

James Delaney is the most famous sportsman in Britain. He's quite old now, but he's done lots of exciting things in his life. Here are some photos in a magazine article about him. Say what James has done and when he did it.

Examples
He's played tennis at Wimbledon. He played tennis there in 1948.
He's taken part in the Olympic Games. He took part (in them) in 1956.

Activity

Have *you* done any exciting or interesting things? Write down one or two. Find out what other people in your class have done.

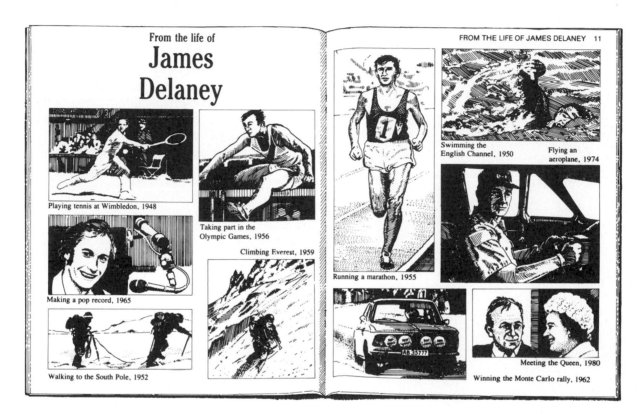

From the life of
James Delaney

Playing tennis at Wimbledon, 1948

Taking part in the Olympic Games, 1956

Making a pop record, 1965

Climbing Everest, 1959

Walking to the South Pole, 1952

FROM THE LIFE OF JAMES DELANEY 11

Swimming the English Channel, 1950

Flying an aeroplane, 1974

Running a marathon, 1955

Meeting the Queen, 1980

Winning the Monte Carlo rally, 1962

19 (3.5)

Complete this conversation by putting the verbs in brackets into the present perfect or simple past.

Rachel Hello, Bob.
Bob Hello. I (not see) you for a long time.
Rachel I (see) you in town two or three weeks ago, but you (not see) me. I (be) on a bus.
Bob Well, how are things? Are you still living over the shop?
Rachel No, I (move) now. I (find) a super flat just before I went on holiday. I (be) there three months.
Bob ... you (pass) your driving test yet?
Rachel Yes, I have. I (pass) in October. I (not buy) a car yet, though. But what about you, Bob? ... anything exciting (happen) to you lately?
Bob No, not really. My mother (not be) very well for a few months now.

Rachel Oh, dear. I'm sorry to hear that.
Bob And my brother's out of work.
Rachel ... he (leave) school in the summer, then?
Bob Yes. He (not do) very well in his exams and he (not find) a job yet.
Rachel Are you still working at Scott's?
Bob Yes. They ... just (give) me a pay rise.
Rachel Well, that's one piece of good news.

Activity

Imagine that you are meeting an old friend who you haven't seen for about a year. Write down three or four items of news about yourself that you can tell your friend.

3.6   The past perfect tense

Compare the tenses:

Present perfect

1   Alan's got no money. He**'s spent** it all.

Past perfect

2   Alan had no money last Sunday. He**'d spent** it all.
I didn't go to see the film last night because I**'d seen** it before.
Had Mrs Williams already **arrived** when you got to the station? ~ No, she **hadn't**.
After we **had looked** round the museum, we went to a restaurant.

Simple past

3   We **looked** round the museum, and then we **went** to a restaurant.

Form

had + the **-ed** form (past participle)

Some past participles end in *-ed*, and some are irregular. ▷ 40

Short forms   **'d** = had   **hadn't** = had not
We form short answers with *had*. ▷ 3.2

Use

1   Remember that we use the present perfect tense to talk about the present result of a past action.

2   When we talk about the past, we sometimes talk about one thing that happened before another. We use the past perfect tense for the thing that happened *first* and the simple past tense for what happened *later*.

3   When one thing happened and then another, we can also use the simple past tense for both actions.

20 (3.6)

Decide the order in which these things happened. Then write two sentences using *after* and the past perfect.

Example

The prisoner ran across the yard.
He jumped out of the window.
He climbed over the wall.

After the prisoner had jumped out of the window, he ran across the yard.
After he had run across the yard, he climbed over the wall.

1 The bank clerk gave it to me.
  She looked at my cheque.
  She counted out the money.

2 The tourists got out of the coach.
  They got back in the coach.
  They took photos.

3 The reporter wrote a report on the accident.
  She interviewed the people there.
  She went to the scene of the accident.

4 The mechanic put a new tyre on.
  He put the wheel back on.
  He took the wheel off the car.

Activity

Write a paragraph describing how you carried out a job such as wrapping a parcel and posting it. (You can use these words: *parcel, paper, wrap, stick, tape, tie, string, post office, assistant, weigh, pay, stamp*). Try to think of a job that you did recently.

21 (3.3–3.6)

Complete this newspaper story about an unlucky man. Put each verb in brackets into the simple past, the present perfect or the past perfect tense.

DISASTROUS DAVID!

David Williams of Milchester (have) such a terrible time this year that he ought to be in *The Guinness Book of Records*. The trouble (start) one morning last January when David (find) that his car (go) from outside his house. He (not see) it since.

In February David's joy at winning £200,000 on the football pools (not last) long — he (forget) to post the letter. In March he (buy) a new car, but he (not have) it more than a week when someone (crash) into the back of it. These disasters (continue) right up to the present time. Two days ago David (sit) on a seat that someone (finish) painting only minutes before. He (have) on a new suit that he (buy) only the previous week.

August (be) the worst month so far this year. David (spend) three days of his holiday at airports because of strikes. When he (arrive) home, he (discover) that someone (break) into his house. His video-recorder and television (disappear).

David doesn't know what he (do) to deserve all this bad luck. He just hopes his luck will change soon.

Activity

Write a letter to the newspaper about a piece of good luck or bad luck that happened to you.

3.7   The past continuous tense

Compare the present continuous and past continuous:

1   What **are** you **doing**? ~ I**'m waiting** for a bus.

2   What **were** you **doing** at six o'clock yesterday evening? ~ I **was waiting** for a bus.

Compare the past continuous and simple past:

3   We **were watching** the news when the telephone **rang**.
The accident **happened** while they **were coming** down the mountain.
What **were** you **doing** when the policeman **came**? ~ I **was** just **making** some coffee.

4a   When the telegram arrived, I **was packing** a suitcase.

b   When the telegram arrived, I **packed** a suitcase.

5   It was a lovely morning. The sun **was shining**, and the birds **were singing** in the trees.

6   While everyone **was talking** and **laughing**, Martha **was crying** quietly in the kitchen downstairs.

7   She **wanted** to be a writer when I **knew** her.

Form

was/were (▷ 3.1) + the -ing form
We form short answers with *was/were*.

Use

1   Remember that we use the present continuous tense to talk about things happening now.

2   We use the past continuous tense to talk about things happening at a time in the past, e.g. *at six o'clock yesterday evening*.

| 5.55 | 6.00 | 6.05 |

I was waiting for a bus.

3   If an action was going on for some time (e.g. *we were watching the news*) and a new, shorter action happened (e.g. *the telephone rang*), we use the past continuous for the longer action.

7.00   7.30
*I was watching
the news.*

The telephone rang.

4a   We use the past continuous tense for a longer action that is interrupted. (The arrival of the telegram interrupted my packing.)

b   We use a simple past tense when one action follows another. (The telegram arrived, and then I packed a suitcase.)

5   We often use a past continuous tense to describe a scene, especially when telling a story.

6   We also use the past continuous tense for two longer actions happening at the same time.

7   Some verbs (e.g. *want, know*) are not normally used in continuous tenses. ▷ 2.5

22   (3.7)

Mr Pratt has a lot of dreams. He's telling a psychiatrist about them. How does Mr Pratt describe his dreams? Look at the pictures and the psychiatrist's notes.

Examples

I was driving a car when a wheel came off.

The Queen walked in when we were eating breakfast.

Activity A

Last night Mr Pratt had these two dreams. How do you think he described them?

Activity B

Have you had any interesting or amusing dreams? Can you describe them?

> drives car — wheel comes off
> eat breakfast — Queen comes in
> walks across bridge — meets tiger
> roof falls in — watch television
> climbs stairs — sees ghost
> looks into mirror — it breaks
> wind blows him over cliff — walks along
>   path
> lie on beach — elephant comes out of sea
> digs garden — finds dead body

3.8   The present perfect continuous tense

1 Peter **has been working** in the garden since ten o'clock this morning, and he's still hard at work. How long **has** he **been digging**? ~ Oh, for hours.

2 Alan, you**'ve been reading** that book all day. ~ Yes, I **have**, but I haven't finished it yet.

3 What **have** you **been doing** this afternoon, Carol? ~ I**'ve been talking** to some friends at the club.

Form

have been/has been + the -ing form
We form short answers with *have/has*. ▷ 2.2

Use

1 The present perfect continuous tense shows that an action began in the past and has gone on for some time. We often use the tense in a question with *How long . . .?* or with *for* or *since*. ▷ 25.7

2 We can use the tense to talk about an action that is still happening.

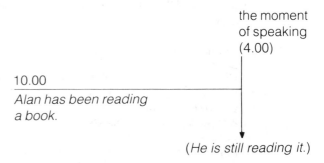

10.00
Alan has been reading a book.

(*He is still reading it.*)

3 We can use the tense to talk about an action that finished a short time ago.

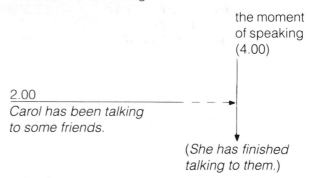

2.00
Carol has been talking to some friends.

(*She has finished talking to them.*)

3.9   Present perfect or present perfect continuous?

1 The lawn looks nice because I**'ve cut** the grass. (The grass is short now.)
I'm tired because I**'ve been cutting** the grass. (The cutting went on for some time.)

2 I**'ve owned** this bicycle since I was fifteen. (something staying the same)
I**'ve been riding** this bicycle since I was fifteen. (something happening)

3a Mrs Dobson **has lived** in Bristol for twenty years and **has worked** at the bookshop for ten years.

b Mrs Dobson **has been living** in Bristol for twenty years and **has been working** at the bookshop for ten years.

The present perfect and present perfect continuous tenses do not have the same uses. Study carefully the differences between them.

1 We use both tenses to talk about an action that finished a short time ago. We use the present perfect to talk about the present result of an action, and we use the present perfect continuous to show that an action has gone on for some time.

2 We use both tenses to talk about things that began in the past and have gone on up to the present. We use the present perfect to talk about something staying the same and the present perfect continuous to talk about something happening.

3 We can talk about some things either as staying the same (a) or as happening (b).

23 **(3.8)**

Twelve students live in a big old house. Today they're all helping to clean it and tidy it up. Read the conversation and say how long they've been doing their jobs. Use a phrase with *for*.

Example

Gary has been throwing away rubbish for an hour and a half.

Adam What are you doing, Gary?
Gary Throwing away rubbish. I started at half past ten, and it's twelve o'clock now, look.
Melanie I'm washing up. I've been doing it since half past eleven.
Adam Sadie and I are tidying up. We started at half past ten.
Lisa Has anyone seen a bucket? I've been looking for one since ten to twelve.
Gary I think Alison and Jason had a bucket. They're working in the garden. They've been there since nine o'clock.
Lisa What's Don doing?
Adam He's cleaning the stairs. He's been doing that since Melanie started washing up.
Emma And I'm repairing this toaster. I started at eleven o'clock, but it still won't work.
Adam Trevor's mending the door bell. He began the job at about twenty to twelve.
Melanie Daniel and Rebecca are brushing carpets. They started at ten.
Gary Let's all go out and have some lunch soon.
Adam Good idea.

Activity

Find out who in your class has been living in the same house or flat the longest.

24 **(3.1–3.9)**

Complete this newspaper article by putting each verb in brackets into the correct past or perfect tense. (Sometimes there is more than one correct answer.)

UNITED WANT SIMMONDS

Manchester United manager Brian Price (go) to Turin for talks with the Juventus club about Wayne Simmonds. Simmonds (join) Juventus a year ago, and he (score) 18 goals for them. Last autumn he (score) almost every week, but he (not play) well recently. English fans would welcome his return, and yesterday everyone at United (talk) about Simmonds. In fact, the club (wait) for some time now for a chance to talk to the player.

At the moment Simmonds is England's greatest footballer, although he (be) in the game for only two years. He (play) amateur football for Mendip Athletic when Bristol City (invite) him to join them. When Arsenal (buy) Simmonds for £750,000, he (spend) only six months with the Bristol club, but he (already play) twice for England Under-21s. Simmonds quickly (become) a big star, and he (now play) five games for the full England team, although he (play) only one game for them since he (leave) Arsenal for Juventus.

Activity

Write a short paragraph about a famous living person summarizing his/her career so far.

3.10   The past perfect continuous tense

Compare the two tenses:

Present perfect continuous
1   We**'ve been working** hard since seven o'clock so we're going to have a rest now.

Past perfect continuous
2   We felt very tired yesterday afternoon because we **had been working** hard since seven o'clock.
How long **had** you **been waiting** when the Browns arrived?
Had Keith **been driving** a van before he got the job at the factory last year? ~ Yes, he had. He**'d been delivering** furniture for three years.

Form

had been + the -ing form
We form short answers with *had*. ▷ 3.2

Use

1   Remember that we use the present perfect continuous tense (▷ 3.8) to talk about an action that has gone on up to the present time.
2   We use the past perfect continuous tense to talk about an action that went on up to a time in the past.

3.11   **used to**

1   We **used to** live in London years ago.
2   **Did** you **use to** go cycling when you were younger? ~ Yes, I **did**.
3a   Tourists **didn't use to** come here.
 b   Tourists **used not to** come here.
 c   Tourists **never used to** come here.
4   Lots of tourists come here nowadays.

Form

1   *used to* + the base form of the verb in all persons.
2   We form questions and short answers with *did*.
3   The negative is
 a   usually *didn't use to*
 b   sometimes *used not to* or
 c   *never used to* (more emphatic)

Use

used to means that something often happened in the past but does not happen now.
4   There is no present tense of *used to*. We use the simple present tense of a normal verb to talk about things that often happen these days.

Note *be used to* (+ -ing form) means to have done something so often that it no longer seems new or strange, e.g. *We're used to living in London now, but everything was new and exciting at first.* ▷ 15.5

25 (3.1–3.10)

A lawyer has made some notes about a traffic accident. Complete them by putting each verb in brackets into the correct past or perfect tense. (Sometimes there is more than one correct answer.)

Traffic accident: Mr Keith Johnson, 44 Grange Rd, Milchester

1 The accident (happen) at 10.47 pm on October 23rd at the corner of Compton St and Brooks Rd, Milchester.
2 Mr and Mrs Johnson (be) on their way home. Mr Johnson (drive).
3 The couple (visit) friends. They (drink), but Mr Johnson (have) only one small whisky. He (finish) this drink at 10.15 pm.
4 It (not rain) at the time, but it (rain) shortly before, and the roads (be) wet.
5 At 10.47 pm Mr Richard Hunter (cycle) north along Brooks Rd. He (have) his lights on.
6 Mr Johnson (not stop) at the 'Stop' sign. As he (turn) into Brooks Rd, he (hit) Mr Hunter and (knock) him off his bike.
7 Mr Hunter (be) not badly hurt, but his bike (be) damaged. Mr Johnson (stop) and (report) the accident.
8 Mr Johnson (drive) for twenty years now. He (not have) an accident before.

Activity

Tell your partner about an accident that once happened to you or one that you saw. It can be a road accident or an accident at work or in the home.

26 (3.1–3.11)

Mrs Vincent is a hundred years old. She's talking to a reporter. Complete their conversation by putting the verbs in brackets into the correct tense. You can use the simple past, the present perfect, the present perfect continuous or *used to*. (Sometimes there is more than one correct answer.)

Reporter How long … you (live) in this house, Mrs Vincent?
Mrs Vincent I (live) here for seventy-five years now.
Reporter And how long is it since your husband (die)?
Mrs Vincent Oh, he (be) dead for forty years. Yes, he (die) a long time ago. I (be) alone since then. It (be) a long time.
Reporter And where … you (live) before you (come) here?
Mrs Vincent Well, before we (get) married I (live) with my parents in William Street. They (knock) the house down now. I (only live) in two houses all my life.
Reporter I expect you (see) a lot of changes in all that time.
Mrs Vincent Oh, yes. Milchester (be) very quiet in my young days. And it (not be) as big as it is today. I (go) for picnics on Long Hill with my brothers and sisters. Now they (build) houses there.
Reporter … you (enjoy) life in those days?
Mrs Vincent Oh, yes. We (have) a wonderful time. People (be) a lot friendlier in those days. We (do) things together. Nowadays people just sit at home and watch television, don't they?

Activity

Write three or four sentences about *your* childhood and the place where you lived then. Ask a partner about his/her childhood.

4 Verbs: Talking about the future

4.1 will

1 Life **will** be very different in a hundred years' time. ~ Yes, it **will**, but I **won't** be here. I**'ll** be dead.
2 I think England **will** win on Saturday. ~ No, they **won't**. They **won't** beat Italy.
3 I think I**'ll** read a book this evening. Or perhaps I**'ll** watch television.

Form

will in all persons. But ▷ 4.2

Short forms
'll = will   **won't** = will not

Short answers
Yes, I/you/he/we/they **will**.
No, I/you/he/we/they **won't**.

Use

1 We use *will* to talk about something in the future (often a long way in the future). It does *not* mean that somebody has decided on an action.
2 We use *will* to talk about things which the speaker cannot control. (We use it to make predictions. ▷ 30.6)
3 If we are talking about things that we have not yet decided to do until the moment of speaking, we can use *will*. ▷ 32.1

▷ 4.4, 7, 10; 7.11; 13.2 sub clauses of future time

4.2 shall

I **shall** be ready in about half an hour.
We **shall** get wet in this rain.
I **shan't** be here next week.
We **shan't** stay long.

Instead of *will* and *won't*, we sometimes use *shall* and *shan't* (*shall not*) to talk about the future, but only in the first person.

▷ 7.11 uses of *will* and *shall*

4.3 be going to

1 We**'re going to** walk up the hill this afternoon. **Are** you **going to** take a picnic? ~ Yes, we **are**.
2 Look at those black clouds up there. It**'s going to** rain.
It **isn't going to** be nice enough for a picnic.
3 We **were going to** go for a walk, but the weather made us change our minds.
It **was** obviously **going to** rain at any moment, so they began to carry the food back into the house.

1 We use *be going to* to talk about people's intentions, things they have already decided to do in the future. ▷ 32.2 intentions
2 We also use *be going to* to make predictions when there is something in the present (e.g. *black clouds*) which tells us about the future (often the near future). ▷ 30.6 predictions
3 We use the past of *be going to* to talk about past intentions or past predictions.

27 (4.1)

There's a programme about the future on television
tonight. Professor Joseph T. Bloomenberg is saying
what the world will be like in fifty years' time. Look at
the Professor's notes and write down what he says.

Examples

People will live longer.
There will be more people in the world.

```
people living longer
more people in the world
robots doing all the hard work
not so many jobs
people having more free time
the weather colder
not very much oil
fish farms under the sea
people flying to other planets
people not very happy
```

Activity

Write a few sentences saying what you think the world
will be like in fifty years' time.

28 (4.3)

The pupils in Class 6F at Parkside School are all
seventeen or eighteen years old. Most of them are
going to leave school soon. Read the information
about them and then say what they're going to do.
Choose the correct phrase from the box below.

Example

Andrew is interested in machines.
Andrew is going to study engineering.

1 Neil wants to be out in the fresh air.
2 Michelle and Kevin are interested in computers.
3 Sharon has already learnt to drive.
4 Simon is good with numbers.
5 Nick and Julie need to take their exams again.
6 Adrian's parents have their own company.
7 Tina would like to work with people.
8 Ian and Jeremy want to get away for a while.

```
become a taxi driver
do electronics
hitch-hike round the world
look for an outdoor job
stay at school another year
study engineering
take a course in banking
train to be a social worker
work for the family business
```

Activity A

If you're still at school or college, say what you're
going to do in the future.

Activity B

Say what you're going to do next weekend. Write
three or four sentences.

4.4   **will** or **be going to**?

will

1   Trains **will** be much faster in the future.
2   Just a minute. I think I**'ll** buy a newspaper.

be going to

3   I**'m going to** read this book. I bought it last week.
4   That boat's full of water. It**'s going to** sink!

will and *be going to* do not have the same uses. Study carefully the differences between them.

We use *will*

1   to talk about things in the future which we cannot control (*not* things that we have decided to do)
2   when we are deciding to do something at the moment of speaking

We use *be going to*

3   to talk about intentions, things we have already decided to do
4   when there is something in the present which tells us about the future

29 (4.1, 4.3)

Bymore's is a big department store. It's quite an old store now. The management of Bymore's have decided to modernize the store. The manager of the store is explaining what they are going to do and what the result will be. Look at the manager's notes and write down what he says.

Example

We're going to have a computer. It'll tell us what people are buying.

1 We're going to put in ... . They'll ...
2 ... employ ...
3 ... put in ...
4 ... play ...
5 ... have ...
6 ... have ... ... be able ...

```
            N  O  T  E  S

  EX   computer to tell us what people
       are buying

  1    new escalators to move people
       around more quickly

  2    more assistants to help our
       customers

  3    cameras to stop people stealing
       things

  4    music to produce the right
       atmosphere

  5    televisions to inform customers
       about things in the store

  6    children's room for parents to
       leave their children
```

Activity

Imagine that you are in charge of your school or college. Discuss with the rest of the class what changes you would like to make in the building. You must make definite decisions, and you have plenty of money to spend. Write down your decisions and say what the results will be.

30 (4.1–4.4)

Graham and his family are going to move from London to Alaska. Janet is asking Graham about the move. Put in *'ll, will, won't, shall, shan't* or a form of *be going to.* (Sometimes there is more than one correct answer.)

Janet Someone told me you and the family ... go and live in Alaska. Is it true?
Graham Yes, it is. I ... work for a building company.
Janet That ... be interesting.
Graham I hope so. It ... be something different. It ... certainly be a lot colder than London.
Janet When ... you ... leave?
Graham On the tenth of next month. We ... be there in three weeks.
Janet Oh, so it ... be long now. Jerry and I ... be sad to see you go.
Graham Oh, we ... be back some time. We ... be there for ever. And you can always come to Alaska and see us.
Janet Well, that isn't a bad idea. We ... visit my sister in Vancouver next summer.
Graham Oh, that's great. We ... see you next summer then.

Activity

Imagine that Janet and Graham live in Birmingham, and Graham, who is single, has got a new job with an oil company in Saudi Arabia starting in two weeks. Rewrite the conversation changing the details where necessary. Then practise the conversation with a partner.

4.5   The present continuous tense with a future meaning

Are you **doing** anything tonight? ~
Yes, I**'m playing** tennis. We've got a game against
another club.
Are you **taking** a holiday this year? ~
Yes, we've just arranged a holiday. We**'re
spending** ten days in Spain.

Form ▷ 2.3

Use

We often use the present continuous tense to talk
about things that people have arranged to do in
the future.
This meaning is almost the same as *be going to*
used for things people have decided to do
(▷ 4.3).

4.6   The simple present tense with a future meaning

What time **does** your plane go? ~
It **leaves** at half past ten on Saturday, and we
arrive in Rome at twelve o'clock.

Form ▷ 2.4

Use

We sometimes use the simple present tense to
talk about a programme or timetable in the future.

4.7   **will be** + -ing form

1   Mr Briggs is 65, so he **will be leaving** the
company next month.
Will you **be staying** late at the office tomorrow? ~
Yes, I **will**. I've a lot of work to do.

2   I've got all the garden to dig—I**'ll be doing** it all
day.
We're washing up now, but this time next week we
won't be washing up—we**'ll be lying** on the
beach in the sun!

1   We use *will be* + -ing form to talk about things
which are fairly certain to happen in the future.
This meaning is almost the same as the present
continuous tense with a future meaning. ▷ 4.5

2   We also use *will be* + -ing form to talk about
actions that will be going on for some time in the
future.

31 (4.5, 4.6)

Charles Dearborn is the managing director of
Ramplus Computers, an international company with
its main offices in London. Mr Dearborn has a busy
life. Describe his schedule for next week. For the
times of arrival and departure use the simple present
form. To describe the other arrangements use the
present continuous form of these verbs: *speak, visit,
open, meet, have, go.*

Example

*On Monday he leaves London at 9.30 and arrives in
Madrid at 12.40. He is speaking at an international
conference.*

Monday	London 9.30 Madrid 12.40
	International conference
Tuesday	Madrid 7.40 Athens 13.55
	Ramplus offices
Wednesday	Athens 8.15 Milan 12.35
	New Ramplus factory
Thursday	Milan 10.10 Strasbourg 11.15
	President of the Common Market
Friday	Strasbourg 10.45 The Hague 11.40
	*Discussions with the Dutch Minister
of Technology*
Saturday	The Hague 9.30 Stockholm 12.25
	Computer show

Activity

Imagine you are the head of a big international
company. You have just met your partner at a party,
and you are telling him/her about a three-day
business trip you are making next week. Think of
some interesting places and important things to do
and tell your partner about them.

32 (4.1–4.7)

Sue and Kate are discussing their holiday plans.
Complete their conversation using *will, 'll, won't, shall*
or *be going to* with the verbs in brackets, or use a
present tense form of the verb. (Usually there is more
than one correct answer.)

Sue Where … you and Ben (go) for your holidays,
Kate?
Kate Morocco. We (spend) ten days in Agadir.
Sue Oh, that (be) nice. When … you (go)?
Kate On Friday night. Our plane (leave) at seven,
and we (arrive) at four in the morning.
Sue You (need) a holiday after that.
Kate Oh, I don't mind night flights. Anyway, we
(enjoy) the sunshine this time next week.
Sue … you (stay) in a hotel?
Kate Yes, a big hotel not far from the beach.
Sue Our holiday (not be) until next month. Jerry and I
(tour) Scotland in the car, we've decided. We (do)
some walking, too. The weather (not be) like Agadir,
of course.
Kate How long … you (go) for?
Sue Two weeks. We haven't been to Scotland
before, so it (be) something different.
Kate … you (take) your caravan?
Sue No, we don't want to take the caravan. We (have
to) find hotels to stay in as we go.
Kate Well, we (be) back from Morocco before you
go.
Sue Have a nice time, Kate.

Activity

Discuss your holiday plans with other people in your
class.

4.8   be to

The American President **is to** visit the Soviet Union later this year.
The two leaders **are to** meet in Moscow.
The Minister travelled to Glasgow, where he **was to** open a factory the following day.

We use *be to* for official arrangements.
We use *be to* mostly in formal written English.

▷   12.6; 31.1 *be to* used for orders

4.9   be about to

I**'m about to** leave for the station. The train leaves in twenty minutes.
I think it**'s** just **about to** start raining.
Robert **was about to** pay for the glass when he noticed a small crack in it.

We use *be about to* to talk about things which are going to happen in the very near future.

4.10   will have + -ed form

Let's go out tonight. ~ All right. I have some work to do, but I**'ll have finished** it by about eight.

Can I have the book back tomorrow, please? Will you have read it by then? ~ No, I **won't**. I **won't have read** all of it until the weekend.

We use *will have* + -ed form (past participle) to talk about something that will be completed at a time in the future.
We often use the verb *finish*.
We often use *by* and (in negative sentences), *till/until*. ▷ 25.5

33 (4.5, 4.8)

These newspaper headlines are all about things in the future. Write the headlines as full sentences using the present continuous tense or *be to*. Sometimes you also need to put in *the, a* or *some*.

Examples

GAS PRICES GOING UP IN NOVEMBER
Gas prices are going up in November.

NEW LONDON CONFERENCE CENTRE TO OPEN SOON
A new London conference centre is to open soon.

1 WORLD LEADERS TO MEET NEXT MONTH
2 DOCK STRIKE STARTING TOMORROW
3 PRIME MINISTER TO VISIT GREECE IN AUGUST
4 QUEEN LEAVING FOR AUSTRALIA TOMORROW
5 CHINESE TOURISTS ARRIVING IN BRITAIN NEXT SATURDAY
6 SHOE FACTORY TO CLOSE
7 EUROPEAN GAMES TO TAKE PLACE NEXT YEAR
8 THREE NEW PLAYERS JOINING LIVERPOOL

Activity

Try to think of news stories that you have heard recently about things arranged to happen in the future. Write two sentences like those in the exercises but about real events.

34 (4.1, 4.7, 4.10)

Madame Zaza is a fortune teller. She's telling Julie what her life will be like. Complete the sentences using *will, will be* or *will have* and a form of the verb in brackets.

1 You (be) on holiday soon. In two weeks from now you (lie) on a beach.
2 You (have) a good life, and you (live) a long time.
3 Your personality is changing all the time. In ten years time you (change) completely.
4 At some time in your life you (have) a bad accident, but you (not die).
5 You (marry) when you are twenty-three.
6 In twenty years from now you (live) on the other side of the world. By that time you (leave) your husband.
7 You (be) rich. When you are thirty-five, you (already make) a lot of money.
8 At this time of your life you (work) very hard. Your life (be) very exciting.

Activity

Imagine you are visiting Madame Zaza. Write three predictions that you would like to hear from her. Use *will, will be* and *will have*.

5 Verbs: *be, have* and *do*

5.1 **be, have** and **do** used as auxiliary verbs

1   I**'m** writing a letter.
    We**'ve** spent a lot of money.

2   I**'m not** working today.
    The programme **hasn't** started yet.
    You **didn't** send me a postcard.

3   **Are** you waiting for someone?
    Have you filled in the form?
    Does Alison take sugar?

4a Emma is coming, **isn't** she? ~ Yes, she **is**.
    Peter plays golf, **doesn't** he? ~ No, he **doesn't**.

b   The letter has come but the money **hasn't**.
    The passengers got out and so **did** the driver.

c   You *are* doing well.
    I *do* like that colour.

We use *be, have* and *do* as auxiliary verbs (helping verbs). Auxiliary verbs help to form tenses.

1   In positive statements we use *be* and *have* to form tenses.

    Note In two tenses only—the simple present and the simple past—we do not use an auxiliary, e.g. *I write a letter every week. We spent ten pounds.*

2   In the negative we use *be, have* or *do* (or a modal verb ▷ 7.1) + *n't/not*. ▷ 8.1

3   In questions we use *be, have* or *do* (or a modal verb) before the subject. ▷ 8.2

4   We also use an auxiliary verb (or modal verb)
a   in question tags ▷ 8.5 and in short answers ▷ 8.4
b   in short additions to statements ▷ 9.1
c   in the emphatic form ▷ 28.2

5.2 Uses of **be**

1   Jane **is** ill. She **wasn't** at school today. She**'s been** in bed since last night.

2   She **wasn't** feeling very well yesterday, but she**'s eating** a little now.

3   This medicine **is** best **taken** after meals. It must **be taken** three times a day.

We use *be*

1   with a complement or adverb phrase ▷ 1.1; 2.1; 3.1

2   as an auxiliary verb (helping verb) in continuous tenses ▷ 2.3; 3.7, 8, 10; 7.14

3   as an auxiliary verb in the passive ▷ 10

For *be to* ▷ 4.8; 31.1

35   (5.1)

A reporter has written a newspaper article about a boy who writes computer games programmes. Put in *is, are, was, were, has, have, had, do, does* or *did.* Sometimes you need a negative form with *n't.*

COMPUTER WONDER-BOY

Mr and Mrs Stokes ... sitting in the garden of their Bristol home when I arrived to interview them and their fourteen-year-old son Carl. But Carl ... working upstairs. 'He ... often leave his room,' his mother explained.

At the moment Carl ... working on a programme for a new computer game. Computers ... become his whole life. In the last year Carl ... earned over £25,000 from writing programmes. A lot of other people ... trying to do the same nowadays, but not many of them ... done as well as Carl.

'When ... he buy the computer?' I wondered. 'We bought it for him eighteen months ago for his birthday,' said Mr Stokes. 'We ... know what we ... doing. Our son ... changed. Eighteen months ago he ... seen a computer. Now he ... talk about anything else. And we ... understand a thing about computers.' 'And ... you think it's good for him?' was my next question. 'No, we .... We worry about him,' said Mrs Stokes. 'He ... have any other interests now. And he ... done any work for his school exams. It's often quite a job to make him go to school at all.'

Carl's parents ... understand computers, but Carl certainly ... . 'I love computers,' he said. 'I soon got tired of playing games, though. I like writing programmes much better. I've got three computers now. I bought two more. I ... earn much at first, but now I .... My parents make me put most of it in the bank.'

Activity

Write a similar short article about a twelve-year-old girl from Coventry called Kerry Pike who writes and sings pop songs and plays the guitar. She earns a lot of money from records and concerts.

5.3   it + be and there + be

it + be

It's after one, isn't it? ~
Yes, **it is**. **It's** quarter past.
(= The time is after one o'clock.)

It wasn't expensive to go to London.
(= The fare wasn't expensive.)

Has it been very wet here?
(= Has the weather been very wet?)

It's a huge stadium, but **it'll be** full tonight.
(= The stadium will be full.)

Form

After *it* the verb is always singular, e.g. *it's*.

Use

We use *it* instead of a noun phrase, e.g. *the time, the fare, the weather*.

▷   20.2 uses of *it*

there + be

There's no time for a meal. ~ No, **there isn't**.
(= No time exists . . . /We have no time . . .)

There weren't any trains on Sundays.
(= Trains didn't run on Sundays.)

Has there been an accident? ~ Yes, **there has**.
(= Has an accident happened?)

There'll be a big crowd here tonight.
(= A big crowd will come tonight.)

Form

If the noun after *there + be* is plural, then the verb is plural too, e.g. *there weren't any trains*.

Use

We use *there + be* to say that something exists. After *there + be* we use a noun phrase, e.g. *no time*, *any trains*, *a storm*, but not usually a noun with *the*.

▷   28.6 emphatic use of *there*

5.4   been to and gone to

1   Have you ever **been to** America? ~
Yes, I went to New York two years ago.

2   Is Judy in America? ~
Yes, she's **gone to** Los Angeles. She'll be back next week.

We sometimes use the past participle of *be* instead of the past participle of *go*.

1   *been to* = gone somewhere and now come back

2   *gone to* = gone somewhere and still there

36 (5.3)

Say what today's weather has been like and what the
forecast is for tomorrow.

Example

*It has been cold in Scotland today. It will be cold again
tomorrow, and there will be snow on the hills.*

TODAY

TOMORROW

Activity

Write one or more sentences describing the weather
where you are. Use *It's* ... and *There's* ...

5.5   Uses of **have**

Auxiliary verb

1   **Have** you **sold** your car? ~
Yes, it **had done** 100,000 miles, you know.

have (got)

2   You **had** a telephone last year. ~
Yes, but we **haven't got** one now.

have (got) to

3   **Have** you **got to** clean the stairs? ~
Yes, we **have to** wash the hall floor, too.

Normal verb

4   **I'm having** a sandwich.
I think **I'll** just **have** a cup of tea.

5   **Are** you **having** a good holiday?
We've **had** some lovely weather lately, haven't
we?

6   Did you **have a look** at the pictures?
The children **didn't have a ride** on the donkey.

1   *have* as an auxiliary verb (helping verb) in perfect tenses. ▷ 3.4, 6, 8, 10; 4.10; 5.1; 7.15

2   *have* (*got*) meaning *own* or *possess*. ▷ 2.2; 3.2; 5.6

3   *have* (*got*) *to* meaning the same as *must*. ▷ 7.4

have as a normal verb with other meanings, e.g.

4   *eat* or *drink* ▷ 31.1 ordering food; 33.1 offering food

5   something happening to us, something that we experience

6   *have a look* = look (verb); *have a ride* = ride (verb) etc.

Note The normal verb *have* can have a continuous form (*Are you having . . .?*) and we form questions and negatives with *do* (*Did you have . . .?*)

▷   10.8 *have something done*

5.6   **have** in American English

1   GB: **Have** you **got** a ticket to London? ~
Yes, I **have**. But my friend **hasn't got** one.

2   USA: **Do** you **have** a ticket to New York? ~
Yes, I **do**. But my friend **doesn't have** one.

1   *have got* is more usual in British English (but we also use *have* especially in the past tense ▷ 3.2).

2   *have* is more usual in American English. Questions, negatives and short answers are with *do*.

▷   7.4 *have* (*got*) *to*

5.7   Uses of **do**

Auxiliary verb

1   What **does** this word mean? ~ I **don't** know.
Did you learn English at school? ~ Yes, I **did**.

2   **Don't** shout. I can hear you all right.

Normal verb

3   What do you **do** in your free time?
What are you **doing** now?
I **did** something interesting yesterday.
What did you **do**?

4   We're **doing** a few odd jobs.
Mike's **done** some wallpapering.

1   As an auxiliary verb (helping verb) in the simple present and simple past tenses. ▷ 2.4; 3.3

2   As an auxiliary verb with the negative imperative. And ▷ 6.1

3   As a normal verb, to talk about an action when we do not know or do not say what the action is.

4   As a normal verb meaning e.g. *work at, finish.* ▷ 15.4

Note We use the auxiliary verb *do* with the normal verb *do* in the simple present and simple past tenses, e.g. *What do you do? What did you do?*

37 (5.5)

It's lunch time. Mike is sitting in the canteen. Paul has just joined him. Complete the conversation using a form of *have*, e.g. *had, are having*. You may need to use negative or question forms.

Paul Hello, Mike. ... you ... a nice time in France?
Mike Hello, Paul. Yes, we did, thanks. We ... very good weather, but we still ... a good time.
Paul ... you already ... your lunch?
Mike Yes, I was early today. And I only ... a sandwich.
Paul You can ... one of my sausages if you like.
Mike No, thanks. I ... only ... light lunches this week. I'm trying to lose weight.
Paul You haven't got anything to worry about.
Mike You're going camping in Wales next week, aren't you?
Paul That's right.
Mike I hope you ... nice weather.
Paul So do I. Did you know Mark and Jane are in Benidorm at the moment? We ... a postcard from them on Friday. They say they ... a marvellous time.
Mike I took some photos in France. You can ... a look at them some time if you like.
Paul Okay.
Mike Come round to our house tonight, and we can ... a talk.

Activity

Act out the conversation with a partner. Then talk to your partner about *your* last holiday.

38 (5.7)

Sue is visiting her cousin Cathy. They're going for a walk in the town where Cathy lives. Complete the conversation using *do, don't, does, doesn't, did, didn't, doing* or *done*.

Cathy Let's go this way past the sports centre.
Sue Oh. I ... know there was a sports centre here. It looks new. When ... it open?
Cathy A few months ago. Since your last visit, anyway. It's very good. You can ... all kinds of sport.
Sue ... you use the centre a lot?
Cathy Quite a lot, yes. There are courses in different sports. I'm ... a tennis course this term. I ... judo last term.
Sue Judo? That's for boys, isn't it?
Cathy ... be silly. Lots of girls ... it as well as boys. I've ... it for ages.
Sue How much ... it cost to go in?
Cathy You have to pay every year to be a member. But it ... cost very much, luckily. You can go in as my guest if you want to.
Sue Oh, good.
Cathy What about a game of badminton some time?
Sue I ... like badminton much. ... they have table tennis?
Cathy Yes, of course. We can have a game this evening.

Activity

Tell a partner either about the subjects you are doing or about your spare-time activities. Mention things you did in the past as well.

6 The imperative and *let's*

6.1 The imperative

1 **Come** here, please, David.
  Go and **stand** over there, Jane.
2 **Help** me with these cases, you two.
3 **Don't drop** the glass.
4 **Do** be careful.
5 **Have** a drink. ~
  Not for me, thanks. But **you have** one.
6 **Go** straight ahead here and then **turn** right at the crossroads.

Form

1 The imperative is the base form of the verb.
2 We use the same form to talk to two or more people.
3 We use *don't* in the negative.
4 We use *do* for emphasis. ▷ 28.2
5 We sometimes use *you* before the imperative.

Use

We use the imperative

1,2 to give orders ▷ 31.1
3,4 to give warnings ▷ 31.7
  5 for informal offers or invitations ▷ 33.1,2
  6 to tell someone how to do something ▷ 31.6

▷ 8.5 question tags; 12.6 reporting orders

6.2 *let's*

1 **Let's** sit down for a minute.
2 Oh, **don't let's** stop/**let's not** stop now.
3 **Do let's** finish the job first.

Form

1 After *let's* we use the base form of the verb.
2 We use *don't let's* or *let's not* in the negative.
3 We use *do* for emphasis. ▷ 28.2

Use

We use *let's* to make suggestions. ▷ 31.4

▷ 8.5 question tags; 33.1 *let me*

7 Modal verbs

7.1 Introduction to modal verbs

1a We **can** find the way all right.
 b I **must** clean this floor.
 c The key **may** be in the drawer.
2 **Can** you drive a car? ~
    Yes, I **could** drive when I was seventeen.
3a I **can't** play the guitar. ~
    But you said yesterday you **could** play.
 b Alan **won't** be at the meeting tonight. ~
    But he told me he **would** be there.
4a It isn't far. We **could** walk, **couldn't** we?
 b A picnic **would** be nice. ~ Yes, it **would**.
 c The rain **might** stop soon. On the other hand it
    might not.
 d Why don't we get a taxi? ~
    Yes, I think we ***should*** get one.
5a It's a holiday tomorrow. You**'ll be able to** have a
    rest.
 b When the manager was away, Mr Fisher **was
    allowed to** use his office.
 c I**'ll have to** take these library books back
    tomorrow.

Form

1 The modal verbs are *can, could, may, might, will,
    would, shall, should, ought to, must, need, dare.*
    A modal verb always has the same form. There is
    no *-s* ending, no -ing form and no -ed form. But
    ▷ 7.13 *dare*
    After a modal verb we use the infinitive without *to*,
    e.g. *find, clean, be.*
2 Modal verbs (and auxiliary verbs ▷ 5.1) come
    before the subject in questions.
3 Modal verbs (and auxiliary verbs) have *n't* or *not*
    after them in the negative.
4 We also use a modal verb (or auxiliary verb)
a in question tags ▷ 8.5
b in short answers ▷ 8.4
c in short additions to statements ▷ 9.1
d in the emphatic form ▷ 28.2

Present, past and future

2 The past form of *can* is *could.*
3 In reported speech *can, will, may* and *shall*
    change to *could, would, might* and *should.* ▷ 12.3
4 But *could, would, might* and *should* also have their
    own meanings. We use them to talk about the
    present and the future too.
5 To talk about ability, permission and necessity in
    the past or the future, we can use *be able to, be
    allowed to* and *have (got) to.* ▷ 7.16

Use

1 We use modal verbs to talk about, for example,
a someone's ability to do an action ▷ 7.2
b an action that is necessary ▷ 7.4
c a situation that is possible ▷ 7.7

7.2 Ability: **can, could, be able to**

1 I **can** swim.
   Sarah **could** play the piano when she was very
   young.
   If we go to town, I**'ll be able to** do some shopping.
   Jim **can't** drive.
   Can your sister dance? ~ Yes, she **can**.

2 The children fell into the water, but luckily they
   were able to hold on to the boat.
   I **was able to** swim back and get help.

3 **Could** you lift the cupboard? ~
   No, I **couldn't**. It was too heavy.
   Were you able to paint the windows? ~
   No, I **wasn't**. It rained all day.

4 We **could see** a man on the roof.
   I **could hear** the traffic on the main road.

5 I **couldn't** do your job. I'm not clever enough.

Use

1 We use *can* and *could* to talk about ability or
   opportunity.

2 We use *was/were able to* to talk about ability or
   opportunity + action in the past. *I was able to
   swim back* means that I really did swim back.
   We do not use *could* to talk about a past action
   which really happened.

3 We can use both *could* and *was/were able to* in
   questions and negative sentences. (But *Could
   you . . . ?* is often a request. ▷ 31.2)

4 We can use *can* and *could* with verbs of
   perception, e.g. *see, hear. could see* = saw.

5 We can use *could* to talk about ability in a situation
   which we are imagining. Here *could* = would be
   able to. For *would* ▷ 7.9.

▷ 7.8 possibility: *could*; 7.16 *be able to*

Form

	Positive	Negative
Present	**can**	**can't/cannot**
	am/are/is able to	**am not/aren't/isn't able to**
Past	**could**	**couldn't/could not**
	was/were able to	**wasn't/weren't able to**
Future	**will be able to**	**won't be able to**

Short answers with **can** *and* **could**

Yes, I/you/he/we/they **can**.   Yes, I/you/he/we/they **could**.
No, I/you/he/we/they **can't**.   No, I/you/he/we/they **couldn't**.

39 (7.2)

Six weeks ago a man and his wife were flying over the jungle when their plane came down in the trees. Last week their bodies were found about twenty miles from where the plane crashed. The woman had written a diary. Read the diary below and say what happened to the two people. Use *could, couldn't* and *was/were able to*.

Example

Thursday
We were able to climb down from the plane. We couldn't think clearly because we were so shocked.

Thursday	Climbed down from plane. Too shocked to think clearly.
Friday	Too hot to sleep. Heard the noise of insects all night.
Saturday	Got water from a stream. Saw some smoke from the south.
Sunday	Too wet to travel. Kept dry.
Monday	Walked several miles along the bank of a river. River too wide to cross.
Tuesday	Killed and ate a monkey. Heard a plane somewhere above us.
Wednesday	Both too ill to walk. Slept for several hours.

Activity

The bodies of the two people were found in a cave. The diary and a bottle half full of water were lying on the ground about fifty metres from the cave. What do you think happened after the woman stopped writing the diary?

40 (7.2)

The Psycho-Clinic in London helps people with their problems. Below is an advertisement for the clinic. Complete the sentences using *can, could, was/were able to, 'll be able to* or their negative forms. (Sometimes more than one answer is correct.)

PSYCHO-CLINIC
The answer to your problems

1 *Rosemary, Manchester*
Psycho-Clinic is wonderful. My problem was that I . . . fly. I was afraid of aeroplanes. As soon as my course was over, I . . . take a flight to the Canary Islands! I had a super holiday. Now I . . . fly where I like. Next summer I . . . go to the West Indies. (I . . . do that every year because I haven't enough money.) I . . . thank Psycho-Clinic enough.

2 *Bernard, Southampton*
Now at last I . . . stand up in front of a group of people! From now on my life will be different. I . . . do my job much better in future. I often have to give talks to sales people at work. I just . . . avoid it. In the old days I . . . sleep for a week before a talk. I . . . hardly do my work. But now I . . . give a talk without feeling too nervous. Last week I . . . get a good night's sleep before talking to a group of twenty people the next day. It's marvellous!

3 *Margaret, Cornwall*
Yesterday someone asked me for my telephone number, and for the first time in my life I . . . give the number without looking in my book. Before I went to Psycho-Clinic I always forgot numbers and names. I . . . remember them at all. Now, thanks to Psycho-Clinic, I . . . remember much more. If I see someone in the street tomorrow, I won't need to hide—I . . . stop and say hello to them.

4 *Eugene, Maryland, USA*
I didn't like crowds of people. I . . . go to the theatre or the cinema. I love horse racing, and I . . . go to the races. But the people at Psycho-Clinic . . . stop me feeling afraid. Now I . . . do all those things. Yesterday I . . . stand in a crowd at a baseball game. I . . . lead a normal life now. There's an interesting show at the local theatre next week, and I . . . see it.

Activity

Imagine that you were once a very shy person. You didn't like meeting people and talking to them. Then you went to Psycho-Clinic. Write a few sentences about what the clinic has done for you.

7.3   Permission: **can, may, be allowed to**

1   People **can** drive/**may** drive/**are allowed to** drive
a car in Britain when they're seventeen.
People **can't** drive/**may not** drive/**are not allowed
to** drive a car before they're seventeen.
My brother is sixteen. He**'ll be allowed to** drive a
car soon.
Were you **allowed to** look round the church
yesterday? ~ Yes, we **were**, but we **weren't
allowed to** take any photos.

2   **Can** I ride your bicycle, please, Jane? ~
Of course you **can**.
May I use your telephone, please, Mr Taylor? ~
Certainly you **may**.

Use

1   We use *can, may* and *be allowed to* (▷ 7.16) to
talk about permission. *may* is rather formal.

2   We use *can* or *may* to ask permission. ▷ 31.3

Form

	Positive	Negative
Present	**can**	**can't/cannot**
	may	**may not**
	am/are/is allowed to	**am not/aren't/isn't allowed to**
Past	**was/were allowed to**	**wasn't/weren't allowed to**
Future	**will be allowed to**	**won't be allowed to**

We use short answers with *can/can't* (▷ 7.2) and
with *may* (▷ 7.7).

7.4   Necessity: **must, have (got) to, needn't, mustn't**

Necessity

1   I'm late. I **must** hurry.
You **must** tell me the truth.
I**'ve got to**/I **have to** go to work today.
Martin **has got to** see/**has to** see the doctor.
We **had to** wait half an hour for the bus.
I**'ll have to** go and get some eggs.

No necessity

2   **Have** we **got to** pay/**Do** we **have to** pay now? ~
No, we **haven't/don't**.
You **haven't got to** answer/You **don't have to**
answer the letter.
We **didn't have to** book a table.

3   I **needn't** wash this shirt. It's clean.
You **needn't** come if you don't want to.

Not allowed

4   You **mustn't** open other people's letters.
I **mustn't** forget my key.

Form

	Positive	Negative
Present		**needn't/need not**
	must	**mustn't/must not** ▷ 7.5
	have/has to	**don't/doesn't have to**
	have/has got to	**haven't/hasn't got to**
Past	**had to**	**didn't have to**
Future	**will have to**	**won't have to**

Use

1   Necessity means that you cannot avoid doing
something. *You must buy a ticket* = You cannot
go without a ticket.
We use *must* and *have (got) to* to talk about
necessity.
must expresses the authority or feelings of the
speaker, and *have (got) to* (▷ 7.16) refers to the
authority of another person or to something the
speaker cannot control. ▷ 31.1 orders

2   We use the negative forms of *have (got) to* when
there is no necessity.

3   We can also use *needn't* when there is no
necessity.
Note We also use the normal verb *need* with *to*,
e.g. *Do we need to pay now? We didn't need to
book a table.* The modal verb and the full verb
have the same meaning.

4   We use *mustn't* when we are not allowed to do
something. *You mustn't forget* = Don't forget.

Short answers with **must, needn't** *and* **mustn't**
Yes, I/you/he/we/they **must**.
No, I/you/he/we/they **needn't**.
No, I/you/he/we/they **mustn't**. ▷ 7.5

41 (7.3, 7.4)

Complete this article about learning to drive in Britain. Put in a positive or negative form of *be allowed to* or *have to*.

In Britain you … drive a car when you're seventeen. You … get a special two-year driving licence before you can start. When you're learning, someone with a full licence always … be in the car with you because you … take the car on the road alone. You … go to a driving school — a friend can teach you. The person with you … take money for the lesson unless he's got a teacher's licence.

Before you … have a full licence, you … take a driving test. You can take a test in your own car, but it … be fit for the road. In the test you … drive round for about half an hour and then answer a few questions. If you don't pass the test, you … take it again a few weeks later if you want to. In 1970 a woman passed her fortieth test after 212 driving lessons! When you've passed your test, you … take it again, and you … go on driving as long as you like, provided you are fit. Britain's oldest driver was a Norfolk man who drove in 1974 at the age of 100.

Before 1904 everyone … drive, even children. Then from 1904 motorists … have a licence. But they … take a test until 1935. In the early days of motoring, before 1878, cars … go faster than four miles an hour, and someone … walk in front of the car with a red flag.

Activity

Write a few sentences about learning to drive in your country.

42 (7.3, 7.4)

Here are some rules and information for campers at the Riverside Camping Centre.

> You must pay on arrival.
> You musn't light fires.
> You musn't play ball games.
> You must leave before ten o'clock in the morning.
> You needn't worry about food—there's a shop at the Centre.

When Paul and Diane arrived at the camp site, they looked at the rules. What did Paul and Diane say?

Example: We have to pay on arrival.

1 We aren't …   2 …   3 …   4 …

When they got home, Paul and Diane told their friends Mike and Wendy about the camp site.

Example: We had to pay on arrival.

5 …   6 …   7 …   8 …

Mike and Wendy decided to stay at the camp site during their next holiday. They talked about it before they went.

Example: We'll have to pay on arrival.

9 …   10 …   11 …   12 …

Activity

Talk to the other members of the class about rules at schools and colleges in your country. When do students have to be there? Are there some things they aren't allowed to bring into class? etc. If you've left school, say what the rules were when you were there.

43 (7.4)

Do you know what these signs mean? Use *You must* … and *You mustn't* … with these words: *turn round, go straight on, overtake, put some money in, smoke, stop, take photos, turn left, turn right, go faster than.*

Examples

You must put some money in.

You mustn't turn left.

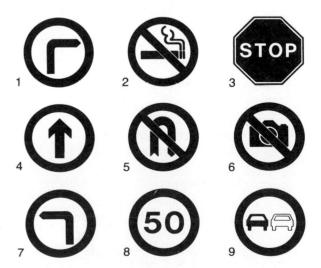

Activity

Can you think of any other signs that say what you must or mustn't do? Describe a sign to your partner and ask him/her what it means.

7.5 **needn't** or **mustn't**?

1a The car's clean. I **needn't** wash it this week.
b It isn't raining. You **needn't** take a coat.
2a The baby's asleep. We **mustn't** make a noise.
b Your father's very ill. He **mustn't** get up.

needn't and *mustn't* have different meanings. It is important to know the difference between them, or there can be misunderstandings.

1 We use *needn't* when there is no necessity to do something, but we can do it if we want to.
2 We use *mustn't* when we are not allowed to do something, or when there is a necessity not to do it.

7.6 Obligation: **ought to, should**

You're not fit. You **ought to** walk more.
You **should** walk more.
I **oughtn't to** eat cakes.
I **shouldn't** eat cakes.
Ought Paul **to** see a doctor? ~
Yes, I think he **ought (to)**.
Should he see a doctor? ~ Yes, I think he **should**.

Form

Positive   Negative
ought to   oughtn't to/ought not to
should   shouldn't/should not

Short answers

Yes, I/you/he/we/they **ought (to)**.
No, I/you/he/we/they **oughtn't (to)**.
Yes, I/you/he/we/they **should**.
No, I/you/he/we/they **shouldn't**.

Use

Obligation means that something is the right thing to do. *You ought to walk* = Walking is the right thing for you to do.
We use *ought to* and *should* to express obligation or to give advice. ▷ 31.5
There is little difference between *ought to* and *should*, but *ought to* is sometimes a little stronger than *should*.

▷ 7.12 other uses of *should*; 35.1, 2 approving and blaming

7.7 Possibility: **may, might**

1 The keys **may** be/**might** be in one of those drawers.
2 Amanda **may not/might not** come tomorrow.
3 Do you think it'll snow? ~ Yes, it **may/might**.

Form

Positive Negative
may   may not
might   might not/mightn't

Short answers
Yes, I/you/he/we/they **may**.
No, I/you/he/we/they **may not**.
Yes, I/you/he/we/they **might**.
No, I/you/he/we/they **might not/mightn't**.

Use

We use *may* and *might* to talk about
1 possibility in the present
2 possibility in the future
There is little difference between *may* and *might*, but a speaker who uses *might* is a little less sure.
3 To ask questions, we use *Do you think . . . ?* and *will*.

▷ 7.15 possibility in the past; 30.5 being sure and unsure; 32.2 intentions

44 (7.4, 7.5)

Helen isn't very well today. She's in bed. She's been sick, and she's quite hot. The doctor has come to see her. Complete what the doctor says. Put in *must, mustn't* or *needn't.*

Doctor Well, I'm going to give you some medicine. You … take it four times a day before meals. And go on taking it even if you feel better. You … stop taking it until you've finished the bottle. You … drink all of it. Now, you … stay in bed today. It's the best place for you at the moment. You can get up tomorrow if you like. You … stay in bed all the time when you start to feel better. But you … go outside this week. It's too cold. And you really … do any work at all. You need absolute rest. You … just relax for a few days. You can eat a little if you like, but you … if you don't want to. But don't forget to keep drinking. You … drink as much water as you can. You'll probably be all right again next week, so you … call me again unless you feel worse. But I'm sure the worst is over.

Activity

Imagine that your partner has a bad cold. What would you recommend him/her to do?

---

45 (7.6, 7.7)

The picture is from a booklet about safety in the home. Say what's wrong and what the dangers are. Use *ought to* and *might.*

Example

There oughtn't to be a cloth on the table. The baby might pull it off.

Activity

Imagine that tomorrow you plan to go on a 15-mile walk in the country with three or four other people in your class. Discuss with them what you ought to wear and what you ought to take with you. Give reasons for your suggestions.

Ex There's a cloth on the table. There's a danger that the baby will pull it off.
1   The pills aren't in a safe place. There's a danger that the baby will eat them.
2   There's a hole in the rug. There's a danger that someone will fall over.
3   The towel is over the cooker. There's a danger that it will catch fire.
4   The drawer isn't shut. There's a danger that it will fall out.
5   There's some broken glass on the floor. There's a danger that someone will step on it.
6   There isn't a plug on the kettle. There's a danger that someone will get an electric shock.

7.8   Possibility: **could**

1   The keys **could** be in one of those drawers.
2   We **could** go out later, **couldn't** we? ~
Yes, why not?

Form

Positive   **could**
Negative   **couldn't/could not**

For short answers ▷ 7.2

Use

We use *could* to talk about

1   possibility in the present (*could* is rather less sure than *may* or *might* ▷ 7.7)
2   possibility in the future, especially in suggestions ▷ 31.4

For the use of *could* to talk about past ability or about a situation which we are imagining ▷ 7.2

▷   7.15 possibility in the past; 31.2 requests

7.9   Imagining situations: **would**

A holiday in the Bahamas **would** be nice. ~
Yes it **would**. I**'d** certainly enjoy a holiday right now.
How much **would** it cost? ~
I don't know, but it **wouldn't** be cheap.

Form

would in all persons.

Short forms
'd = would   **wouldn't** = would not

Short answers
Yes, I/you/he/we/they **would**.
No, I/you/he/we/they **wouldn't**.

Use

We use *would* to talk about a situation which we are imagining (= thinking about) but which is not really happening.

▷   7.12 other uses; 16.2 *would like*; 30.8 having ideas

7.10   Certainty: **will, must, can't**

He left half an hour ago, so he**'ll** be home by now.
(= he is certainly home by now)
No one's answering the phone. They **must** be out.
(= They are certainly out.)
This story **can't** be true.
(= It is certainly untrue.)

We use *will*, *must* and *can't* to say that something is logically certain.

▷   30.5 being sure and unsure

46 (7.9)

Sadie is doing a test to find out what kind of personality she has. She has to answer a lot of questions about what she would do in different situations. Here are some of the questions with Sadie's answers. Say what Sadie *would* and *wouldn't* do.

Example

She would go to the party. She wouldn't go to the cinema.

100 You want to go out one evening. You decide to go to a cinema. Then a friend invites you to a party. Where would you go?

 ☐ to the cinema   ☑ to the party

101 You are walking through a forest on a warm day when you come to a wide river. You can either swim the fifty metres across the river or walk an extra kilometre to the nearest bridge. Which would you do?

 ☐ swim   ☑ walk

102 You find a £10 note in the street. What would you do with it?

 ☑ keep it   ☐ take it to the police

103 You are on a bus. There are two people sitting and talking in front of you. You don't know them. You hear your name mentioned in the conversation. What would you do?

 ☑ listen   ☐ move to another seat

104 You have to choose between two jobs. One is interesting but not well paid. The other is boring but well paid. Which would you choose?

 ☐ the interesting job   ☑ the well paid job

105 You are travelling on a plane to England. The man sitting next to you offers you £5,000 to take a small packet through Customs for him. What would you say?

 ☐ yes   ☑ no

106 You are driving along a country road when you see a car by the side of the road. The driver is standing and waving at you. He wants you to stop. What would you do?

 ☐ stop   ☑ drive on

Activity A

Say what *you* would do in these situations.

Activity B

There's a television programme in Britain called 'Jim'll Fix It'. A man called Jimmy Savile appears on the programme. People write to him and say what they would like to do but have never been able to do. People want to parachute from aeroplanes, sing in a pop group, play tennis at Wimbledon, and so on. Jim fixes it so that they can do these things, and we see their wishes coming true on television. Imagine that it's your turn to do what you like. What would you do?

---

47 (7.8, 7.10)

Milena and Ahmed are students of English. They're doing this crossword. Milena is reading out the clues, and Ahmed is suggesting possible answers.

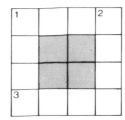

Across

1 You write with it.
4 Past tense of 'be'.
6 It carries things by road.

Down

1 Person learning something.
2 Opposite of 'old'.
3 You pay to ride through the streets in it.
5 Planes travel in it.

Complete their conversations about each clue. Write the sentences with *It could ...* , *It can't ...* and *It must ...* . Here are the words that Ahmed suggests: *bus, taxi, new, young, pen, pencil, sky, air, student, pupil, van, lorry, was, were.*

Example

Milena *One across. You write with it.*
Ahmed *It could be 'pen' or 'pencil'.*
Milena *It can't be 'pencil'. It must be 'pen'.*

1 **Milena** Four across. Past tense of 'be'.
  Ahmed It could be ... .
  Milena It can't ... . It ... .

Go on.

Activity

Do this crossword with a partner. Discuss the possible answers together.

Across

1 Give information.
3 A number.

Down

1 It's bigger than a village.
2 Like very much.

7.11   Uses of **will** and **shall**

will

Future	Juliet **will** be 20 next month.	▷ 4.1
Deciding	I think I**'ll** buy it.	▷ 4.1
Requests	**Will** you shut the window, please?	▷ 31.2
Invitations	**Will** you/**Won't** you sit down?	▷ 33.2
Promises	I **will** write, I promise.	▷ 32.5
Refusing	The car **won't** start. What's wrong with it?	▷ 32.4
Certainty	I sent the parcel last week, so they**'ll** have it by now.	▷ 7.10
Strict orders	You**'ll** do as I tell you.	▷ 31.1

shall

Suggestions	**Shall** we go out this evening?	▷ 31.4
Offering	**Shall** I carry your bags for you?	▷ 33.1
Promises	You **shall** have the goods by next week.	▷ 32.5
Future with I/we	I **shall** be on holiday in July.	▷ 4.2

7.12   Uses of **would** and **should**

would

Imagining situations	It **would** be nice to have a party here one weekend.	▷ 7.9
	If I had a lot of money, I**'d** travel round the world.	▷ 11.1
Wishing	I**'d** like to meet your brother.	
	I wish this rain **would** stop.	▷ 34.5
Requests	**Would** you write your address here, please?	▷ 31.2
Invitations	**Would** you like to come to dinner?	▷ 33.2
Preferences	I**'d** rather have tea than coffee.	▷ 34.6
Reporting **will**	She said she **would** come tomorrow.	▷ 12.3

should

Obligation	We **should** help other people.	▷ 7.6
Advice	I think you **should** go by air. It's much quicker.	▷ 31.5
In if-clauses	If you **should** be late, I'll wait for you.	▷ 11.2

Exercises

48 (7.1–7.12)

Adam, Lisa, Don and Melanie are students. They were on their way to visit some friends last week in Adam's car when it broke down. Complete the conversation by putting in one of the following: *can, can't, could, must, mustn't, needn't, ought to, should, might, 'll, will, won't, shall, would.* (Sometimes more than one answer is correct.)

Lisa What's the matter? Why have you stopped?
Adam There's something wrong. It isn't going properly.
Don Let's have a look.
Lisa We … be out of petrol, I suppose.
Adam We … be out of petrol. We only got some half an hour ago.
Lisa Well, if there is something wrong, … you put it right, do you think?
Adam Give me a chance. I don't know what the trouble is yet.
Melanie Look at this steam. The engine … be too hot.
Don Don't take the cap off the radiator. You … do that. You … get boiling water all over you.
Adam If it's too hot, we … have to wait until it cools down.
Lisa And how long … that take?
Don We … wait about half an hour before we go on.
Melanie I suppose there … be something else wrong with it.
Lisa We passed a garage about a mile back. I suppose they … come and have a look at it if we ask them.
Adam The car … be all right. Our local garage has just serviced it. I paid £30 for a full service.
Don You … worry. I'm sure it's just got too hot. Let's wait a bit.
Lisa We … be late now, I expect.
Melanie There's some coffee in the back of the car. … we have some while we're waiting? There are some sandwiches, too.
Don I'm starving. I … have something to eat.
Melanie … you like a sandwich, Lisa?
Lisa No, thanks. I … eat bread. I'm on a diet.
Adam We … phone Matthew if we're going to be late.
Don We … be very late, I don't think.
Melanie You … buy a new car, Adam.
Adam Well, it … be nice if I had the money. But I'm afraid we … have to put up with this old thing for a little longer.

Activity A

Act out the conversation in groups of four.

Activity B

Work in groups of four again. Imagine that you are about to go on a 300-mile car journey along a motorway. Discuss what to do about food on the journey.

7.13   dare

1   **Dare** you climb the ladder? ~ No, I **daren't**.
    I **daren't** go near the dog.
    The guests **dared not** complain.

2   **Do** you **dare (to)** climb the ladder? ~ No, I **don't**.
    I **don't dare (to)** go near the dog.
    The guests **didn't dare (to)** complain.

Form

1   We can use *dare/dared* as a modal verb.
    We use the infinitive without *to* after the modal verb.

2   We can use *dare* as a normal verb with *do/did*.
    We use the infinitive with or without *to* after the normal verb.

Use

dare means not to be afraid to do something.
We use *dare* mostly in questions and negative sentences.

7.14   Modal verbs + **be** + -ing form

Obligation
Why are you sitting here watching television?
You **ought to be doing/should be doing** some work.

Possibility
Elaine **may be coming/might be coming** to tea tomorrow.

Certainty
What's that noise? ~ It's Mr Greaves. He **must be repairing** his motorbike.

Imagining
I'm glad it's a holiday. I**'d be working** if it wasn't.

We can use a modal verb + *be* + -ing form to talk about obligation, possibility, etc.

▷   4.7 *will be* + -ing form

7.15   Modal verbs + **have** + -ed form

Necessity
Not many people came to the party—we **needn't have bought** so much food. (= It was not necessary to buy so much food, but we had bought it.)

Obligation
Peter and Susan didn't come. They **ought to have told/should have told** us. (= They had an obligation to tell us, but they didn't tell us.)

Possibility
They **may have forgotten/might have forgotten** about it. (= It is possible that they forgot about it.)

But Susan mentioned the party yesterday. She **couldn't have forgotten** about it. (= It isn't possible that she forgot about it.)

Imagining
It **would have been** nice to see them here.
(= . . . if we had seen them here.)

We use a modal verb + *have* + -ed form (past participle) to talk about necessity, obligation etc. in the past.

Note We *needn't have bought* so much food.
(= We bought too much.)
We *didn't need to buy* much food.
(= We didn't buy much because there was no need.) ▷ 7.4

▷   4.10 *will have* + -ed form; 11.1 if-clauses

49 (7.14)

Emma and Sadie are students. They've both got exams tomorrow. Complete their conversation using a modal verb + *be* + the -ing form of each verb in brackets. Use the modal verbs *ought to*, *might*, *must* and *would*.

Example

You (do) some work.
You ought to be doing some work.

Emma Hello, Sadie. Aren't you doing any work? You (revise) for the exams.
Sadie I (read) my notes if I had them, but I've lost them.
Emma Good Lord! How awful! Do you want to look at mine?
Sadie No, thanks. It's okay. Don't worry, Emma. Exams aren't important.
Emma Not important! You (joke)! I (look) everywhere if my notes were lost.
Sadie Well, I'll probably find them before tomorrow.
Emma Have you seen Lisa? She's got a book of mine.
Sadie She was in here not long ago. Perhaps she's outside. She (sit) in the garden.
Emma I'll go and have a look. Then I (go). I have to get to the library before it closes.
Sadie What are you doing tonight, Emma?
Emma Revising, of course. Aren't you?
Sadie I (play) tennis with Rebecca. If the weather stays fine, that is. It'll be too late for revision tonight.

Activity

Say what you would be doing at the moment if today was a different day of the week. Find out what the other members of the class would be doing (or might be doing) if it was a Saturday or a Sunday.

50 (7.15)

Last night Lord Milton was found dead in his study at his home in Devon. Someone shot him. Detectives are trying to find out who the murderer is. Read what the detectives are thinking and add a sentence with a modal verb + *have* + -ed form. Use *must*, *might*, *couldn't* or *shouldn't*.

Example

Lord Milton was shot in the head from about two feet. He certainly died instantly.
He must have died instantly.

1 His wife Lady Evelyn found the body. She picked the gun up from the carpet. It was a mistake to touch it.
2 The doors and windows were locked. The murderer was certainly one of the five people in the house.
3 Lord Milton had made a new will. He wanted to leave some money to his secretary Warren Digby. It's a pity he told anyone about it.
4 We can't find the will. Perhaps the murderer took it.
5 Lord Milton's daughter Barbara was ill last night. It was impossible for her to walk to the study.
6 The writer Felicity Gray is staying in the house. She's writing the life story of Lord Milton. Why would she kill him? But it's possible.
7 It doesn't make sense for Warren Digby to take the will. It's impossible.
8 Barbara's husband John was in London yesterday. Lady Evelyn says he rang her in the evening from his club. It's certain he was in London.

Activity

Discuss the murder and write three or four more sentences about it using a modal verb + *have* + -ed form.

7.16   **be able to, be allowed to** and **have (got) to**

1   *Simple tenses*
I**'m able to** visit my father quite often.
The visitors **were allowed to** go inside.
You **don't have to** wait.

2   *Perfect tenses*
I **haven't been able to** find their address.
We**'ve had to** sit here in the dark all evening.
Children **had** always **been allowed to** play on the
grass before.

3   *After* **will, may** *etc.*
We**'ll be able to** have a rest soon.
I **may have to** go to the bank.
They **might not be allowed to** leave early.
You **ought to be able to** find the answer.

1   We can use *be able to* (▷ 7.2), *be allowed to*
(▷ 7.3) and *have (got) to* (▷ 7.4) in the simple
present and simple past tenses.

2   We can also use them in the present perfect and
past perfect tenses.

3   We can also use them after *will* and other modal
verbs.

51 (7.16)

Aldo, Jan and Lila are foreign students at an English-speaking university. Put each verb in brackets into the simple present, simple past or present perfect.

Aldo I'll be sad to leave here. But I (have to) leave at the end of my course.
Jan I still don't know if I can stay longer or not. I (not be able to) make any plans during the last two years.
Lila My problem was getting in here. I (have to) get a visa before I left home. I wanted to come here a year earlier, but I (not allowed to).

Aldo Money is a problem, too. I (not be allowed to) work since I came here.
Jan Ever since I came here, I (have to) report to the police every week.

Activity

What rules do governments usually make about people entering their country? Are there different rules for tourists, for students, and for people who want to live and work there? Discuss with other members of your class.

---

52 (7.1–7.16)

Nils and Oskar are spies. They're sitting in a car near the border between Silonia and Omagua. They're waiting for Harry. Put in a modal verb, (positive or negative), *be able to*, *be allowed to* or *have to*. (Sometimes more than one answer is correct.)

Nils Where's Harry, then? I … see him.
Oskar Yes, we said seventeen hours. He … be here by now.
Nils He might not … find the place. He … have crossed the border in the wrong place.
Oskar Impossible! Harry … have made a mistake. You know Harry.
Nils Well, I hope he comes soon.
Oskar It's the most important job he's ever done for us. He absolutely … get the information.
Nils I've often wondered about Harry. You don't think he … be working for the other side?
Oskar No, I don't. Harry is one of us.
Nils Well, I just think this job has been easy for him so far. Too easy. Perhaps the Omaguans know all about Harry. Someone … have told them about the job. They … have a man in our organization.
Oskar I don't believe it. They're not clever enough. But Harry is clever.
Nils But you … be sure. What if it was true?
Oskar It … be the end for us, of course. But it isn't true.
Nils Harry takes a lot of risks. He does dangerous things. The boss lets him do what he wants. Harry shouldn't … put other people in danger. I told the boss, but he didn't listen. He … have listened to me.
Oskar Shut up, will you? Harry is a good man. Only Harry … do this job.
Nils It's seventeen oh two. We're late.
Oskar You're right. We … go at once. We … stay here any longer.

Nils We've waited and he hasn't come. We … have driven here at all.
Oskar We had to be here. Harry … have come. He … have done if he'd been able to.
Nils Just a minute. There's someone behind that tree. Two men, I think. They … be watching us. Why else … they be here?
Oskar Right. Have your gun ready. We may … **shoot** our way out.
Nils OK, I'm ready.
Oskar Let's go then. Come on!
Nils The car … start! Oh, my God! Where's my gun? Give me my gun!
Oskar Put your hands up. Get out of the car! Lie down!
Nils It was you, Oskar! You told the Omaguans about Harry, didn't you? You … be mad. Oh, my God!

Activity

Imagine that it is fifteen minutes after the start of your lesson and the teacher still hasn't arrived. Discuss the situation and decide what to do.

8 Negatives, questions and tags

8.1 Negative statements

1a I**'m not** leaving yet. I **haven't** packed my bag.
 b We **can't** stop now or we **won't** get there in time.
 c I **don't** remember that party. I **didn't** go to it.
2a There are **no** lights on.
  (= There aren't any lights on.)
 b Peter isn't here, and **neither** is Jane.
  (= Peter isn't here, and Jane isn't either.)
 c There was **nobody** in the house.
  (= There wasn't anybody in the house.)
 d I've **never** been here before.
  (= I haven't ever been here before.)

1 In a negative statement we use *n't/not* after
a the auxiliary verbs *be* or *have* ▷ 5.1
b a modal verb ▷ 7.1
c the auxiliary verb *do* in the simple present and simple past ▷ 2.4; 3.3
2 We can also make a negative statement with
a *no* and *none* ▷ 20.23
b *neither* and *nor* ▷ 9.1; 20.23; 27.5
c *no one, nobody, nothing* and *nowhere* ▷ 20.16
d *never* ▷ 24.7

8.2 Questions

Yes/no questions

1 **Are** you looking for someone?
  Has the new supermarket opened yet?
2 **Shall** we have lunch now?
  Will John have time?
3 **Do** you normally come here?
  Did you see Jennifer yesterday?
4 You saw Jennifer yesterday?

Wh-questions

1 Where **are** you going?
  Which book **have** you read before?
2 How **can** we get there?
  When **must** you be back?
3 Why **does** Mr Gray leave so early?
  Who **did** you see in George Street?
  (You saw somebody.)
5 Who **saw** you in George Street?
  (Somebody saw you.)

Alternative questions

6 **Are** you going on Monday **or** Tuesday?
  Shall we have lunch now **or** later?
  Did you take a bus **or** did you walk?

In questions we put one of these verbs before the subject:
1 the auxiliary verbs *be* or *have* ▷ 5.1
2 a modal verb ▷ 7.1
3 the auxiliary verb *do* in the simple present and simple past ▷ 2.4; 3.3 (but see note 5)
1–3 Yes/no questions begin with an auxiliary or modal verb, and we can answer them with *yes* or *no*. ▷ 8.4
 Wh-questions begin with a question word (▷ 21) and an auxiliary or modal verb.
4 In informal spoken English we sometimes ask a yes/no question by using the same word order as in a statement but with a rising intonation. We do this to check that our information is correct. ▷ 8.5
5 When *who* or *what* asks about the subject, the verb is the same as in a statement, e.g. *Who saw you . . .?* ▷ 21.2
6 Alternative questions begin with an auxiliary or modal verb and have *or* (▷ 27.5) before the last alternative.

53 (8.1)

People are going to vote for a new government soon. Tony and Jackie are arguing about who to vote for. Complete the conversation, replying to a positive statement with a negative one each time.

Example

Jackie I like Betty Root.
Tony *I don't like her.*

Jackie Betty Root would be a good Prime Minister. People should vote for her.
Tony They … for her, you mean. She'd be no good. George Wright's party is the best.
Jackie It …, you know. Betty Root's party is the best. Her people have got the right ideas.
Tony … at all. Remember what happened when Root was Prime Minister? She made mistakes.
Jackie … . She did well. She took the right decisions.
Tony I'm afraid … .

Jackie Things were OK in Betty Root's time.
Tony … you know. They were terrible.
Jackie Betty understands our problems.
Tony … . But George Wright does. He's been a good Prime Minister.
Jackie … . He's been awful.
Tony George is popular. People like him.
Jackie …, I tell you. They're tired of him.
Tony George Wright will win.
Jackie … . Betty Root will. I'm sure of that.

Activity

Comment on these three statements and say in what way they are wrong.

1 London is the biggest city in the world.
2 A person can live for weeks without food or water.
3 The Americans sent the first satellite into space.

54 (8.2)

Earlier this evening a man walked into Dixie's wine store, held a gun to the manager's head and got away with £3,000. The police have a description of the man and of the car he was driving. They think the gunman was someone called Lennie Walsh. A detective is questioning Lennie. Complete the conversation, putting in the questions.

Detective Think back to half past six this evening, Lennie. … ?
Lennie Where was I? I don't know. I was walking somewhere. Yes, I went for a walk.
Detective … for walks?
Lennie No, not often, but I did tonight.
Detective … ?
Lennie No, I didn't go to Dixie's wine bar.
Detective … ?
Lennie Yes, of course I've got a car. It's a Mavis Corona.
Detective … ?
Lennie Blue. Look, … ?
Detective I'm asking you all these questions because there's been a robbery. Now, the number of the car. … ?
Lennie No, I don't know it. I can't remember numbers.
Detective Well, I can help you. I think it's BDX 25S. … ?
Lennie Well, you *may* be right. I'm not sure.
Detective … the car?
Lennie No, I didn't. I never steal.
Detective I'm very interested in your car, Lennie. … ?
Lennie I don't know. I've no idea where it is. Someone's borrowed it.
Detective Well, … ?
Lennie A man I know.

Detective … ?
Lennie No, I can't. I can never remember names.
Detective You forget names too, do you? Well, let's talk about your walk. … ?
Lennie I went to the park.
Detective … ?
Lennie No, no one saw me. Well, I don't *think* anyone saw me.
Detective … ?
Lennie No, I didn't see anyone I know.
Detective …, Lennie?
Lennie What do you mean — am I going to tell you the truth? I'm telling it *now*.
Detective You went out for a walk! No one saw you!
Lennie Well, *someone* saw me. I've just remembered.
Detective … ?
Lennie It was a policeman. He's called Phil Grady. He spoke to me in the park. I know him well — he's arrested me twice.
Detective … this?
Lennie Oh, about half past six, I think.
Detective Just a minute. I'm going to make a phone call.

Activity A

Act out the interview with a partner.

Activity B

Imagine that *you* are the detective. You discover from Phil Grady that Lennie's story is true — Grady spoke to him at half past six. What questions would you now ask Lennie?

8.3   Negative questions

1   Who **hasn't** arrived yet?
    Why **aren't** I on the list?

2   Why **don't** we ask Sarah to the party?
    Why **doesn't** she come on the bus?

3   You were reading that book last month. **Haven't**
    you finished it yet? ~ No, it's taking me a long time.
    Don't you like it? ~ Oh, yes, I like it very much.

4   **Didn't** the Romans build this road?
    (= The Romans built this road, didn't they?)

5   **Haven't** you done well!

Form

In negative questions we use an auxiliary or modal
verb + *n't*.

1   In the first person singular we use *aren't I?*

1   We can use a question word in a negative
    question to ask for information.

2   We can use *Why don't/doesn't . . .?* to make a
    suggestion. ▷ 31.4, 11

3   A negative question can express surprise. *Haven't
    you finished it?* = I am surprised that you haven't
    finished it. ▷ 34.7
    We use *no* to agree with a negative question, e.g.
    Haven't you finished it? ~ No, I haven't finished it.
    We use *yes* to disagree with a negative question,
    e.g. *Don't you like it? ~ Yes, I like it very much.*

4   We can use a negative question to ask if a person
    agrees with a statement. ▷ 8.5

5   We can use a negative question form with a falling
    intonation in exclamations. ▷ 34.1

8.4   Answering questions

Yes/no questions
Have you seen the photos?
1 Yes.   2 Yes, I have.   3 Yes, I have seen them.
Will you be here tomorrow?
1 No.   2 No, I won't.   3 No, I won't be here.

Wh-questions
Who wants a drink?
1 Me.   2 I do.   3 I want a drink.
Where did you buy those jeans?
1 In the market.   3 I bought them in the market.

We can answer questions
1   in one word or phrase
2   often with a short answer using an auxiliary or
    modal verb
3   with a full sentence

Short answers are much more usual than full
sentences.

▷   31.2, 4 answering requests and suggestions;
    33.1, 2 answering offers and invitations

55 (8.2, 8.3)

Yesterday a Puffco petrol tanker crashed into a house and exploded, killing four people. The Daily Talk is looking into the accident, which happened in the village of Hamleigh. Look at the information that the newspaper has found and ask some questions.

Examples

Why was the fire station at Upstone closed last year?
Why didn't the fire brigade arrive until twenty minutes after the accident?

Activity

What questions might the Daily Talk ask about a fire at a dance hall in which thirty young people died?

EX There was once a fire station at Upstone, two miles away. <u>It was closed last year.</u>

The fire brigade were slow. <u>They didn't arrive until twenty minutes after the accident.</u>

1 Puffco are trying to save money. <u>Their tankers aren't serviced until they break down.</u>

2 The driver was breaking the law. <u>He had been on the road for nine hours.</u>

3 The warning sign was knocked down a month ago. <u>It wasn't put up again.</u>

4 There's no speed limit, even for lorries. <u>They're allowed to go as fast as they like.</u>

5 The villagers have protested. <u>The police haven't taken any notice of them.</u>

6 A by-pass was planned thirty years ago. <u>It hasn't been built.</u>

7 Puffco told their drivers not to use the route. <u>They still use it.</u>

8 There have been accidents in the past. <u>We haven't learned any lessons from past accidents.</u>

8.5   Question tags

1a   It's lovely today, **isn't it**? ~ It certainly is.
 b   You'll be on holiday next week, **won't you**? ~
      No, we've had our holiday.
 c   Bob likes this weather, **doesn't he**? ~
      Yes, he does.

2a   We haven't had a nice summer for ages, **have
      we**? ~ No, we haven't.
 b   The dog can't get out, **can it**? ~ I don't think so.
 c   You didn't buy these drinks, **did you**? ~
      No, David did.

3   Ann isn't here. ~ Oh, she's working, **is she**?
      I won't be long. ~ You'll be back soon, **will you**?
      Jennifer was there. ~
      You saw Jennifer yesterday, **did you**?

4a   I'd better answer these letters, **hadn't I**?
 b   You'd rather sit in the garden, **wouldn't you**?

5a   Let's have some fresh air, **shall we**? I'll open the
      window, **shall I**?
 b   Open the door, **will you**?/**would you**?/**can
      you**?/**could you**?

6a   It's lovely today, ⬉ **isn't it**?
      We haven't had a nice summer for ages, ⬉ **have
      we**?
      I'd better answer these letters, ⬉ **hadn't I**?
 b   You'll be on holiday next week, ⬈ **won't you**?
      The dog can't get out, ⬈ **can it**?
      Let's have some fresh air, ⬈ **shall we**?
      Open the door, ⬈ **will you**?

Form

1, 2   We form question tags with
 a   the auxiliary verbs *be* or *have*
 b   a modal verb, or
 c   the auxiliary verb *do* in the simple present or
      simple past
      In a negative tag we put *n't* after the auxiliary or
      modal verb.
      After the verb (+ *n't*) there is a pronoun. The
      pronoun refers to the subject of the sentence.

Use

1   After a positive statement we use a negative tag to
      ask if a person agrees with the statement. ▷ 30.2
2   After a negative statement we use a positive tag to
      ask if a person agrees with the statement.
      ▷ 34.7 showing surprise
3   After a positive statement we can use a positive
      tag when we have just found out or just
      remembered some information and we want to
      ask or check if it is correct. ▷ 34.7 showing
      interest
4a   After *had better* we use a tag with *had*.
 b   After *would rather* we use a tag with *would*.
5a   After suggestions with *let's* and after offers, we
      use a tag with *shall*.
 b   After an imperative we use a tag with *will, would,
      can* or *could*.
6a   We use a falling intonation when we think the
      statement is true and we are asking someone to
      agree with it. (But he/she may disagree.)
 b   We use a rising intonation when we are not so sure
      that the statement is true. A tag with a rising
      intonation is almost the same as a real yes/no
      question. ▷ 8.2
      We often use a rising intonation in suggestions,
      offers and requests.

56 (8.5)

All the pupils who left Parkside School twenty years ago are having a reunion. They're meeting to talk about the old days when they were younger. Put in the missing tags.

Roger Hello. You're Wendy, … ?
Wendy Yes. I remember you, too. You're Roger Cowley.
Roger That's right. We were in the same class, … ? But it's easy to forget people, … ?
Wendy I think I remember most of the people here. Jessica Squires is over there. She reads the news on Television North-West, … ?
Roger Yes, she's on television quite often. She's done well, … ?
Wendy We had a lot of fun at school, … ?
Roger Er, yes. Don't turn round, but Malone's looking this way.
Wendy Mike Malone?
Roger Yes, you can remember him, … ?
Wendy Oh, yes.
Roger I hated him. Oh, no! He's coming over here.
Wendy Well, it is a reunion. We ought to be friendly, … ?
Mike Hello, Roger. Nice to see you again.
Roger Nice to see you too, Mike.
Mike This reunion was a good idea, … ?
Roger Yes, I'm enjoying it. Mike, do you remember Wendy?
Mike Yes. She's my wife.
Roger Oh!

Activity

Imagine that in twenty years' time you are at a reunion with the other members of your class. Think of three or four sentences with question tags that you might say to your partner.

57 (8.5)

Peter, Sue and Bob are football fans. They're talking about the World Cup. Complete their conversation by putting in the question tags.

Peter Did you see Holland and Mexico on television last night?
Bob Yes, it was a great game, … ? Holland were marvellous.
Sue They won't find it so easy against Poland, … ?
Bob No, they won't. Poland have got a good team, … ?
Peter Lobak looks good, … ? The Austrians couldn't stop him, … ?
Bob It'll be an interesting game, … ?
Sue England haven't been very good, … ?
Bob Luck hasn't been on our side, … ?
Sue But why is Bodger playing? He isn't very good, … ?
Peter He didn't play very well against Peru, … ?
Bob He doesn't play as well now as he used to, … ?
Peter Well, we should beat Nigeria, … ?
Sue I don't know. Anything could happen, … ?
Bob The West Germans are good, … ? They don't take any risks, … ?
Peter They're playing Hungary tonight. You'll be watching, … ?
Bob Yes, of course.

Activity A

Talk to a partner about a sporting event. Try to use a few positive and negative tags in your conversation.

Activity B

If you aren't interested in sport, talk to your partner about a television programme you both watch or about world events which have been on the radio lately.

9 Replacing words and leaving out words

9.1 Short additions to statements

1 I like cats. ~ **So do** I./I **do, too**.
The old man is very ill, and **so is** his wife./ and his wife **is, too**.

2 We've never been here before. ~
Neither have we./**Nor have** we./We **haven't either**.
The shops won't be open, and **neither will** the banks./and **nor** will the banks./and the banks **won't either**.

3 The girls helped with the washing-up. The boys **didn't**, though.

4 My brother can't swim, but I **can**.

5 My sister's going to Japan. ~ Oh, **is** she?

1 We make positive additions to positive sentences with *so* or *too* and an auxiliary or modal verb.

2 We make negative additions to negative sentences with *neither/nor* or *either* and an auxiliary or modal verb.

We also use an auxiliary or modal verb for

3 negative additions to positive sentences

4 positive additions to negative sentences

5 short questions after statements. ▷ 34.7 showing interest

9.2 **so** and **not** after a verb

1 Someone must have stolen your bicycle. ~
Yes, I suppose **so**.

2 Will the police get it back for you? ~
I don't think **so**.

3 Will you be able to buy a new one? ~
No, I'm afraid **not**.

1 We can use *so* after some verbs instead of a whole clause. *I suppose so* = I suppose someone must have stolen my bicycle.

2 We can use *so* after the negative form of some verbs, e.g. *think, suppose, expect, imagine*.

3 We can use *not* to give a negative answer after some verbs, e.g. *be afraid, suppose, hope, believe, guess* (USA).

Note We do not use *so* or *not* after *know* or *be sure*, e.g. *Yes, I know. Yes, I'm sure.*

58 (9.1)

Look at the notes about three cars in the table below.

First, write eight sentences (1–8) giving information about the cars. Use *but* in those sentences.

Examples

The Prince isn't easy to drive, but the Delta and the Swift are.
The Prince and the Swift feel comfortable, but the Delta doesn't.

1 The Prince and the Delta … . (Go on in this way.)

Then write another eight sentences (9–16). In each sentence mention the two cars which have the same answer. Use *so* or *neither*.

Examples

The Delta is easy to drive, and so is the Swift.
The Prince feels comfortable, and so does the Swift.

9 The Prince …, and neither … . (Go on in this way.)

Activity

Think of some similarities and differences between the capital of your home country and London. Talk about the two cities using *so*, *neither* and *but*.

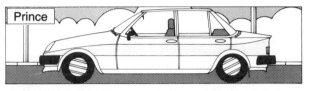

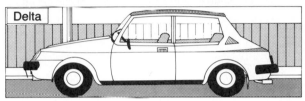

	Prince	Delta	Swift
Is it easy to drive?	no	yes	yes
Does it feel comfortable?	yes	no	yes
Does it look good?	no	no	yes
Can it do 150 kilometres an hour?	no	no	yes
Does it use less than ten litres of petrol per 100 kilometres?	no	yes	no
Is it cheap to repair?	yes	yes	no
Has it got four doors?	yes	no	yes
Has it got a lot of room inside?	no	yes	yes
Did it win a 'Road' magazine prize last year?	yes	no	no
Is it good value?	yes	no	no

59 (9.2)

Paul and Diane are going to Tony's party. Complete their conversation using the verbs in brackets. Do not put a whole clause after the verb. Use *so* or *not* if necessary.

Example

No, (expect).   *No, I don't expect so.*

Diane I hope this party's good.
Paul (hope), too. I don't know how we're going to get there.
Diane Is the car still out of action?
Paul (be afraid).
Diane What's the matter with it?
Paul (be sure), but I think it's something electrical.
Diane Haven't you taken it to the garage yet?
Paul (be afraid). I haven't had time.
Diane Well, Martin will be going, won't he? We can ask him for a lift.

Paul Yes, (suppose). I don't imagine there's a bus.
Diane I (expect). Not in the evening.
Paul OK, I'll ring Martin. He might be taking Richard, of course.
Diane Oh, (hope). That man talks about horse racing the whole time. He's so boring.
Paul Yes, (know).
Diane Do we have to take a bottle to this party?
Paul No, (think). Tony didn't say.
Diane We'd better take some wine. There's a bottle in the cupboard.

Activity

React to these three questions using similar sentences with *hope*, *think* etc.

☐ Is there going to be a Third World War?
☐ Have people from other planets visited the earth?
☐ Is there life after death?

9.3   Leaving out words [A]

My sister plays the piano and my brother the guitar.
(= . . . and my brother **plays** the guitar.)
I like the music but not the words.
(= . . . but **I do**n't **like** the words.)
Someone's borrowed that record and I don't know who.
(= . . . and I don't know who**'s borrowed it**.)

We can leave out words instead of saying them again if the meaning is clear without them.

▷   8.4 answering questions; 14.12 the verb after *to*; 18.4 the possessive form; 20.21 quantifiers without a noun

9.4   Leaving out words [B]

Enjoying the music? ~ Sounds great.
(= **Are you** enjoying the music? ~ **It** sounds great.)

In informal speech we can leave out words from the beginning of a sentence if the meaning is clear without them.

The words which we leave out are usually a pronoun and/or an auxiliary verb.

60 **(9.3)**

A British reporter is at the Olympic Games. Look at her notes and combine each pair of sentences into one. Use *and* or *but* and leave some of the words out.

Examples

The Russians are first in the medals table.
The Americans are second in the medals table.
The Russians are first in the medals table and the Americans second.

The British team have won three silver medals.
They haven't won a gold medal.
The British team have won three silver medals but not a gold medal.

1 Polinski won the long jump.
   McCall won the high jump.
2 Ivor Ketapov won't be running in the 100 metres.
   No one knows why he won't be running in it.
3 He holds the 200 metres world record.
   He doesn't hold the 100 metres world record.
4 British runners have broken records.
   British swimmers haven't broken records.
5 A Frenchman is leading in the marathon.
   A Swede is leading in the cycle race.
6 There were big crowds on Tuesday.
   There weren't big crowds on Wednesday.

Activity

Write similar sentences on these topics.
Use two clauses linked with *and* or *but*.

☐ Corsica and Sardinia
☐ John F. Kennedy and Edward M. Kennedy
☐ dinosaurs

61 **(9.1–9.3)**

Milena and Ahmed are students. They're going to take an English exam soon. Their English is correct, but they could improve it by replacing or leaving out words. Can you help them to make the underlined sentences shorter? Use short additions to statements, use *so* and *not* after a verb, or leave out words instead of saying them again.

Milena It's the English exam in two weeks. Have you done any work for it?
Ahmed No, I'm afraid I haven't done any work for it. I haven't had much time lately.
Milena And I haven't had much time. I've been very busy.
Ahmed I've been to all the classes, though. And I've done the homework.
Milena I haven't done the homework. I always have so many other things to do in the evenings.
Ahmed There's an oral exam, isn't there?
Milena Yes, I think there's an oral exam. Mrs Moss mentioned it last week in one of our lessons.
Ahmed I can do written work all right, but I can't do oral work.
Milena Oh, nonsense. Your spoken English is very good. You can hold conversations in English, can't you?
Ahmed Yes, I suppose I can hold conversations in English. Perhaps I'll do all right. Are we allowed to use dictionaries in the exam, do you know?
Milena I don't think we're allowed to use them. Why don't you ask Mrs Moss?
Ahmed Yes, I will ask her. She'll know, won't she?
Milena I expect she'll know.
Ahmed I really must pass the exam.
Milena Will you need English in your job?
Ahmed I'll need it to get a good job.
Milena I'll need it, too. But don't worry, Ahmed. Your English is fine. You're going to pass.
Ahmed Well, I hope I'm going to pass. I know you will pass.
Milena I wish I could be so sure. I'm certainly not looking forward to it.
Ahmed And I'm not looking forward to it. I'll be glad when it's over, in fact.
Milena I'll be glad, too.

Activity A

When you have improved the conversation, act it out with a partner.

Activity B

Talk to your partner about the English exam you will both take or about whether you will need to use English in your job or as a visitor to an English-speaking country.

10 The passive

10.1 The passive: simple tenses

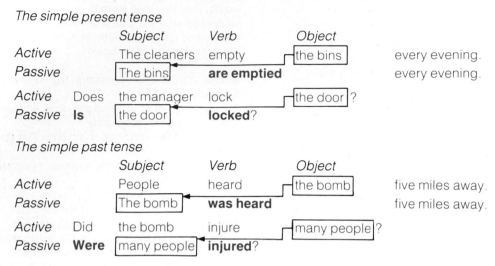

The simple present tense

		Subject	Verb	Object	
Active		The cleaners	empty	the bins	every evening.
Passive		The bins	**are emptied**		every evening.
Active	Does	the manager	lock	the door ?	
Passive	**Is**	the door	**locked**?		

The simple past tense

		Subject	Verb	Object	
Active		People	heard	the bomb	five miles away.
Passive		The bomb	**was heard**		five miles away.
Active	Did	the bomb	injure	many people ?	
Passive	**Were**	many people	**injured**?		

Form

We form the passive with *be* and the -ed form (past participle), e.g. *are emptied, is locked, was heard, were injured.*

The object of an active verb becomes the subject of a passive verb, e.g. *the bins, the door.*

If the subject of a passive verb is plural, then the verb is also plural, e.g. *the bins are emptied.*

The subject of the active verb (the agent) is left out of these passive sentences. ▷ 10.2

Use

We use the passive to make the object of the active verb more important. We put the object of the active verb at the beginning of the passive sentence because we want to talk about e.g. *the bins* not about *the cleaners*, or about *the bomb* not about *people.*

Note We can also use the past participle as an adjective to describe the result of an action, e.g. *The door is locked at the moment.* ▷ 17.1

62   (10.1)

These pictures show what happens when you post a letter. Write a sentence for each picture using the passive voice.

Example

A letter is posted.

Ex posting a letter

1 emptying the post box

2 postmarking the stamps at the post office

3 sorting the letters into the different towns

4 loading the mail into the train

Activity

Describe in a few sentences the process that leads to a tin of Australian peach slices being on the shelf of a British supermarket.

5 unloading the mail bags after their journey

6 taking the bags to the post office

7 sorting the letters into the different streets

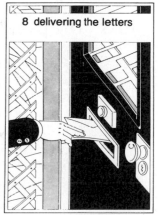

8 delivering the letters

63   (10.1)

Complete this short article about the ship 'Mary Rose'. Put the verb into the correct simple past form. Some verbs are active, and some are passive.

The warship Mary Rose (build) in the years 1509–10. In 1544 England (start) a war against France, and in 1545 French ships (send) across the Channel towards England. Some English ships (go) out from Portsmouth to meet them. One of these ships was the Mary Rose. It was carrying 91 guns and 700 men — twice as many as normal. It (sink) quickly to the bottom of the sea even before it (attack) by the French. About 650 men (die). This terrible accident (see) by the king of England himself.

The next month an attempt (make) to raise the Mary Rose, but it (fail). The ship (forget) for hundreds of years.

In the 1970s new plans (make) to raise the ship. Thousands of objects (bring) up from the ship by divers. Then, on 1st October 1982, the Mary Rose (lift) out of the sea. Many people (see) the raising of the ship on television. Finally the Mary Rose (take) into Portsmouth dock 437 years after she had sunk.

Activity

Use these notes to write a paragraph about a ship called the 'Cutty Sark'.

famous sailing ship – built in the 1860s – brought tea from China – later wool from Australia – owned by many different people – finally brought into dry dock in London in 1954 – made into a museum

10.2 **by** + agent

		Subject	Verb	Object	(agent)
1	Active	The birds	eat	the food.	
	Passive	The food	**is eaten**		**by** the birds
	Active	Picasso	painted	the picture.	
	Passive	The picture	**was painted**		**by** Picasso
2	Active	Someone	stole	the car.	
	Passive	The car	**was stolen**.		
3	Active	The police	arrested	the driver.	
	Passive	The driver	**was arrested**.		

1   The subject of the active verb is the *agent*, the person or thing that does the action.
The agent can come after a passive verb in a phrase with *by*, e.g. *by the birds, by Picasso*.
We put in the agent if it is important to mention it.

2   We can leave out the agent if we do not know it, e.g. *The car was stolen*. (We do not know who stole it.)

3   We can leave out the agent if we do not need to mention it, e.g. *The driver was arrested*. (We know that the police arrested him or her.)

10.3   The passive: perfect tenses

The present perfect tense

Active   They have opened two new motorways.
Passive   Two new motorways **have been opened**.

Active   How much has the government spent on them?
Passive   How much **has been spent** on them?

The past perfect tense

Active   They had delivered the furniture while I was out.
Passive   The furniture **had been delivered** while I was out.

Form

We form the passive of perfect tenses with *have/has been* + past participle and *had been* + past participle.

Use ▷ 10.1

64 (10.2)

Answer the quiz questions using the passive and *by* + agent.

Example

Who invented radio?
Bell, Edison or Marconi?
It was invented by Marconi.

1 Who won the World Cup at football in 1982?
Brazil, Italy or West Germany?
2 Who wrote stories about a French detective called Maigret?
Agatha Christie, Ellery Queen or Georges Simenon?
3 Who killed Martin Luther King?
John Wilkes Booth, Lee Harvey Oswald or James Earl Ray?
4 Who invented television?
John Logie Baird, Alexander Graham Bell or Thomas Edison?
5 Who built the pyramids?
The Egyptians, the Greeks or the Romans?
6 Who directed the film Gandhi?
Attenborough, Fassbinder or Hitchcock?
7 Who spoke the words 'To be or not to be?'
Alexander, Hamlet or Julius Caesar?
8 Who played James Bond in the first Bond film?
Sean Connery, George Lazenby or Roger Moore?

Activity

Discuss possible answers to these questions.

☐ How are road accidents caused?
☐ Who buys expensive pictures?
☐ How do department stores and industrial companies lose a lot of goods that are never paid for?

65 (10.3)

Write the newspaper headlines as sentences using the present perfect. Some sentences are active and some are passive.

Examples

COST OF LIVING GOES UP
The cost of living has gone up.

GOODS DAMAGED IN FIRE
Some goods have been damaged in a fire.

1 MAN KILLED IN MOTORWAY ACCIDENT
2 OLYMPIC GAMES BEGIN
3 CHILDREN INJURED IN GAS EXPLOSION
4 PICTURE STOLEN FROM MUSEUM
5 CHARLES AND DIANA ARRIVE IN INDIA
6 SECRET PAPERS LOST
7 FAMOUS HOUSE SOLD TO AMERICAN
8 RAY JENKS WINS IMPORTANT RACE
9 DEAD BODY FOUND IN PARK
10 50 'STYLE' SHOPS BOUGHT BY WILSON-MCARTHUR GROUP

Activity

Think of some items of news, or find them in a newspaper. Write five or six sentences about things that have happened recently. Use present perfect active and passive sentences.

10.4   The passive: continuous tenses

The present continuous tense

Active   They're painting the bridge today.
Passive   The bridge **is being painted** today.

The past continuous tense

Active   The farmer was milking the cows when
we arrived.
Passive   The cows **were being milked** when we
arrived.

Form

We form the passive voice of continuous tenses
with *am/are/is being* + past participle and
was/were being + past participle.

Use ▷ 10.1

10.5   The passive: **will** and other modal verbs

Breakfast **will be brought** to your room.
Meals **cannot be served** after 11.00 p.m.
Your key **should be given** in before 11.30 a.m.
Must the bill **be paid** in cash?
The room **has (got) to be cleaned**.

Form

After modal verbs we use *be* + past participle to
form the passive.

Use ▷ 10.1

66 (10.5)

Electrobrit is a company that makes washing machines. At the moment it isn't selling enough machines. The Directors are having a meeting to discuss the problem. Write down their words as they might be reported in a written summary of the meeting. Use the passive.

Example

'We all know we can expect a difficult time, of course.'
A difficult time can be expected.

1 'We have to reduce costs, you know.'
2 'Of course we must keep the factory open.'
3 'We all agree then that we must take action.'
4 'We should warn the staff, of course.'
5 'We ought to make things clear to them.'
6 'Everyone agrees then that the company will employ no more new staff.'
7 'We all know we can't allow the situation to continue.'
8 'We'll hold the next meeting on May 8th, then.'

Activity

Discuss with other members of your class what you think should be done about the problem of heavy traffic in towns. The following points can be included in your discussion.

☐ road-building
☐ public transport
☐ air pollution
☐ the future of oil as a fuel

67 (10.1–10.5)

Below is a short article about computers. Put the verbs in brackets into the passive voice. Choose the correct tense, or use the modal verb if one is given.

Examples

These machines (control) by computers nowadays.
These machines are controlled by computers nowadays.

Programmes (can/record) on cassette.
Programmes can be recorded on cassette.

Computers then and now

The world's first electronic computer (build) at the University of Pennsylvania in 1946, although computer-like machines (build) in the 19th century. Computers (sell) commercially for the first time in the 1950s, and a lot of progress (make) since then. Computers are now much smaller and more powerful, and they (can/buy) much more cheaply.

Computers (use) in many fields — in business, science, medicine and education, for example. They (can/use) to forecast the weather or to control robots which make cars. The computer's memory is the place where information (keep) and calculations (do).

A computer cannot think for itself — it (must/tell) exactly what to do. A lot of difficult calculations (can/do) very quickly on a computer.

And computers don't make mistakes. Stories (hear) sometimes about computers paying people too much money or sending them bills for things they didn't buy. These mistakes (make) by the programmers — the people who give the computer its instructions. Some years ago, a computer-controlled rocket belonging to the USA went out of control and (have to/destroy). The accident (cause) by a small mistake in one line of the programme. This mistake cost the USA $18 million.

Criminals have found out that 'computer crimes' are often a lot easier than robbing banks. Hundreds of millions of dollars (steal) from American businesses every year by people changing the information in computers.

Large numbers of home computers (sell) recently, especially in the USA and Britain. People know more about computers than they used to, and computers are playing a bigger part in our lives. Progress (make) all the time. Many people believe we can look forward to the day when even our household jobs like cleaning (do) by computer-controlled robots.

Activity

Write a short paragraph about any one of these things. Use the passive in some of your sentences.

☐ the pocket calculator
☐ the video recorder
☐ the aeroplane

10.6 The passive: direct and indirect objects

Direct object

1 They sent a telegram to the winner.
A telegram was sent to the winner.

Indirect object

2 They sent a telegram to the winner.
The winner was sent a telegram.

Direct object

3 They promised the workers better conditions.
Better conditions were promised to the workers.

Indirect object

4 They promised the workers better conditions.
The workers were promised better conditions.

The subject of a passive sentence can be either

1,3 the *direct object* of an active sentence or

2,4 the *indirect object* of an active sentence.

10.7 The passive with **get**

1 Lots of people **get injured** in the home.
The cake **got burnt** in the oven.
How did this clock **get broken**?

2 I had to **get dressed** in the dark.
Without a map we soon **got lost**.
When did they **get married**?

We use *get* in the passive instead of *be*

1 sometimes in informal English, especially to talk about something happening by accident

2 in certain expressions, e.g. *get dressed, get washed, get lost, get married*

10.8 **have/get something done**

1 **have something done**
We **had** this room **decorated** last year.
I**'m having** my hair **cut** tomorrow.
Did you **have** your suit **cleaned**?

2 **get something done**
We **got** this room **decorated** last year.
I**'m getting** my hair **cut** tomorrow.
Did you **get** your suit **cleaned**?

Form

1 *have* + object + past participle

2 *get* + object + past participle

have and *get* can have a continuous form (*I'm having/getting it cut*), and questions and negatives are with *do* (*Did you have/get it cleaned?*).
For e.g. *I had decorated this room* ▷ 3.6 the past perfect tense
For e.g. *We decorated this room ourselves* ▷ 20.9

Use

I had/I got the car repaired = I asked someone to repair the car (and they repaired it).
get is a little more informal than *have*.

10.9 **it** + passive verb + clause

1 *Active* People say that the company is in difficulties.
Passive **It is said** that the company is in difficulties.

2 *Active* They decided to appoint a new manager.
Passive **It was decided** to appoint a new manager.

We can use *it* and the passive voice

1 before a clause with *that*. We can use these verbs: *say, think, feel, believe, know, expect, suppose, report, consider, agree, decide, arrange*

2 before an infinitive. We can use these verbs: *agree, decide, arrange*.

▷ 20.2 uses of *it*

68 (10.6)

The sentences below are from an article about the money paid to famous sports people. Rewrite each sentence beginning with the phrase in bold type.

Examples

They paid the racing driver Bobby Kraft **£200,000** when he won the Grand Prix.
£200,000 was paid to the racing driver Bobby Kraft when he won the Grand Prix.

Their club have promised **the AC Milan team** a new house each if they win the European Cup.
The AC Milan team have been promised a new house each if they win the European Cup.

1 They gave **the tennis player Kathy Duprey** £50,000 for winning a competition.
2 A company has paid the skier Anne Stolberg **£40,000** to advertise ski trousers.
3 A TV company gave **the ice hockey team Phoenix Flyers** $20,000 each to play in front of the cameras.
4 His club pays footballer Wayne Simmonds **£250** for every goal he scores.
5 A company offered **the cyclist Luigi Delgado** £25,000 to advertise a soft drink.
6 Henry Lane will pay **the boxer Howard Duke** $3 million for his next fight.
7 They've promised the London Wonders basketball team **a holiday in the West Indies** if they win the league.

Activity

Talk about jobs and money. Which people are paid a lot of money? Which are paid very little? Which people are given extra things in addition to their pay?

69 (10.8, 20.9)

Mark and Jane are going to buy a house. It's quite cheap, but it isn't in very good condition, so they've had a report made on it. In the report there's a list of what they'll have to do to the house. They've ticked the things they can do themselves. Say which jobs they can do and which they'll need to have done by someone else.

Examples

They can clear the gutters themselves.
They'll need to have the roof repaired.

```
 ┌─────────────────────────────────────────┐
 │  Summary of work needed                  │
 │  Clear the gutters. ✓                     │
 │  Repair the roof.                         │
 │  Re-build the garage wall.                │
 │  Replace the broken glass. ✓              │
 │  Lay a new floor in the dining-room.      │
 │  Repair the bedroom ceiling.              │
 │  Put in a new kitchen window.             │
 │  Paint the outside of the house. ✓        │
 │  Decorate all the rooms. ✓                │
 │  Check the electrical wiring.             │
 └─────────────────────────────────────────┘
```

Activity A

Say which of the jobs in the list you would do yourself and which you would have done by someone.

Activity B

Say what you can have done at these places.

☐ a laundry   ☐ a photographer's studio
☐ a hairdresser's   ☐ a dry cleaner's
☐ a garage   ☐ a dentist's

11 if-clauses

11.1 The main types of if-clause

1   Type 1: **if** + the simple present tense,
    + **will, can** or **may/might**

Probable actions in the future
If you **leave** before ten, you**'ll catch** the train.
If you **don't hurry**, you **might miss** it.
That bowl **will break if** you **drop** it.
I **can get** some more milk **if** there **isn't** enough.

2   Type 2: **if** + the simple past tense,
    + **would, could** or **might**

a   *Less probable actions in the future*
If we **saved** £500, we**'d have** enough for a holiday next year.
We **might save** enough **if** you **worked** overtime.

b   *Unreal actions in the present*
If we **were** rich, I**'d travel** round the world.
We **could buy** a new car **if** you **didn't spend** so much on clothes.

3   Type 3: **if** + the past perfect tense,
    + **would have, could have** or **might have**

Impossible actions in the past
If it **had rained** yesterday, there **wouldn't have been** many people here.
If I **hadn't been** ill, I **could have gone** yesterday.
I **might have bought** some trousers **if** I**'d seen** some.
Peter **would have rung if** there**'d been** anything wrong.

1   We use Type 1 to talk about future situations that the speaker thinks are probable. *If you leave before ten* means that it is quite probable that you will leave before ten.

2a We use Type 2 to talk about future situations that the speaker thinks are possible but not very probable. *If we saved £500* means that it is possible that we will save £500 but not very probable.

b   We also use Type 2 to talk about unreal situations in the present. *If we were rich* means that we are not rich.

3   We use Type 3 to talk about past situations that did not happen. *If it had rained* means that it did not rain.

Types 1–3

The if-clause can come before or after the main clause. We often put a comma when the if-clause comes first.

Note *'d* is the short form of *had* and of *would*. *If you'd asked me, I'd have told you* = If you had asked me, I would have told you.

▷   31.7, 9 warnings and threats

70 (11.1)

Charlotte works for an advertising company. She's made some notes about different products. Write sentences with *if* + the simple present + *will* to advertise the products.

Examples

wash your hair with Glam – it looks super
If you wash your hair with Glam, it'll look super.

feel better – take Panadex
You'll feel better if you take Panadex.

1 choose a Sunspot holiday – have a great time
2 sleep a lot better – sleep in a Dreamway bed
3 people notice you – wear Rodeo jeans
4 shop at Kwikbuy – save money
5 use Luxidor paint – your house looks beautiful
6 know what's happening – read the Daily Talk
7 wash with Whizz – your clothes cleaner
8 drive a Delta – not want to drive any other car

Activity

Write a few sentences advertising some other products. Use if-clauses. You can choose real products.

71 (11.1)

Amanda is a secretary. She's grumbling about her new job and her boss. Match each sentence in the first box with one in the second. Rewrite the sentences using *if* + the simple past tense + *would/could*.

Examples

If my boss didn't play golf, he wouldn't be out of the office so much.
If he told me where he was, I could contact him.

> My boss plays golf.
> He doesn't tell me where he is.
> 1 The pay isn't good.
> 2 He gives me so much work.
> 3 His writing is so awful.
> 4 He doesn't listen to me.
> 5 The offices are such a long way from here.
> 6 There aren't any cafés nearby.

> I can't afford a nicer flat.
> I can't contact him.
> I can't read it.
> I have to tell him everything twice.
> I have to stay late.
> I have to take sandwiches.
> I spend so much time on the bus.
> He's out of the office so much.

Activity

What kind of things do parents say to their children when they aren't doing very well with their school work and are getting low marks? Think of three or four sentences with *if* and the simple past tense.

72 **(11.1)**

Hilary Lester works for an organization called Food for the Third World. She's talking on television about the situation in Omagua. Put the verbs in brackets into the correct tense, or use *will* or *would* or their short forms.

Interviewer Miss Lester, what is the situation in Omagua?

Hilary Well, it's very bad. Thousands of people have died, and thousands more (die) soon if they (not get) help. The people have very little food or water. And if we (not do) something soon, things (get) much worse. There will simply be nothing left to eat.

Interviewer Is the British government doing anything to help? If they (send) food, that (help) to save lives, wouldn't it? After all, Omagua was once a British colony.

Hilary Yes, indeed. And the country is very poor, of course. But our government refuses to do anything quickly. They say they need time to find out about the problem. But we haven't got any time. It (be) too late if they (not do) something soon.

Interviewer Well, it doesn't look as if Omagua is going to get any help for the moment. So what next? What (happen) if the country (not get) enough food or enough money to buy food?

Hilary Well, if our government (not be) willing to help, we (have to) ask people to send us money. In fact, we're asking them now.

Interviewer How much are you asking people to give?

Hilary We're asking them just to send what they can. Even small amounts will be welcome. We (be) very grateful if people (send) what they can afford. After all, if everyone in the country (give) just 10p, we (have) a lot of money, wouldn't we? I'm sure if people (know) exactly what things were like in Omagua, they (want) to help.

Interviewer And are you hopeful that **people will** send money?

Hilary Oh, yes. If people (hear) about the problem, as they're doing now, then they (help), I'm sure. They always have done before.

Interviewer Is there still time to get food and money to the people who need it, Miss Lester?

Hilary Oh, yes. We'll put the money to good use immediately. If people (post) money to us tomorrow, the food (be) in Omagua by the end of the week.

Interviewer Well, it's certainly a good thing that you're able to help the Omaguans. If your organization (not exist), things (be) much less hopeful. Now, can you tell us the address where people should send money? ...

Activity

Graham and Miranda are on holiday in East Africa. They're in a safari park, and their car has run out of petrol. They're three miles from the nearest filling station, which is just outside the park. They've got a petrol can. There are no other cars in sight. It is very hot, and they have no water. There are lions in the safari park, although they can't see any at the moment.

Discuss possible answers to their problem using if-clauses.

73 **(11.1)**

Below is the story of what happened when four people went on a long walk last week. Read the story and rewrite the underlined parts using if-clauses type 3.

Examples

If it hadn't rained most of the morning, it would have been a pleasant walk.
They wouldn't have decided to go if the forecast had been bad.

Last Saturday Trevor, Alison, Gary and Emma went on a twenty-mile walk over the Norland Hills. Trevor likes walking, and it was his idea. They walked from Oscroft at the eastern end of the hills to Raveley in the west. The day didn't go at all as planned. It rained most of the morning, so it wasn't a very pleasant walk. The weather is often wet in the Norland Hills, in fact. But they decided to go because the forecast wasn't bad. Trevor and Alison wore their anoraks, but Gary and Emma got wet because they didn't have their anoraks. The four friends had other problems too. They forgot to bring a map, and they lost the way. They wanted to stop for lunch in the village of Rydale. They finally got there at two o'clock. They were late because they didn't go the right way. They had planned to eat at the café in Rydale, but they weren't able to eat there because the cafe was closed for the day. It was very annoying. They didn't have any food with them, so they were hungry. But the weather was better by this time, and they decided to go on to Raveley. Five miles further on Alison had an accident. She fell and hurt her leg. So they had to go more slowly after that. They lost even more time. They missed their bus home because they got to Raveley so late. There wasn't any other transport, so they rang their friend Adam. Luckily he was at home, so he was able to come and fetch them in his car. They were glad to get home.

Activity

Here is part of a newspaper report about a motorway accident. Read it and then write three or four sentences about the accident using if-clauses type 3. You can use your own words as well as the words in the report.

---

30 DIE IN COACH DISASTER

There was a terrible accident on the motorway near Gondolfo last night when a coach overturned and caught fire. Thirty people died, all of them British. There were only four survivors, who managed to get out through a broken window. Luckily the motorway was quiet and no other vehicle was involved in the crash. The coach, owned by Gladway Tours of London, was on its way to Athens. According to the survivors, the driver had been at the wheel of the coach for fourteen hours and had probably fallen asleep. The coach left London two hours late, and the driver was

---

74 (11.1)

David, Lynn, Angela and Martin live in a town on a busy main road. They're talking about a plan to build a by-pass round the town.

Complete the conversation by putting the verbs in brackets into the correct form. Use *will* or *would* if necessary.

David I think a new road is a good idea. It (keep) the traffic out of the town if they build a by-pass. The traffic in the High Street is terrible. If they'd had any sense, they (build) a by-pass years ago.
Lynn But what about the shopkeepers? If there was a by-pass, then people (not stop) here. And there'll be fewer customers in the shops if there (be) less traffic in the town.
Angela I don't agree. I think more people (want) to shop here if it's quieter and pleasanter.
Martin Tourists (not come) into the town if there's a by-pass.
David If the High Street (be) less busy, it would be a lot easier to cross the road.
Angela There (be) less noise if there were fewer heavy lorries.

David And the traffic doesn't do the buildings any good. Everything shakes when a heavy lorry goes past. Do you remember those old houses in West Street? They had to knock them down because of damage by lorries. If there (be) a new road ten years ago, they (not have to) do that. And cyclists have been knocked off their bikes by lorries. One man was killed. That (not happen) if the lorries hadn't had to use the High Street.
Martin Don't forget that if you (improve) the road system, then the traffic may simply increase. Or you'll just move the problem to another town.
Angela But look at the situation now — dozens of lorries moving very slowly through the town. It (save) a lot of time if they travelled more quickly along a by-pass.
Martin The by-pass would use up good farmland that we can't afford to lose.
Lynn The route goes right through Gordon Bentley's farm. It (cut) his farm in two if they build it there. He only bought the farm three years ago.
David Well, if that (happen), they'd pay him for the land.
Lynn He told me yesterday he (not buy) the farm in the first place if he (know).
Angela But a by-pass is for the whole town.
Lynn Well, if I (be) Gordon, I (be) angry about it.
David I'm angry now about the traffic in the High Street. If they (not give) us a by-pass, there'll be trouble, I can tell you.

Activity

Complete these sentences in your own words.

Discuss your answers with other members of the class.

If all goes well, …
If I had a million pounds, …
If there was only one day left before the end of the world, …
If I had lived … hundred years ago, …

11.2　Other types of if-clause

1　**if** + *a present tense,* + *the imperative*
If it**'s raining**, take a coat.
Don't wear those shoes **if** you **want** to go walking.

2　**if** + *the simple present tense,*
　 + *the simple present tense*
If you **mix** blue and yellow, you **get** green.
If the temperature **falls** below zero, water **freezes**.

3　**if** + *the present continuous/present perfect tense,*
　 + *a modal verb*
If you**'re planning** a holiday, I**'ll tell** you about ours.
If you **haven't been** to Wales, you **ought to go** there.

4　**if** + *a modal verb,* + *a modal verb*
If you **can't find** a cup, there **might be** one in the cupboard.
Well, David **can't use** this kitchen **if** he **won't wash** up.

5　**if** + **will/would**, + *a modal verb*
If you**'ll give** me your address, I **can send** you the information.
If you **would** kindly **wait** a moment, please,
Mr Barnes **won't be** long.

6　**if** + **should**, + *a modal verb/the imperative*
I think it's going to be nice, but **if** it **should rain**, we **can have** the meal inside.
I'll probably arrive on time, but **if** I **should be** late, please **don't wait** for me.

1　To give orders etc. ▷ 6.1
2　To talk about things that are always true.
3　Many uses, e.g. offering, giving advice.
4　Many uses, e.g. suggestions, permission.
5　To make a request. ▷ 31.2
6　To talk about future actions which the speaker thinks are not very probable.

For the three main types of if-clause ▷ 11.1. There are many other types of if-clauses with different verb tenses. These six types here are some of the most usual ones.

75   (11.2)

There are some 'laws of life' hidden in this table. For each sentence on the left, there is one on the right that follows on from it. Find the pairs of sentences and write the laws. Use *if* and the simple present tense.

Example

If something begins well, it often ends badly.

Something begins well.	They're usually short.
You've got a job to do.	You're probably wrong.
You're in an accident.	You usually make it worse.
You want to buy something.	It often ends badly.
You're absolutely sure about something.	It always takes longer than you think.
You type your own letters.	It's the other person's fault.
You try to make a difficult situation better.	They usually don't make it any more.

Activity A

Discuss the 'laws of life' in the table above and say if you think they are true.

Activity B

Complete these simple 'scientific laws' and write two or three more.

If you mix blue and yellow, you get … .
If air gets warmer, … .
… a piece of glass with a hammer, … .

76   (11.2)

Arthur worries all the time. He worries most of all when he's going on holiday. Look what Arthur is thinking and write sentences with *If … should … might …* .

Example

What if the holiday company goes bankrupt?
(lose my holiday)

If the holiday company should go bankrupt, I might lose my holiday.

1 What if it's foggy at the airport?
    (plane not able to take off)
2 What if my luggage was put on the wrong plane?
    (never see it again)
3 What if my house is broken into?
    (lose everything)
4 What if I lost my money?
    (have to come home early)
5 What if I lost my passport?
    (not be able to get home)
6 What if I had an accident?
    (have to go into hospital)
7 What if it rains all the time?
    (have a terrible holiday)
8 What if everything goes well?
    (have nothing to worry about)

Activity

Give some advice to a group of people who are going for a walk across wild and lonely country. Include some *if-* clauses with *should*. e.g. *If the weather should get worse …*

12 Reported speech

12.1 Reporting verbs

1 Statements

Direct speech   'There's a game this evening.'
Reported speech   Peter **says** (**that**) there's a
game this evening.
There's a game this evening,
Peter **says**.

Direct speech   'It begins at eight o'clock.'
Reported speech   Jane **told** me (**that**) it begins
at eight o'clock.
It begins at eight o'clock, Jane
told me.

1 *say* and *tell* are reporting verbs which report statements or thoughts. We also use e.g. *mention, explain, answer, agree, write, think, know, be sure*. And ▷ 12.7

say does not have an indirect object when used as a reporting verb. *tell* must have an indirect object, e.g. *me*.

The reporting verb (e.g. *says*) usually comes before the reported clause (e.g. *there's a game this evening*), but the reported clause can come first. When the reporting verb comes first, we can use *that* or leave it out. Leaving it out is more informal.

When the reporting verb comes after the reported clause, we cannot use *that*.

2 Questions

Direct speech   'What time is the game?'
Reported speech   Andrew **asked** me what time
the game was.

2 *ask* is a reporting verb which reports questions. We also use e.g. *wonder, enquire, want to know*.

▷   12.6 reporting orders and requests;
39.3, 6 punctuation

12.2 Reporting in the present tense

Michael is reading Simon's letter and reporting what he reads to a friend.
'I'm having a great time in New York.'
Simon says he's having a great time in New York.
'My girl-friend likes it here, too.'
He mentions that his girl-friend likes it there, too.
'We'll be home next Tuesday.'
He says they'll be home tomorrow.

When the reporting verb is in the present tense (*says, mentions*), then the tense of the verb in direct speech (*'m having, likes, 'll be*) does not change.

Sometimes pronouns, adjectives and adverbs change in reported speech, e.g. *I →he, my →his, here →there, next Tuesday →tomorrow*.

We have to change these words when the situation has changed, e.g. New York is *here* for Simon but *there* for Michael because Michael is in England; the day when Simon comes home is *next Tuesday* for Simon but *tomorrow* for Michael because Michael reads the letter on Monday.

Exercises

77 **(12.2)**

Find out what the horoscope on the right says about the people in the list below.

Examples

Helen (18th November)
It says she is having a difficult time, but there will be some surprises for her.

Paul (6th July)
It says he will have money problems, so it isn't the time to plan his holiday.

1 Bob (13th February)
2 Kate (14th September)
3 David (22nd April)
4 Janet (30th November) and Jerry (10th December)
5 Sarah (3rd October)
6 Tom (12th April)
7 Diane (18th March)
8 Jane (29th May)
9 Mr Johnson (8th January)
10 Sue (4th August) and Peter (20th August)

Activity

Find your horoscope in a newspaper or magazine and tell the other people in your class what it says. If possible, find different horoscopes and compare them.

What the stars say – your horoscope

Aries (21st March – 20th April)
You are worrying a lot, but your problems aren't very great.

Taurus (21st April – 21st May)
You will meet someone interesting, and your life may change suddenly.

Gemini (22nd May – 21st June)
Your boss or teacher will not be pleased with you, but it won't be your fault.

Cancer (22nd June – 23rd July)
You will have money problems, so it isn't the time to plan your holiday.

Leo (24th July – 23rd August)
Everything is going well for you, but you must think before you make any decisions.

Virgo (24th August – 23rd September)
You will have problems at work and you should ask your friends for help.

Libra (24th September – 23rd October)
Your life is getting more exciting, but you must control your feelings.

Scorpio (24th October – 22nd November)
You are having a difficult time, but there will be some surprises for you.

Sagittarius (23rd November – 21st December)
You are feeling rather unhappy, but you will hear some interesting news.

Capricorn (22nd December – 20th January)
You should spend more time with your friends because you are working too hard.

Aquarius (21st January – 19th February)
You will have lots of energy, and you may have to travel.

Pisces (20th February – 20th March)
Your life feels empty, but you will find romance.

12.3   Reporting in the past tense [A]

Martin is reporting Barbara's words to Stephen.

1   'We **need** Stephen.'
Barbara said they **needed** you.

2   'I**'m starting** a pop group.'
She told me she **was starting** a pop group.

3   'I **haven't found** anyone who can play the guitar.'
She said she **hadn't found** anyone who could play the guitar.

4   'I**'ll be** at the club.'
She told me she**'d be** at the club.

5   'The group **is going to** meet there.'
She said that the group **was going to** meet there.

6   'I **must** talk to Stephen.'
She said she **had to** talk to you.

7   'He **played** in a group once.'
She mentioned that you **had played**/that you **played** in a group once.

8   'It **would** be great if he **could** play in our group.'
She said it **would** be great if you **could** play in their group.

If the reporting verb is in the past tense (e.g. *said, told*), then the verb in direct speech usually changes from the present to the past tense, e.g.

1   *need → needed*
2   *am → was*
3   *haven't → hadn't*
4   *will → would*
5   *is → was*
6   *must → had to*
7   If the verb in direct speech is in the past tense, it either changes to the past perfect tense (e.g. *played → had played*) or it stays the same.
8   *would, could, should, might* and *ought to* stay the same.

12.4   Reporting in the past tense [B]

Paul is reporting Sarah's words.

'Horses are my favourite animals.'
Sarah said horses **were** her favourite animals.
Sarah said horses **are** her favourite animals.

'I can ride.'
She told me she **could** ride.
She told me she **can** ride.

After a reporting verb in the past, there is usually a tense change. ▷ 12.3

But sometimes the verb in direct speech stays in the same tense if the words are still true when someone reports them, e.g. it is true that horses are still Sarah's favourite animals.

Even if the words are still true, *we can always change the tense* into the past after a past tense reporting verb.

78 (12.3)

Stanley Arnold, the multi-millionaire businessman and head of Arnold Motors, has just died. He wasn't a very popular man. Below are some examples of what the press said about him during his lifetime. Write down what they said.

Example

'Arnold is not a very nice person.' – Today Magazine
Today Magazine said that Arnold was not a very nice person.

1 'Arnold Motors has never paid any tax.' – News Extra
2 'Arnold spends the company's money at a Las Vegas casino.' – Newsday Magazine
3 'When he dies, he will probably leave more than $500 million.' – International News
4 'Stanley Arnold never speaks to his children.' – Modern World
5 'He is planning to leave his money to a dogs' home.' – The Daily Free Press
6 'Arnold has friends in the Mafia.' – World Magazine
7 'The police ought to ask Stanley Arnold some questions.' – The Saturday Reporter
8 'No one will be sorry when he's gone' – The Daily Talk

Activity

Complete the sentences by reporting what people might say in these situations.

After winning a million pounds in a competition, Mrs Grout of Birmingham said …
A plane crashed into the sea, and fifty people were killed. There was one survivor. He told reporters afterwards that …
On the day he became Prime Minister, Mr Wright said …

79 (12.3)

The American pop group *Thunder* left Britain yesterday after their first tour of the country. At the airport they spoke to reporters. How did the British newspapers report what they said?

Example

Lena said they wanted to thank their fans.

Activity

You were sent to interview *Thunder* when they arrived at the airport to begin their British tour. What questions did you ask? Make up the story and write it for a newspaper.

12.5 Reporting questions

Mrs Todd is reporting a telephone conversation to her husband.

1   *Yes/no questions*

'Is your husband in?'
He asked **if** you were in.
'Has he gone to London?'
He wanted to know **whether** you'd gone to London.

2   *Wh-questions*

'Which train did he take?'
He asked me **which** train you'd taken.
'When does he usually get home?'
He asked **when** you usually got home.

1   We report yes/no questions with *if* or *whether*.
2   In wh-questions we use question words (e.g. *which, when, what, who* and *how*) both in direct speech and in reported speech.

Verbs in reported questions change in the same way as in reported statements. ▷ 12.3

The word order in a reported question is the same as in a direct statement (not a direct question), e.g. *you were in, you'd gone to London, you'd taken, you usually got home.*

80   (12.5)

Tina has left school but she hasn't got a job yet. Yesterday she had an interview for a job at a pet shop. A man and a woman interviewed her. The next day Tina told her friend Sharon what they had asked her. Give Tina's words.

Examples

They asked me how old I was.
They asked me if I'd had a job before.

Activity A

Think of a job and imagine that you were interviewed for it yesterday. Tell the class what questions you were asked. They have to guess the job.

Activity B

Imagine that you can invite anyone in the world to be your dinner guest. Write down three questions you would like to ask your guest. Tell the other members of your class who you would invite and what you would ask him or her.

81   (12.3, 12.5)

Adam does his shopping at Brisco supermarket. Yesterday a woman who works for Brisco stopped him on his way out and asked him some questions. She wrote the answers on the form below. Later Adam told his friend Don about it. Give Adam's words.

Examples

She asked me how often I shopped at Brisco, and I told her I shopped there twice a week.
She asked me if I was happy to shop there, and I told her I was.

Activity A

Has anyone ever stopped you in the street or knocked on your door to ask you questions? Have you ever had an interview for a job? Has a reporter or a policeman ever asked you questions? Report the interview to the class.

Activity B

Imagine that one student in your class has won a TV quiz contest. The student tells the class how he/she answered the questions, e.g. 'I said it was Sofia.' You say what the student was asked, e.g. 'Oh, so you were asked what the capital of Bulgaria was.'

Practise the game with a group of other students. Take it in turns to think of an answer to a quiz question.

12.6　Reporting orders and requests

1　'Take the pills before meals.'
The doctor **told me to** take the pills before meals.
'You mustn't smoke.'
He **told me not to** smoke.

2　'Would you mind not leaving your car here?'
Someone **asked me not to** leave the car there.

3　I **was told to** take the pills before meals.
You **were asked not to** leave the car there.

4　The doctor said I **must** take/I **had to** take/I **was to** take the pills before meals.
He said I **mustn't** smoke/I **was not to** smoke.

5　'Can I have some water please?'
A motorist **asked me for/asked for** some water.

6　He **asked if** he could have some water.

1　We report orders (▷ 31.1) with *tell* + object + infinitive.

2　We report requests (▷ 31.2) with *ask* + object + infinitive.

3　The reporting verb can be in the passive. ▷ 14.9

4　We can also report orders with a form of *must* or *be to*.

5　We report a request to have something with *ask for*.

6　We can also report requests which are in question form (e.g. *Can I . . .?*) in the same way as other yes/no questions. ▷ 12.5

12.7　Reporting suggestions, advice etc.

Suggestions	'Let's go out.' Tony **suggested going** out.	▷ 31.4
Advice	'You'd better phone the police.' Mrs Dell **advised** me **to phone** the police.	▷ 31.5
Warnings	'Don't be late.' I **warned** you **not to be** late.	▷ 31.7
Threats	'If you don't go, I'll call the police.' I **threatened to call** the police.	▷ 31.9
Insisting	'We simply must take a taxi.' Mr and Mrs Beal **insisted on taking** a taxi.	▷ 31.10
Refusals	'I'm not going to wait any longer.' Mrs Janner **refused to wait** any longer.	▷ 32.4
Promises	'I'll send you a postcard.' He **promised to send** us a postcard.	▷ 32.5
Offers	'Can I get you a taxi?' Eric **offered to get** the visitors a taxi.	▷ 33.1
Invitations	'Would you like to have lunch with us?' The Updikes **invited** us **to** lunch.	▷ 33.2

82   **(12.6)**

Every summer there's a ten-mile 'Fun Run' around Milchester for people who want to keep fit. Last year the organizers gave all the runners a list of rules. Sarah did the run last year, and she's telling a friend what the rules were. Look at the rules and give Sarah's words. Use *tell* or *ask*.

Examples

They asked us to arrive at the start between 1.45 and 2.15.
They told us to be there by 2.30 at the latest.

> Milchester Fun Run
>
> **Rules for runners**
>
> Please arrive at the start between 1.45 and 2.15.
> You must be there by 2.30 at the latest.
> Please do not park in the centre of Milchester.
> You must show your ticket.
> You must wear your number on your shirt.
> Please wear running shoes.
> You must not carry any bags or bottles during the run.
> You must follow the correct route.
> Please run on the left.
> Please do not leave litter.

Activity

What does your English teacher like you to do? Say if he/she tells or asks you to do these things.

☐ work hard
☐ bring a dictionary to the English lesson
☐ write new words down in a vocabulary book
☐ listen to English programmes on the radio

83   **(12.3, 12.5, 12.6)**

The Anglian bus company wants to stop its service between Milchester and Little Wittering village. An Anglian manager, Mr Budge, is at a meeting in the village. Report what is said.

Examples

'The service is losing money.'
Mr Budge explained that the service was losing money.

'Please try to understand our position.'
He asked the villagers to try to understand the company's position.

1 'Lots of people use the buses.'
  Mr Crane said that …
2 'How can we get to town?'
  Mrs Manston asked …

3 'Most people in the village have got a car.'
  Mr Budge replied that …
4 'You must keep quiet and listen, everyone!'
  The chairman told everyone …
5 'What's going to happen to the school bus?'
  Mrs Davis asked …
6 'It will continue to run.'
  Mr Budge answered that …
7 'The village needs a bus service.'
  Mr Rice said that …
8 'Can you start your own service?'
  Mr Budge wondered …
9 'Can everyone please protest to the government?'
  Mr Hepplestone asked everyone …

Activity

Can you remember the last phone call you made? Tell the other students what was said during the call.

84   **(12.7)**

Magundian soldiers have entered Bingozi, a part of Silonia where a lot of Magundians live. The newspapers are reporting what the Magundians and Silonians are saying. Write down the sentences using *have suggested, have advised* etc.

Example

Magundi Would you like us to sign a peace agreement?
The Magundians have offered to sign a peace agreement.

1 **Silonia** We aren't going to give away Bingozi. It's quite out of the question.
2 **Magundi** We will give full rights to Silonians in Bingozi.
3 **Silonia** You had better think again.
4 **Magundi** Why don't we meet for discussions?
5 **Silonia** You can expect trouble, we're warning you.
6 **Magundi** Would you like to come to Magundi to discuss the problem?
7 **Silonia** If you do not leave Bingozi, we will start a war.
8 **Magundi** It's absolutely essential that we look after our people in Bingozi.

Activity

If you bought a second-hand car that broke down next day and needed expensive repairs, you would probably go back and speak to the salesman you bought it from. What should the salesman offer to do? If the salesman was dishonest, what would he do? What would you do if the salesman didn't want to do anything? Have you any suggestions or advice for people buying second-hand cars?

13 Tenses in sub clauses

13.1 Sequence of tenses

Why didn't you read what the notice **said**?
I thought he **was** an engineer.
We had already decided to buy the house
because we **liked** it so much.

If the main verb is in the past tense, then the verb in a sub clause is often in a past tense too.
Even if the words are still true (the notice still says something), we can use a past tense in the sub clause.

▷   12 reported speech

13.2 Sub clauses of future time

We'll start the meeting when everyone**'s** here.
If I **hear** any news, I'll phone you.
They're going to give a prize to the first person who **finds** the answer.

If the main verb has a future meaning, then we use the simple present tense in most sub clauses of future time.

▷   11 if-clauses

13.3 The unreal present and past

1   Just suppose we **had** enough money.
(= but we haven't enough money)

He acts as though he **was** the boss.
(= but he isn't the boss)

It's time we **went**.
(= but we haven't gone yet)

2   I wish you**'d said** something.
(= but you didn't say anything)

I'd rather we **hadn't come**.
(= but we have come)

If we**'d booked** seats, we'd have been more comfortable.
(= but we didn't book seats)

1   We use the past tense to talk about the unreal present.

2   We use the past perfect tense to talk about the unreal past.

We can do this after certain words and phrases, e.g. *suppose, imagine, if, as if, as though, it's time, wish, if only, would rather.*

▷   11 if-clauses; 30.8 having ideas; 34.5 wishing

85   (13.3)

Edith is talking to a friend about an old man called Arthur who lives near her. Arthur is a rather sad old man. He has a lot of regrets about what happened in the past and about his present life. Read what Edith says about him and then say what Arthur's regrets are.

Examples

Arthur wishes he didn't live in an old caravan.
He wishes he had married.

Edith Arthur lives in an old caravan. He never married, you know. He can't find work. Well, he left school when he was twelve. He never had a real job of course. And his health isn't good. He hasn't got any friends, poor man. People don't like him. The children are afraid of him. He got into trouble with the police, you know. Well, he never even knew his parents. He had a bad start in life.

Activity

Is there anything in your past that you regret?
Is there anything in your present life that you wish was different? Tell the other members of your class.

86   (13.2, 13.3)

A dangerous criminal called Dan Givens escaped from Maxley Prison a week ago. The police still haven't found him. Detectives Prosser and Jeffs are helping with the search. Complete their conversation, putting the verbs in brackets into the correct tense. Use the simple present, simple past or past perfect tense.

Prosser It's time we (find) Givens, isn't it? And we've still no idea where he is. The way things are going, it'll be Christmas before we (catch) him.
Jeffs I wish Maxley Prison (look) after him a bit better last week.
Prosser If they (discover) the escape more quickly, we'd have had a better chance of getting him.
Jeffs And now we haven't got enough men. If we (have) more men, we'd probably find him.
Prosser We don't even know where his girl-friend is.
Jeffs If only we (know) where she lives now. I bet he's with her.
Prosser We'll get him in the end.
Jeffs I wish they (not let) him escape in the first place.
Prosser When we finally (find) him, he'll probably have a gun.
Jeffs Of course. So we'll just have to be careful. He won't have a chance if he (try) to shoot his way out.

Activity

A tiger has escaped from a zoo and is being hunted by soldiers. What do you think the soldiers might say? Write three or four sentences with *it's time, if only, when* etc.

14 The infinitive

14.1 The infinitive with **to** and without **to**

1a Are you ready **to go** now?
 b Don't forget we've a bus **to catch**.
 c I don't want **to be** late.
 d They expect us **to arrive** at seven.
 e Do you know where **to go**?
2a I must **finish** this homework.
 b Our English teacher makes us **work** very hard.
 c I'd better **do** it tonight, although I'd rather **go** out.

The infinitive is the base form of the verb, e.g. *go, catch, be*. We use it with *to* or without *to*.

1 The infinitive is with *to* after
a adjectives ▷ 14.2
b nouns ▷ 14.3
c verbs ▷ 14.4
d verb + object ▷ 14.5
e question words ▷ 14.11
2 The infinitive is without *to* after
a modal verbs ▷ 7.1
b *make/let/see/hear* + object ▷ 14.8; 16.3
c *had better* ▷ 31.5 and *would rather* ▷ 34.6

14.2 The infinitive after adjectives

1 I'm **glad to see** you all.
 The game was **exciting to watch.**
2 It would be more **interesting to go** out.
 The Top Club is the **easiest to find**.
3 This piano is **too heavy to move**.
 I'm not **strong enough to lift** it.
4 It's **good of you to come**.
 It was **silly of Peter not to tell** anyone.

1 The infinitive after an adjective is with *to*.
2 We can also use the comparative and superlative of adjectives (e.g. *more interesting, easiest*).
3 We can also use adjectives with *too* or *enough*.
4 We can use a phrase with *of* after adjectives like *good, kind, nice, helpful, silly, stupid, wrong.*

14.3 The infinitive after nouns and pronouns

Have you got **a book to read**?
(= a book you can read)
You'll need **something to eat**.
(= something you can eat)
I have **some letters to write**.
(= letters I must write)

The infinitive after a noun or pronoun is with *to*.

14.4 The infinitive after verbs

I've **decided to do** a course in nursing.
I **hope to get** a job near here.
I **want to find** somewhere to live.
I've **arranged to look** at a flat tomorrow.

For a list of verbs + infinitive with *to* and verbs + -ing form ▷ 16.1.

87 (14.2, 14.3)

Sally works for an advertising agency. She's made some notes about a number of products. Look at her notes and write two sentences to advertise each product. The first sentence has an infinitive after a noun, and the second has an infinitive after an adjective.

Example

Have you got some clothes to wash? It's best to wash them with Brite.

EX Washing some clothes?
    – best with BRITE

1 Mowing a lawn?
   – easier with a SWISH machine

2 Cleaning your shoes?
   – best with GLEEM polish

3 Doing a dirty job?
   – sensible in ATKINSON'S work clothes

4 Taking some luggage?
   – easier in a car like an ALTON SAHARA

5 Feeding a dog?
   – better to feed CHOMP

6 Doing some sums?
   – quicker with a NUMEREX calculator

---

102 The infinitive

14.5 The infinitive after

Andy's father won't
I **persuaded my b**
No one **expecte**
Jill's aunt invit

14.6 **want s**

Do yo
I'd

14

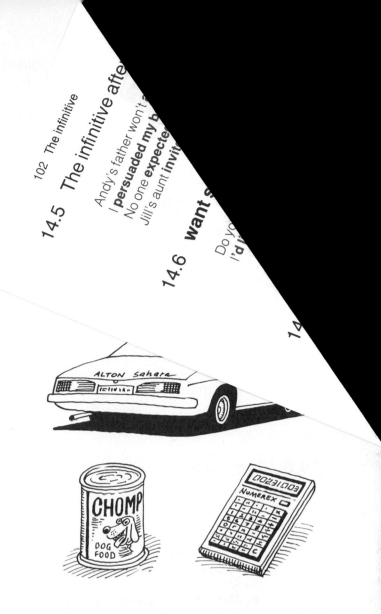

Activity

Think of some inventions that make work easier or quicker to do. Write a few sentences like *If you've got a carpet to clean, it's easier to use a vacuum cleaner.*

verb + object

...**llow him to use** the car.
...**oss to pay** me more money.
...**him to win**.
...**d her to stay** for the weekend.

Some other verbs which can have an object and an infinitive with *to* are: *tell*, *ask* (▷ 12.6), *want* (▷ 14.6), *warn*, *advise*, *remind*, *teach*, *force*.

▷ 14.9 passive

...omeone to do something

...u **want me to cook** the dinner?
...**ke you to help** if you can.

want and *would like* can have an object and an infinitive with *to*.

We cannot use a clause with *that* after *want* or *would like*.

.7 Verb + infinitive with and without a noun phrase

We want to visit the Wilsons. (*We* visit the Wilsons.)
I expected to get a letter from them. (*I* get a letter.)
We want **the Wilsons** to visit us. (*The Wilsons* visit us.)
I expected **them** to write to us. (*They* write to us.)

We put a noun phrase (e.g. *the Wilsons*, *them*) before the infinitive when the subject of the sentence (*We* want, *I* expected) is not the same as the subject of the infinitive.

14.8 The infinitive without **to**: **make** and **let**

The government **forced** companies **to hold** down wage increases.
The government **made** companies **hold** down wage increases.
They **allowed** workers **to have** only a 5% increase.
They **let** workers **have** only a 5% increase.

The verbs *force* and *allow* +object have the infinitive with *to*. ▷ 14.5

The verbs *make* (= force) and *let* (= allow) + object have the infinitive without *to*.

▷   16.3 after *see*, *hear* etc.

14.9 The infinitive after the passive

The gunman forced the cashier to hand over the money.
The cashier **was forced to hand** over the money.
The teachers made everyone take the exam.
Everyone **was made to take** the exam.
The manager let Mr Jones leave early.
Mr Jones **was allowed to leave** early.

After the passive verb the infinitive is always with *to*.

We can also use these verbs in the passive: *tell*, *ask* (▷ 12.6), *warn*, *advise*, *teach*, *persuade*, *expect*, *invite*.

We do not use the verb *let* in the passive. We use *allow* instead.

88 (14.5–14.8)

Granby United is a very successful football club. It's got a good club chairman and the team manager, Bill Grace, is one of the best in the country. Tim Bennett of the Daily Talk is interviewing people at the club. He's going to write an article about United. Write out Tim's notes as full sentences using verb + object + infinitive. Put *to* with the infinitive if necessary.

Examples

the players don't miss a training period – Bill doesn't allow it
Bill doesn't allow the players to miss a training period.

they train five days a week – he makes them
He makes them train five days a week.

1 they work very hard – Bill makes them
2 they take the game seriously – he forces them
3 the players feel proud of the club – Bill wants that
4 they play well together – Bill teaches them
5 they watch films of other teams – he makes them
6 they can relax after a game – Bill lets them
7 the players have to behave – the club expects it
8 they don't go to night-clubs – Bill doesn't allow it
9 the team does well – the fans want that
10 the club can't win everything – but that's what the fans would like!
11 schoolboys visit the club – Bill invites them
12 local companies are giving money to the club – the chairman has persuaded them

Activity

Discuss the function of a teacher in a class of students. What do you expect a teacher to do? How does a teacher want students to behave? What should a teacher make students do or allow them to do?

89 (14.9)

Six members of an organization called Food for the Third World are in Omagua. The group were kidnapped by guerrillas a month ago but have just been released. The leader of the group, Miss Hilary Lester, is telling reporters what happened. Write the sentences as they appear in the newspapers. Use the passive and an infinitive. Remember not to use *let* in the passive.

Examples

'The guerrillas asked me to give them some publicity.'
Miss Lester was asked to give the guerrillas some publicity.

'They made us discuss politics.'
The group were made to discuss politics.

1 'The guerrillas forced us to go with them.'
2 'They made us walk fifty miles to the guerrilla camp.'
3 'The guerrillas didn't let me send a message to anyone.'
4 'They made me carry a heavy bag.'
5 'They expected us to look after injured guerrillas.'
6 'The guerrillas allowed us to move around the camp.'
7 'They let us talk to each other.'
8 'The guerrillas warned me not to try to escape.'

Activity

Up to the year 1865, slavery was allowed in the USA. Write a few sentences saying what a slave's life was like. Use the passive and an infinitive.

14.10 **for** + noun phrase + infinitive

1 It was easy **for the player to kick** the ball into the empty goal.
(= The player easily kicked the ball into the empty goal.)

2 It was a mistake **for Helen to marry** Bob.
(= Helen married Bob, which was a mistake.)

3 We are still waiting **for them to reply**.
(= They have not replied yet.)

We use *for* + noun phrase + infinitive after

1 an adjective, e.g. *easy, important*
2 a noun phrase, e.g. *a mistake, a good idea*
3 a verb which usually has *for* after it, e.g. *wait for*

14.11 The infinitive after question words

I don't know **how to open** this bottle.
(= how I can open this bottle)
Can you tell me **where to buy** a ticket?
(= where I can buy a ticket)
Do you know **what to say**?
(= what you should say)
I've no idea **which bus to take**.
(= which bus I must take)
I can't decide **whether to go** or not.
(= whether I should go or not)

We can use the infinitive after question words and after *whether*.

90 (14.10)

Kelly is a seven-year-old girl whose parents have been killed in a road accident. She's living in a children's home, but she isn't happy there. Two social workers, Valerie and Roy, are talking about Kelly. Rewrite the underlined parts using *for* + noun phrase + infinitive.

Examples

It'll be the best thing for her to live in a family.
It's been very hard for her to accept the situation.

Valerie We've found a family who will have Kelly.
Roy That's excellent. It'll be the best thing if she lives in a family.
Valerie She hasn't accepted the situation. It's been very hard for her.
Roy She hasn't felt at home here. It's been impossible, I'm afraid. Will it take long before the boss gives us a definite decision?
Valerie Well, I've arranged that the psychologist is going to see Kelly on Friday. Then we'll have to wait until she writes her report.
Roy But we're sure, aren't we? There isn't any reason why we should keep her here any longer.
Valerie Oh, it won't be long. It's quite usual that children are in here for months, you know. It would be a mistake if everything happened in a big hurry.
Roy Well, I hope we can explain to Kelly. I think it's important that the children here know about our plans for them.

Activity

Use *for* + noun phrase + infinitive to talk about parties. Do you enjoy parties? Do people have parties in your country? Say what they're like. (*It's usual …*) What makes a good party? (*It's best … / It's important …*) What makes a bad one? (*It's a mistake …*).

91 (14.11)

In 1983 two people from the distant planet Chupron visited the earth. Their names were Kepal and Enis. They looked much like humans. They learnt English before they set off. They travelled in a small spaceship made to look like a Cadillac. They toured the USA pretending to be Canadian tourists. They spoke English the whole time. One day they left the spaceship in West 57th Street, New York while they went for a walk in Central Park. When they came back, it had gone. Look at their conversation and describe their thoughts.

Example

Kepal What shall we do?
Enis I've no idea.
They had no idea what to do.

1 **Enis** How can we get the spaceship back?
 Kepal I don't know.
2 **Kepal** Where should we look?
 Enis I can't think.
3 **Enis** Shall we wait in the street?
 Kepal I'm not sure.
4 **Enis** Where shall we go?
 Kepal I've no idea.
5 **Kepal** Do you think we ought to hide?
 Enis I don't know.
6 **Enis** How can we contact Chupron?
 Kepal I've no idea.
7 **Kepal** Should we go to the police?
 Enis I'm not sure.
8 **Kepal** What do you think?
 Enis I don't know.

Activity

Make similar sentences about these people:

☐ a man who had just finished a meal in a restaurant and discovered that he had forgotten his money
☐ a woman who saw a man on the other side of the street suddenly burst into flames as he was walking along
☐ a man who arrived home from work and unexpectedly found a huge pile of new bricks in his garden completely blocking the way to the door of the house

14.12 Leaving out the verb after **to**

Did you look round the castle? ~
We wanted **to**, but we weren't allowed **to**.

We can leave out the verb after *to* if the meaning is clear without it.

14.13 Other forms of the infinitive

1 *Continuous infinitive*
Those men seem **to be repairing** the road.
They oughtn't **to be making** so much noise on a Sunday.

2 *Perfect infinitive*
I should like **to have gone** for a walk, but it's been raining.
We ought **to have spent** our holiday somewhere warmer.

3 *Passive infinitive*
I'm going **to be interviewed** next week.
I hope **to be offered** a job.

Form

1 *to be* + -ing form
▷ 7.14 modal verbs + *be* + -ing form

2 *to have* + -ed form (past participle)
▷ 7.15 modal verbs + *have* + -ed form

3 *to be* + -ed form (past participle)
▷ 10.5 modal verbs in the passive

92 (14.1–14.11)

David has just met an old friend of his called Nigel. They're having a cup of coffee together. Nigel has some bad news. Complete the conversation by putting in an infinitive with *to* or without *to*.
Use these verbs: *answer, borrow, catch, do, find, go, hear, know, lend, look, make, pay, see, spend, stay, think.* (You will need to use some of the verbs more than once.)

David Are you still working for Electrobrit, Nigel?
Nigel No, I'm not. I'm afraid I lost my job there. And Polly's lost her job too. We're having rather a difficult time at the moment.
David Oh, dear. I'm sorry … that.
Nigel I've been out of work for six months now. I expected … a new job fairly quickly, but it isn't so easy, I've discovered.
David Jobs are hard … these days.
Nigel With Polly not working we've very little money … . After I lost my job I managed … my bank manager … us some money, but he won't let us … any more now. And there are lots of bills … . I really don't know what … .
David Do you think you might … a job if you moved somewhere else?
Nigel Well, perhaps. We've talked about it of course. We've even wondered whether … abroad. We could always … a fresh start in a different country. Polly wants me … for a job in America. And I've written to Australia House, although I'm still waiting for them … .
David Do you like the idea of living abroad?
Nigel I don't know really. I think on the whole I'd rather … here if I had a job. But the situation has made us … carefully about our future. We decided we ought … out what opportunities there are. I've agreed … about all the possibilities.
David Well, I hope you find something soon.
Nigel I simply must … a job soon, or I don't know what we shall … .
David Well, let me … what happens, won't you? Look, here's my new address and phone number. Give me a ring some time.
Nigel OK, David. I'd better … now. I've got a bus … .
David I hope … you again soon.
Nigel 'Bye, David.

Activity

Complete these sentences in your own words.

I hope to …
It would be nice to …
I don't know wh… to …
Why won't they let us … ?
Men/Women are always expected to …

93 (14.13)

Complete this newspaper report in the Daily Talk about the racing driver Chuck Loder. Put the verbs in brackets into an infinitive form. Use the continuous infinitive (e.g. *to be doing*), the perfect infinitive (e.g. *to have done*) or the passive infinitive (e.g. *to be done*).

LODER OUT OF HOSPITAL SOON

Racing driver Chuck Loder, who had a bad accident in last year's Grand Prix, is likely (come) out of hospital soon. He agreed (interview) by our sports reporter, although he has refused (photograph), as his face still shows the marks of the accident.

Chuck was very cheerful when he spoke to us. His health now seems (improve) slowly. He expects (sit) at the wheel once again before very long.

Many people think that last year's race at Bruckheim ought never (take) place. It was the last race on the old track, which is going (re-build) soon. The owners of the track expect (complete) the work in time for next season.

Chuck hopes (drive) in next year's Grand Prix. We wish him luck. Read his personal story of the Bruckheim accident in next week's Daily Talk.

Activity

Write a similar story about a yachtsman called Brendan Stiles who was badly injured when his experimental new yacht overturned and sank during an international yacht race which is held every year off the west coast of Australia.

15 The -ing form (verbal noun)

15.1 Introduction to the -ing form

1a **Smoking** isn't allowed here.
b I find **reading** difficult on a bus.
c This is a good place for **fishing**.
2 **Driving** a car isn't as comfortable as **travelling** by train.

1 We can use the -ing form as a verbal noun in the same way as we use other noun phrases. We can use it
a as a subject
b as an object
c after a preposition
2 After an -ing form we can put an object (e.g. *a car*) or an adverb phrase (e.g. *by train*).

▷ 31.1 orders

15.2 The -ing form after conjunctions and prepositions

1 **After working** all evening, John felt tired.
On hearing the news, they left at once.
We like a hot drink **before going** to bed.
I always have the radio on **while doing** the housework.
Judy hasn't found a job **since leaving** school.
Although feeling tired, David didn't want to stop.
In spite of trying so hard, I always make mistakes.
2 Can't you help **instead of** just **standing** there?
You won't pass the exam **without doing** any work.
You need a special tool **for cutting** glass.
Jane stayed awake **by drinking** black coffee.

The clause with the -ing form can come either before or after the main clause.
1 Using the -ing form to express time or contrast is a little formal. In speech we often use a clause with a subject, e.g. *after he'd worked all evening, as soon as they heard the news, before we go to bed.*
▷ 17.2; 27.2 clauses of time; 27.7 clauses of contrast
2 We use the -ing form after *instead of, without, for* and *by* even in informal speech.

▷ 27.9 clauses of purpose; 25.8 means; 31.4; 33.2 *What about/how about . . .?*

15.3 The -ing form after verbs

Have you **finished writing** the letter?
Barry **suggested going** for a walk.
I don't **mind waiting** a few minutes.
We **enjoy listening** to music.

For a list of verbs + -ing form and verbs + infinitive ▷ 16.1

15.4 The -ing form after **do**

Who's going to **do** the **cooking**?
You ought to **do** some **studying**.
I **did** a bit of **shopping** this morning.

We can use *do* with an -ing form to talk about a job of work, e.g. *cleaning, washing, ironing, typing.*
▷ 17.5 the -ing form after *go*

94 (15.1)

Look at the objects and say what sports or activities they are used in. Use these verbs: *camp, climb, fish, ride, sail, skate, ski.*

Example

1 *boxing*

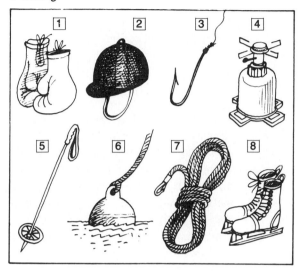

Activity

Talk about the different sports and activities with a partner. Say if you like them.

Example

I like swimming. What about you? ~
Well, swimming's OK, I suppose.

Use sentences like these: *I like swimming. Swimming's OK. I don't mind swimming. I don't like swimming much. I hate swimming. Swimming is something I don't do very often.*

95 (15.2)

This is an article about a woman who is head of a supermarket group. Rewrite the sentences with underlining. Use an -ing form after a conjunction or preposition instead of the underlined parts.

Example

After leaving school at 18, Elaine studied business management at Granby Polytechnic.

Elaine Archer is a 34-year-old woman in a very important job. She's head of the huge Brisco Supermarkets group.

Elaine left school at 18 and then studied business management at Granby Polytechnic. She left the Polytechnic, but she didn't take any exams. Elaine decided to see the world and then to make her home in Britain. She spent four years in the USA. She thought about her career during the time she was filling shelves in a supermarket.

As soon as she returned to Britain, Ms Archer bought a small food store. She was soon the owner of a dozen stores in south-east England. She made her stores a success because she pleased the customers. When Brisco took over Archer Stores, Elaine became south-east area manager of Brisco. She has risen to be head of the company in spite of the fact that she is a woman in a man's world. We certainly have not heard the last of her.

Activity

Find out some details of the life of a famous person. Write three or four sentences about the person, using the -ing form.

---

96 (15.3, 15.4)

Wendy and Diane are talking about how much help they get from their husbands with the housework. Complete the conversation by putting the verbs in brackets into the -ing form. Put *the* in front of the -ing form where necessary.

Wendy Mike's not much good around the house. Do you get any help from Paul?
Diane Yes, he doesn't mind (help) usually.
Wendy Mike sometimes does (shop), but that's all, really. I have to do all (clean) of course.

Diane Paul does (iron) quite often — that's a great help, because I hate (iron). And he's a very good cook. He usually does (cook) at weekends. We both enjoy (cook), in fact.
Wendy I like (cook) too, but Mike's no good at it. I do (cook) in our house. And I do all (wash). Mike doesn't even know how to use the washing-machine!

Activity

Talk to a partner. Say what jobs you do (or don't do) around the house. Say if you like doing them.

15.5 The -ing form after verb/adjective + preposition

1 *Verb + preposition + -ing form*
I'm **thinking of buying** an electric toothbrush.
My brother's **talking about starting** a pop group.
We **succeeded in finding** the place.

2 *Adjective + preposition + -ing form*
Sarah's **fond of doing** crosswords.
You're **good at drawing**.
I'm a postman. I'm **used to walking**.

1 More examples of verb + preposition which can take an -ing form: *agree with, believe in, feel like, insist on, look forward to, take part in, worry about.*
▷ 26.3 prepositional verbs

2 More examples of adjective + preposition which can take an -ing form: *afraid of, bored with, excited about, interested in, keen on, proud of, tired of.*
▷ 25.12 adjective + preposition

15.6 The -ing form with a subject

1 We've stopped **watching** television.
(= We don't watch television any more.)
I insist on **having** a rest.
(= I insist that I have a rest.)

2 We've stopped **the children watching** television.
(= The children don't watch television any more.)
I insist on **you having** a rest, Sarah.
(= I insist that you have a rest.)

3 I insist on **your having** a rest.
I'm afraid of **Sarah's doing** too much.

1 When the subject of the sentence (*We*'ve stopped, *I* insist) is the same as the subject of the -ing form, we do not repeat the subject before the -ing form.

2 When the subject of the sentence is *not* the same as the subject of the -ing form (*The children* don't watch television, *You* have a rest), then we give the -ing form its own subject, too.

3 The subject of the -ing form can be a possessive form (e.g. *your, Sarah's*), but usually only if it is a pronoun or a name. A possessive form is more formal than e.g. *you, Sarah.*

97 (15.3, 15.5)

Look at what these people are saying and complete the sentences using an -ing form. Put a preposition before the -ing form if necessary.

Example

They're worried about losing their jobs.

Activity

Complete the following sentences in your own words using an -ing form.

I enjoy …   I'm afraid …
I believe … I get bored …

They're worried …   1 They insist …   2 He thinks it's wrong to risk …   3 They're tired …

4 She doesn't agree …   5 He wants the government to stop …   6 They believe …   7 She's keen …   8 He doesn't …

---

98 (14.5, 15.6)

Amanda is a secretary. She's got a new job, but she doesn't like her boss. She's telling her friend about him. Rewrite each sentence or pair of sentences using an infinitive or -ing form.

Examples

The boss insists on everyone being in the office at nine o'clock.
He doesn't allow us to make personal phone calls.

Amanda Everyone has to be in the office at nine o'clock. The boss insists on it. And we can't make personal phone calls because he doesn't allow it. We don't have coffee breaks because he's stopped that.

We have to work hard — that's what he's always telling us. People can't work at their own speed; he doesn't agree with that. I have to work late because he quite often wants me to. If he asked me occasionally, I wouldn't mind. But I have to spend my life at the office. He seems to expect it. And he watches me all the time, which I don't like. People can't be friendly with him — he hates that.

Activity

Write three or four similar sentences about your boss or about your parents. Say what they expect (or don't expect) you to do, or what they insist (or don't insist) on you doing, and so on.

15.7   The passive -ing form

Visiting people is nicer than **being visited**.
He was afraid of **being seen** by the police.
I don't like the dog **being shut** up in the house.

Form *being* + -ed form (past participle)

16   The infinitive and the -ing form

16.1   The infinitive and the -ing form after verbs

I **wanted to visit** England.
I **enjoy travelling** around.

After some verbs we use the infinitive with *to*
(▷ 14.4), and after some verbs we use the -ing
form (▷ 15.3).
Here are some of the most common verbs of both types.

+ *the infinitive with* **to**			+ *the -ing form*	
agree	fail	plan	avoid	miss
arrange	forget ▷ 16.2	prepare	can't help	practise
attempt	have ▷ 7.4	promise	dislike	risk
be ▷ 4.8	hope	refuse	enjoy	stop ▷ 16.2
can afford	learn	seem	finish	suggest
choose	manage	used ▷ 3.11	go on	*And*
dare ▷7.13	need ▷ 7.4	want	imagine	it's no fun
decide	offer	wish	keep	it's no good
expect	ought ▷ 7.6		mind	it's no use
				it's worth

99 (15.3, 15.7)

Max Finkel is a famous film director. Max is giving some advice to a friend of his who is going to make a film starring Melinda Burns. Complete what Max says about Melinda using *like, enjoy, love* or *hate* and an active or passive -ing form.

Examples

You might find she makes trouble.
Melinda enjoys making trouble.

Don't ever tell her she's wrong.
She doesn't like being told she's wrong.

1 Let her talk to the press. She …
2 You'd better let them photograph her. Melinda …
3 Don't laugh at her. She …
4 Try to arrange things so that she doesn't have to wait around. Melinda …
5 You'll have to look after her. She …
6 She won't get up early. Melinda …
7 It doesn't matter if people stare at her. She …
8 Never ignore her. She …

Activity

Here is a list of things that many people are afraid of. Are you afraid of them too?

☐ drowning
☐ being bitten by a dog
☐ being stuck in a lift
☐ speaking to a large group of people
☐ being killed in a plane crash

Use *I'm (not) afraid of …, I'm terrified of …* or *I (never) worry about …* . Add more things to the list if you can.

---

100 (16.1)

Complete the newspaper article by putting in the infinitive or the -ing form of the verbs in brackets.

NELLIE WILL STAY

Milchester Council has decided (let) 82-year-old Mrs Nellie Battle go on (live) at her home at 29 Croft Street. The Council had wanted (knock) down all the old houses in the street because they were planning (build) a new car park there. The future of this plan is now uncertain.

The story began five years ago when the people of Croft Street agreed (move) to new homes. Unfortunately the Council forgot (ask) Mrs Battle. When they finally remembered her, everyone else had already gone. But the Council failed (persuade) Nellie to do the same. 'My grandson's just finished (decorate) the sitting-room for me,' she said at the time. 'I can't imagine (leave) now.'

The Council offered (pay) Mrs Battle £500 and promised (give) her a new house, but she still refused (move). 'I can't help (like) it here,' she told our reporter. 'I miss (see) the neighbours of course. I enjoyed (talk) to them.' Croft Street has stood almost empty for the last five years. There seemed (be) no way anyone could move Nellie from number 29.

Now comes the Council's new decision. Mrs Battle is very pleased. 'I kept (tell) them I wouldn't move,' she said today. 'I don't mind (be) on my own any more.

And I expect (live) till I'm a hundred. I hope (be) here a long time yet.'

We have also heard this week that the Council cannot now afford (build) the car park. One or two of the people who used (live) in Croft Street have suggested (repair) the old houses so that they can move back into them. They dislike (live) in the new houses they moved into five years ago.

Activity

Read this paragraph about the Electrobrit company

> The union and management at Electrobrit can't agree. The union wants a five per cent increase in wages. The management say the company hasn't got enough money. If they paid higher wages, they might go bankrupt. But they can give the workers an extra week's holiday next year. The union thinks the wages are very low, and the workers may go on strike.

Think of some sentences that might be spoken during the discussion. Write two or three of the union's sentences and two or three of the management's. Use an infinitive or an -ing form after e.g. *Why do you refuse …, We can't go on …, We're offering …, We can't risk …, We've promised …* .

16.2   The infinitive and the -ing form: special cases

1   Mrs Scott **began to eat/began eating** her dinner. She **intended to go/intended going** out later.

2   I **like to have/like having** tea in front of the television. I **love to read/love reading** at meal times.

3   I **like to go** to the doctor every year. I **like to know** if there's anything wrong with me.

4   Dick **would like to stay** in, but I'd prefer to sit outside.

5   He **remembered to bring** the drinks. He **didn't forget to bring** the drinks.

6   I **remember having** a picnic here years ago. I'**ll never forget having** a picnic here years ago.

7   I'**m trying to get** brown in the sun.

8   Why don't you **try putting** some cream on your back?

9   I **stopped to get** some aspirin as I was driving from the hotel.

10   Your tooth will **stop hurting** if you take two of these.

1   After *begin, start, continue* and *intend*, we use either the infinitive or the -ing form.

2   After *like, love, prefer* and *hate*, we use either the infinitive or the -ing form. ▷ 34.3 likes; 34.6 preferences. But see the special use in 3.

3   We use an infinitive after *like* to talk about something a person chooses to do but may not enjoy doing.

4   After *would like* (= want), *would love, would prefer* and *would hate*, we use the infinitive. ▷ 34.5 wishes; 34.6 preferences

5   We use an infinitive after *remember* or *not forget* when we remember that we have to do something.

6   We use an -ing form after *remember* or *not forget* when we remember something that happened in the past.

7   We use an infinitive after *try* when *try* means to make an attempt, to do your best to succeed.

8   We use an -ing form after *try* when *try* means to make an experiment, to do something as a test to see if it will succeed.

9   We use an infinitive after *stop* when someone stops in order to do something. ▷ 27.9 clauses of purpose

10   We use an -ing form after *stop* to talk about something finishing, something that no longer happens.

16.3   The infinitive without **to** and the -ing form after **see, hear** etc.

1   We saw a group of people. They climbed the hill. We saw a group of people **climb** the hill. (= We saw them do the whole climb to the top.) We heard a man. He shouted. We heard a man **shout**. (= He shouted once, and we heard the shout.)

2   We saw a group of people. They were climbing the hill. We saw a group of people **climbing** the hill. (= But we did not see them do the whole climb.) We heard a man. He was shouting. We heard a man **shouting**. (= He shouted a number of times, and we heard some of the shouts.)

1   We use the infinitive without *to* after verbs of perception (*see, hear* etc.) and with *watch* and *listen to* to talk about a complete action.

2   We use the -ing form after these verbs to talk about part of an action, but not the whole action from beginning to end.

101 (16.2)

Peter and Sue are in the shopping centre. Complete their conversation by putting the verbs in brackets into the infinitive or the -ing form.

Peter Have we done all the shopping now?
Sue Yes, I think so. I must remember (post) this letter.
Peter I remember (pass) a postbox somewhere.
Sue Just a minute, where's my purse? It isn't in my handbag.
Peter Did you forget (bring) it?
Sue No, I had it not long ago. And my credit card is in there. Oh, my God, what are we going to do?
Peter Just stop (worry) and think. You must have put it down somewhere and forgotten (pick) it up. Try (remember) when you had it last.
Sue I remember (have) it in the shoe shop.
Peter Then you stopped (buy) a newspaper …
Sue Oh, it's all right. It's here in the shopping bag. Sorry. I can't remember (put) it there.
Peter You could try (chain) it to your hand next time.

Activity A

Can you remember things you did when you were very young? Give examples of things you remember doing.

Activity B

Do you ever forget to do things such as turning off lights or locking doors? Give examples.

Activity C

What advice would you give to someone who wants to stop smoking? Use the verb *try*.

102 (16.3)

Mr Pratt often has strange dreams. The pictures on the right show what he dreamed about last night. Describe each dream using *see* or *hear* and either the infinitive without *to* or the -ing form.

Examples

He heard a bomb explode.
He saw a girl running along a beach.

Use these verbs: *burn, crash, fly, jump, ring, scream.*

1 He … . It went on for a long time.
2 … into the sea.
3 … in the sky.
4 … . He thought she would never stop.
5 … out of a car as it was moving.
6 …

Activity A

Write two or three sentences saying what you can see and hear when you look out of your window in the morning.

Activity B

One student imagines that he/she was in a certain place yesterday evening, e.g. at a restaurant or at the circus. The student gives clues, e.g. *I could hear people talking quietly. I saw an acrobat do a somersault.* You guess where he/she was.

17 The -ing form and the -ed form (participles)

17.1 The -ing form and the -ed form used as adjectives

1 The men ran out to the **waiting** car.
There were three people inside the **burning** house.

2 The **injured** man was taken to hospital.
The **stolen** money was in **used** notes.
She tried to open the door, but it was **locked**.

1 The -ing form (present participle) describes an action (the car was waiting).

2 The -ed form (past participle) describes the result of an action (something had injured the man).

For e.g. *the car waiting outside* ▷ 22.11
For the -ed form in the passive ▷ 10.1, 2

17.2 The -ing form in clauses of time

1 Jane ate her supper while she was sitting in front of the television.
She heard the telephone and got up to answer it.

2 Jane ate her supper **while sitting** in front of the television.
On hearing the telephone, she got up to answer it.

3a **Sitting** in front of the television, Jane ate her supper.

b **Hearing** the telephone, she got up to answer it.

c Jane ate her supper **sitting** in front of the television.

1 To talk about two actions that happen at the same time or that happen one after the other, we can use two clauses.

2 We can replace one of the clauses by an -ing form after a conjunction or preposition. ▷ 15.2

3a We can use an -ing form without a conjunction or preposition to talk about an action that happens at the same time as another action.

b We can also use an -ing form without a conjunction or preposition to talk about an action that happens just before another action. The -ing form comes before the main clause.

c If the actions happen at the same time, the -ing form can come after the main clause.

An -ing form before the main clause is rather formal, and we normally use it only in writing.

17.3 The perfect -ing form in clauses of time

Compare the use of the past perfect and the -ing form:

1 After she had counted the money, she locked it in a drawer.

2 **After counting** the money, she locked it in a drawer.

3 **Having counted** the money, she locked it in a drawer.

Form *having* + -ed form

Use

1 Remember that we use the past perfect tense to talk about the first of two actions in the past. ▷ 3.6

2 We can use *after* + -ing form in the same way. ▷ 15.2

3 We can also use the perfect -ing form without *after* to talk about the first of two actions in the past.

The sentences with -ing forms are used much more in writing than in speech.

103 (17.1)

Complete the newspaper story about an earthquake in a city called Kitamo. Put in either an -ing form or an -ed form. Use these verbs: *break, burn, cry, damage, fall, frighten, injure, smoke.* (You have to use one of the verbs twice.)

KITAMO EARTHQUAKE

There was an earthquake in the Kitamo region at ten o'clock yesterday morning. It lasted about a minute. Many buildings collapsed. … people ran into the streets. Many were injured by … bricks and stones. After the earthquake, buildings in many parts of the city caught fire. The heat was so great that firemen could not get near many of the … buildings. Hundreds of people have died. The hospital is still standing, but there aren't enough beds for all the … people. Things look very bad in Kitamo now. There are hundreds of badly … houses, and those that caught fire are now just … ruins. The streets are covered with … glass, and … trees block the way. Everywhere there is the sound of … children.

Activity

Imagine that instead of suffering an earthquake, Kitamo and the villages around it were flooded when snow on the mountains suddenly melted, and the River Nor burst its banks after heavy rain. Write a short report on the floods. Try to use -ing forms and -ed forms as adjectives. You can use the verbs in the exercise as well as some of these verbs: *abandon, continue, expect, float, flood, melt, rise, ruin, shiver, worry.*

---

104 (17.2, 17.3)

In this story, a British government agent is following a man who he thinks is a spy. Rewrite the sentences under the pictures using an -ing form or a perfect -ing form.

Examples

He left the office carrying a briefcase.
Crossing the road, he bought a newspaper.
Having looked at an inside page, he started walking along Oxford Street.

When he left the office, he was carrying a briefcase.

He crossed the road and bought a newspaper.

After he had looked at an inside page, he started walking along Oxford Street.

1 As he was hurrying along the street, he suddenly stopped outside a travel agency.

2 As he was standing outside, he looked twice at his watch.

3 After he had waited five minutes, he continued along Oxford Street to Hyde Park.

4 He ate a sandwich. He was sitting on a seat.

5 After he had looked again at the paper, he put it in a litter bin.

6 He left the park and stood at the side of the road.

7 He ran into the road and stopped a taxi.

Activity A

Using the pictures on the right, write two more sentences saying what the man did next.

Activity B

Write about a journey you have made recently or about a walk in the country. Include sentences like *Walking through the wood, we saw a fox* or *Having filled up with petrol, we set off.*

In Victoria Street …   Half an hour later …

17.4 The -ing form and the -ed form in clauses of reason

1a   They didn't know the way, so they soon got lost.
b   Not **knowing** the way, they soon got lost.
2a   The plane was delayed by bad weather, so it took off three hours late.
b   **Delayed** by bad weather, the plane took off three hours late.
3a   I had got up early, so I felt pretty tired.
b   **Having got up** early, I felt pretty tired.

We can use the -ing form and the -ed form to give a reason. We can use these forms:

1b   the -ing form
2b   the -ed form (which has a passive meaning)
3b   the perfect -ing form ▷ 17.3

We use the -ing form and the -ed form to give a reason more often in writing than in speech.

17.5 The -ing form after **go**

We **go dancing** every weekend.
The boys **went swimming** yesterday.
Are you **going sailing** again soon?

We can use *go* + -ing form to talk about things we go out to do, especially in our free time, e.g. *walking, climbing, fishing, riding, skating, shopping.*

▷   15.4 the -ing form after *do*

105 (17.4)

A reporter has made some notes about a fire on a passenger aircraft. Combine each pair of sentences. Use the -ed form, -ing form or perfect -ing form.

Examples

The plane was delayed by technical problems. It took off one hour late.
Delayed by technical problems, the plane took off one hour late.

The passengers saw smoke. They became alarmed.
Seeing smoke, the passengers became alarmed.

The pilot had travelled only a short distance from Heathrow. He decided to turn back.
Having travelled only a short distance from Heathrow, the pilot decided to turn back.

1 The airport fire service was warned by air traffic control. It prepared to fight a fire.
2 The passengers believed the aircraft was going to crash. Some of them shouted in panic.
3 The pilot brought the plane down safely. Then he felt very relieved.
4 Everyone was worried by the risk of fire. They hurried to get out.
5 The firemen used chemicals. They soon put out the fire.
6 Most of the passengers had had enough excitement for one day. They put off their journey.

Activity

Write a paragraph telling the story of a group of people who were picked up from the sea by lifeboat men after the boat on which they were passengers had sunk. Some of these words and phrases may be useful: *passenger, alarmed, captain, radio message, life jacket, lifeboat, shocked, experience, hospital.*

106 (17.1–17.5)

Complete the story in the Mudford Gazette about a girl who paints pictures. Put each verb in brackets into the *-ing* form or *-ed* form.

MUDFORD GIRL IS WINNING ARTIST

13-year-old Annabel Waites of Mudford has won first prize in a national art competition. Her (win) picture is a painting of Mudford Hill.

I talked to Annabel at her home in Embury Road. At the moment she has a (break) arm, which she got (play) netball. Fortunately it's her left arm, so she can still paint. Annabel usually listens to music while (paint). And she always paints (stand) up because she feels more comfortable that way. 'I often feel very tired after (finish) a picture,' she told me. 'It takes a lot out of me.'

Annabel was working on a half-(finish) picture of horses in a field. And on the wall was a beautifully (draw) portrait of her dog Beezer. (Be) an animal lover, Annabel often paints pictures of animals. On another wall I noticed a picture of a lawn (cover) with (fall) leaves.

(Encourage) by her success, Annabel hopes to make painting her career, although she knows it will not be easy. But (help) by her art teacher, Mrs Emma Goodenough of Portway School, she has developed an individual style.

Annabel has many other hobbies, and she often goes (skate) with her friends.

Activity

Find one or more ways of completing each sentence. Use either an *-ing* form or *-ed* form.

I often listen to music while …
Three people were killed, but the lorry driver suffered only a …
I'd love to go …
The workers refused to do overtime …

18 Nouns

18.1 Regular plurals of nouns

my coat	our coat**s**	a bus	three bus**es**
a book	book**s**	a dish	some dish**es**
a dog	some dog**s**		
one day	two day**s**		

The regular plural ending is -*s*/-*es*.
We use -*es* after [s], [z], [ʃ] etc. ▷ 38.2

▷   38.1 pronunciation

18.2 Irregular plurals of nouns

1 a potato — some potato**es**
   a tomato — a pound of tomato**es**

2 a pony — a lot of pon**ies**
   the factory — both factor**ies**

3 a knife — the kni**ves** [vz]
   the shelf — the shel**ves** [vz]

4 his mouth — their mouths [ðz]
   a path — two paths [ðz]

5 a house — a lot of houses [zɪz]

6 her child [tʃaɪld] — her child**ren** [ˈtʃɪldrən]
   an ox — two ox**en**

7 a sheep — some sheep
   an aircraft — two aircraft

8 a foot — six feet [fiːt]
   a tooth — teeth [tiːθ]
   the goose — the geese [giːs]
   a mouse — some mice [maɪs]
   the woman — the women [ˈwɪmɪn]
   a man — two men [men]
   a policeman — three policemen [mən]
   (+ postmen, milkmen etc.)

9 one penny — ten pence/ten pennies
   a person — people/persons
   a fish — a lot of fish/three fishes

1 We add -*es* after *o* in *potato*, *tomato*, *hero*. But *photo*, *piano*, *radio* have -*s* (*photos*, *pianos*, *radios*).

2 After a consonant, *y* changes to *ies* in the plural ▷ 38.6, but when *y* comes after a vowel, the plural is regular, e.g. *keys*, *boys*, *ways*.

3 *f* and *fe* change to *ves* in *knife*, *shelf*, *wolf*, *thief*, *calf*, *half*, *wife*, *life*, *leaf*, *loaf*. But *chief*, *cliff* and *roof* are regular (*chiefs*, *cliffs*, *roofs*).

4 [θ] becomes [ðz] in *mouth*, *path*, *bath*, *youth*. But *birth*, *death* and *month* are regular [θs].

5 *house* [s] becomes *houses* [zɪz].

6 *child* and *ox* have plurals in -*ren*, -*en*.

7 *sheep*, *deer*, most names of fish (e.g. *salmon*, *trout*) and *aircraft*, *spacecraft* and *hovercraft* have the same singular and plural forms.

8 In some words the vowel changes and there is no -*s*.

9 *ten pence* is an amount of money ▷ 36.10; *ten pennies* means ten penny coins.
   people is the normal plural; *persons* is formal.
   fish is the normal plural; *fishes* is less usual. *three fishes* can mean three different kinds of fish.

▷   18.12 pair nouns; 18.13 nouns with a plural form; 23.10 nationality words

18.3 Direct and indirect objects

What did Debbie give her mother/her father?

1a Debbie gave **her mother a scarf** for Christmas.
 b She gave **her a scarf**.

2a She bought **her father some cigars**.
 b She bought **him some cigars**.

Who did she give the scarf/the cigars to?

3a She gave **the scarf to her mother**.
 b She gave **it to her mother**.
 c She gave **it to her**.

4a She bought **the cigars for her father**.
 b She bought **them for her father**.
 c She bought **them for him**.

1,2 The indirect object without *to* or *for* comes before the direct object.

3,4 The indirect object with *to* or *for* comes after the direct object.

3 We use *to* with *give*, *hand*, *lend*, *offer*, *owe*, *pass*, *pay*, *promise*, *read*, *sell*, *send*, *show*, *take*, *teach*, *tell* and *write*.

4 We use *for* with *buy*, *cook*, *fetch*, *find*, *get*, *leave*, *make*, *order*, *reserve* and *save*.
   With *bring* we can use *to* or *for*.

   We can use a pronoun

1b,2b instead of an indirect object

3b,4b instead of a direct object

3c,4c instead of both an indirect and a direct object

▷   10.6 passive

107   (18.1, 18.2)

Complete these paragraphs from a geography book. Put the words in brackets into the plural.

This small country is mostly farmland. The (animal) seen most often are (cow) and (sheep). Most (farm) have a few (goose), too. There are (donkey), but not many (horse). There's a lot of wheat and (potato), and there are (tomato) on the south side of the hills. In summer the (man), (woman) and (child) work together in the (field) seven (day) a week. The (person) work hard all their (life).

The only two (factory) in the country are in the capital. One makes (toy) and (game), and the other makes (knife) and (fork). All these (thing) are for export.

The east of the country is thick forest, the home of wild (pony), (deer) and (wolf).

(Photo) of the (cliff) along the coast show how beautiful the country is. But not many (tourist) visit it because the airport is too small for most (aircraft).

Activity

One student says e.g. *One apple.* The next says *One apple and two books.* The next says *One apple, two books and three cats*, and so on. Each student adds a plural noun beginning with the next letter of the alphabet. If you like, you can use only one type of noun, e.g. the names of animals or things in the house. You can also give points for irregular plurals said correctly.

108   (18.3)

At Christmas time in Britain, people usually give presents to their family and to their close friends. It's three weeks before Christmas now. Here is Mrs Bailey's list of presents. There is a tick (√) by those she has already bought. Say what she has bought or is going to give people at Christmas.

Examples

She's bought Kelly an umbrella.
She's going to give Joanne a cassette.
She's bought some chocolates for Jamie.
She's going to give some notepaper to Sadie.

```
Kelly - umbrella       ✓
Joanne - cassette
chocolates - Jamie     ✓
notepaper - Sadie
Alan - football
Shaun - watch          ✓
camera - Emma
Nick - book            ✓
hankies - Angela       ✓
Matthew - game
perfume - Gillian      ✓
scarf - Laura
```

Activity

Say if people in your country give presents at Christmas or if they give them at other times of the year. Tell the other students about presents you have given or received recently or that you intend to give.

18.4 The possessive form of nouns

1 *Singular nouns*
That's my brother**'s** watch.
Whose chair is that? ~ It's Ben**'s**.

2 *Plural nouns*
Is that a girl**s'** school or a boy**s'** school?
The Atkinson**s'** house is for sale.

3 *Irregular plural nouns without* **-s/-es**
The men**'s** toilets are over there.
There's a children**'s** playground in the park.

Form

1 With singular nouns we use an apostrophe + *s*.
2 With plural nouns we put an apostrophe after the *s*.
3 With irregular plural nouns that do not end in *-s/-es* we use an apostrophe + *s*.

We can leave out the noun if the meaning is clear without it, e.g. *It's Ben's* = It's Ben's chair.

Use

We use the possessive form with persons to show that something *belongs* to somebody or that something is *for* somebody (*a girls' school* = a school *for* girls). But ▷ 18.5–7

▷ 38.1 pronunciation; 38.6 with *-y*

18.5 The possessive form in phrases of place

Have you been to the chemist**'s**?
I've been at the Wilson**s'** all afternoon.

the chemist's = the chemist's shop
the Wilsons' = the Wilsons' house/the Wilson family's house

18.6 The possessive form in phrases of time

I read about the strike in **yesterday's** paper.
The workers have lost a **week's** wages.
They want five **weeks'** holiday.
It's a 15 **minutes'** drive to the factory.

yesterday's paper	=	the paper that came out yesterday
a week's wages	=	wages for a week
five weeks' holiday	=	a holiday that lasts five weeks
a 15 minutes' drive	=	a distance that we can drive in 15 minutes

For *15-minute drive* ▷ 37.7

18.7 **of** used instead of the possessive form

1 *With things*
There were people picnicking on **the bank of the river**.
It was **the beginning of the holidays**.

2 *With people*
We could hear **the voices of children** playing in the water.
I walked in **the footprints of the man** in front of me.

1 We normally use *of* instead of the possessive form (▷ 18.4) before the name of a *thing*. We use it to show that something (e.g. *the bank*) belongs to or is part of another thing (e.g. *the river*).

2 We also use *of* instead of the possessive form with *people* when the noun has a phrase or clause after it which describes the noun, e.g. *children playing in the water*.

For *the river bank* ▷ 37.2

Exercises

109 (18.4, 18.7)

Give the titles of these pictures in an art gallery. Use the possessive form or *of*.

Examples

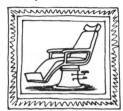 

chair/dentist
The dentist's chair

club/boys
The boys' club

end/game
The end of the game

1 dog/farmer

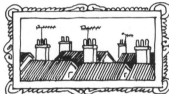 

2 roofs/houses

3 room/directors

4 supper/children

5 edge/lake

6 rest/walker

7 side/hill

Activity A

Find similar titles for these pictures.

Activity B

In a department store you often see signs like WOMEN'S SHOES or CHILDREN'S BOOKS. Think of some other things that are just for men, women, children, girls or boys.

18.8 Countable and uncountable nouns

1 *Countable nouns*
a We need **a teapot** and **some cups**. We don't need **spoons**.
b Here's **the teapot**, and here are **our cups**.
c There are **two cups**.

2 *Uncountable nouns*
a We need **some milk** and **some tea**. I don't take **sugar**.
b Here's **the milk**, and here's **our tea**.
c There are **two bottles of milk**.

1 *teapot*, *cup* and *spoon* are countable nouns. Countable nouns have a plural form, e.g. *cups*. We can say
a *a cup, some cups, cups*
b *the cup, the cups; my cup, our cups* etc.
c *two cups, three cups* etc.
2 *milk*, *tea* and *sugar* are uncountable nouns. Uncountable nouns do *not* have a plural form (but ▷ 18.10). We can say
a *some milk, milk*
b *the milk; my milk, your milk* etc.
c We cannot use a number + uncountable noun. To say *how much* milk, we use a countable noun + *of* e.g. *two bottles of milk*. ▷ 18.9

▷ 19.2 *a/an, the*; 20.17 *a lot of, many, much*

18.9 Countable and uncountable nouns: **of** in phrases of quantity

1 *Countable nouns*
a box **of** matches
two packets **of** cigarettes
a kilo **of** apples
six pounds **of** potatoes

2 *Uncountable nouns*
a bottle **of** milk
two tins **of** meat
half a pound **of** tea
five litres **of** oil
a drop **of** water
two pieces **of** paper
a bar **of** chocolate
six loaves **of** bread

We use a noun (e.g. *box, packets*) + *of*
1 with a countable noun when it is easier to say how many e.g. boxes or kilos than to say how many e.g. matches or apples
2 with an uncountable noun (e.g. *milk, meat*) whenever we need to say how much milk or meat

▷ 20.22 quantifiers + *of*

18.10 Uncountable nouns made countable

1 Two cups of tea and one cup of coffee, please. **Two teas** and **one coffee**, please.
2 We had different kinds of wine and cheese. We had different **wines** and **cheeses**.

1 We sometimes use uncountable nouns as countable nouns when we are ordering drinks or food.
2 We can also use uncountable nouns as countable nouns when we are talking about *a kind of* or *kinds of* wine, cheese, fruit, wool etc.

18.11 Uncountable nouns: **information, news, advice, work** etc.

1 I've got **some information**.
Steven's heard **some** exciting **news**.
Can I give you **some advice**?
2 I've got two **pieces of information**.
Steven's heard an exciting **bit of news**.
Can I give you a **piece of advice**?
3 We've got **work** to do.
We've got **a job** to do.

1 *information*, *news* and *advice* are uncountable nouns. Note the following words, which are also uncountable:
furniture, luggage, progress, research, weather, work, homework, housework, travel, money.
2 To make these noun phrases countable, we can use *piece* or *bit* + *of*.
3 Sometimes there is a countable noun with a similar meaning, e.g. *work/a job, travel/a journey, money/a coin* or *a note*.

110 (18.8, 18.9)

Mr and Mrs Johnson are going to do some shopping. Mrs Johnson is telling her husband what they need, and he is writing a list. Look at the list and give Mrs Johnson's words.

Examples

'a steak pie'
'some flour'
'a pound of tomatoes'

```
steak pie
flour
1 lb tomatoes
2 jars marmalade
eggs
pineapple
5 lbs potatoes
sugar
pkt cornflakes
loaf
bananas
3 tins beans
washing powder
```

Activity

One student says e.g. *Yesterday I went shopping and I bought some coffee.* The next student says e.g. *Yesterday I went shopping and I bought some coffee and a tin of soup.* Each student adds one item to the list. You can either memorize the list or you can take notes, but you must write your list like Mrs Johnson's without using *a, some* or *of.*

111 (18.11)

Complete the conversation by putting in *a, an* or *some*

Martin Hello, Geoffrey. How are you?
Geoffrey OK, thanks, but I'm fed up with this rain.
Martin Yes, let's hope we get … better weather soon.
Geoffrey And how are you?
Martin I'm fine thanks. You're at college now, aren't you?
Geoffrey Yes, I'm doing … course on farming. I'm just going to the library, actually. We've got … homework, … essay on farm management, and I have to do … research.
Martin And how is the course going?
Geoffrey Oh, fine. I made a rather bad start, but my tutor gave me … good advice. I think I'm making … progress now.
Martin Good.
Geoffrey And where are you going?
Martin To the travel agent's. I need … information about flights to Malrovia. My brother's out there at the moment.
Geoffrey How is he getting on?
Martin Very nicely. I had … letter from him yesterday with … news. He's got … job drilling for oil.
Geoffrey Than sounds … exciting job.
Martin Well, I must go. I've got lots to do. I've just moved into … new flat. It's very nice, but I need … new furniture — I haven't even got … table.
Geoffrey Well, good luck.

Activity

Explain the difference between these things.

homework and housework
a coin and a note
belongings and luggage
news and information

18.12 Pair nouns

1   I need **some trousers**.
    My **glasses are** broken.
    These tights are expensive.

2   I need **a pair of trousers**.
    Luckily I've got **two pairs of glasses**.

1   Pair nouns (e.g. *trousers*, *glasses*) are always plural in form.

2   If we want to say how many, we use *pair(s) of*.

    Other pair nouns: *pyjamas*, *shorts*, *pants*, *jeans*, *spectacles*, *binoculars*, *scissors*, *pliers*, *scales*.

18.13 Other nouns with a plural form

1   *With a plural verb*
    His clothes were old and dirty.
    The goods are still at the docks.

2   *With a singular verb*
    Mathematics is a difficult subject.
    The news is at ten o'clock on ITV.

3   *With a plural or a singular verb*
    The company's **headquarters is/are** in Leeds.
    The cheapest **means** of transport **is** the bicycle/**are** the bicycle and the motorcycle.

Here are some other nouns that have a plural form but no singular form:

1   with a plural verb: *riches, thanks, contents, troops, earnings, savings*

2   with a singular verb: *measles, politics, athletics, gymnastics*

3   with a plural or a singular verb: *works* (= factory)

18.14 Collective nouns

1   **The family has** lived here for hundreds of years.
    The government isn't very popular.

2   **The family have** all gone on holiday.
    Manchester United aren't playing very well.

3   **The police are** questioning two men.

1   We use the singular form of the verb after a collective noun (e.g. *family*) if we are thinking of the group as a whole.

2   We use a plural verb if we are thinking of the group as a number of individual people.

3   The verb is always plural after *police* and *cattle*.

    Other collective nouns: *group, gang, club, team, crowd, audience, public, class, committee, army, company; Liverpool, the BBC, Esso* and other names of sports teams, organizations and companies.

18.15 Noun phrases of measurement

Five hundred miles is a long way.
£35 seems a lot of money for a shirt.

We use the singular form of the verb after a noun phrase of measurement or amount.

18.16 Apposition

1   **The playwright William Shakespeare** was born at Stratford.

2   He was born at **Stratford, a small town in the English Midlands**.

3   It was a special day yesterday for **14-year-old schoolboy Mark Jones**.

We can use two noun phrases one after the other to refer to the same thing. The phrases are in apposition.

1   When the second phrase defines the meaning of the first (e.g. tells us *which* playwright), we do not use a comma.

2   When the second phrase adds extra information about the first but does not define it, we use a comma.

3   *the* is often left out of the first phrase, especially in newspaper reports.

112 (18.11–18.15)

Complete this newspaper article. Choose the correct singular or plural forms in the brackets. Begin like this: *The Clayton Clothing Company is going to build a new factory in Milchester. This news …*

CLAYTON FACTORY FOR MILCHESTER

The Clayton Clothing Company is going to build a new factory in Milchester. (This/These) (new/s) (was/were) announced by company chairman Mr David Clayton yesterday. Mr Clayton spent the morning in Milchester before returning to the Clayton (headquarter/s) at Granby.

The Clayton company (has/have) been in existence for 130 years and (is/are) famous for its 'Polymode' (good/s). The slogans 'You're never alone with a pair of Polymode (trouser/s)' and 'Polymode (jean/s) (is/are) the (one/s) for you' are well known. The company's profit last year of £2 million (was/were) the highest in the clothing business.

Mr Clayton will not say how (much/many) new (job/s) there will be, but my (information/s) (is/are) that there will be about 500. The (new/s) (is/are) very welcome because (work/s) (is/are) hard to find at the moment, and 2,000 unemployed people (is/are) a high figure for a small town.

Activity A

Make a list of all the clothes you own, e.g. *four coats, about five pairs of trousers, …*

Activity B

Write sentences saying what you think of these things: maths, physics, athletics, economics, politics.

Example: Maths is quite interesting.

113 (18.12–18.15)

Someone is talking about Ben, a tramp who begs in the town centre. Put in *is* or *are*.

'You know old Ben, who sits outside the bus station every day and begs for money? Well, he must be a rich man. His clothes … old and dirty, his hair … never washed, and his glasses … broken, but his earnings … more than enough to buy new clothes. Someone told me he takes £10 a day in summer. People … generous, aren't they? Now £10 … not much to live on, but he never spends any of it, you see. His savings … hidden away somewhere. He's been begging there in the same place for twenty years, which … a very long time. And it's against the law, you know. But obviously the police … quite happy about it.'

Activity

A Milchester company called Welton Engineering, which produces spectacles and binoculars, is going to close with a loss of 200 jobs. Write a short newspaper report about this news. You can invent the details.

19 The articles: *a/an* and *the*

19.1 The pronunciation of the articles

a/an		the	
a song	[ə] + [s]	**the** song	[ðə] + [s]
a new bed	[ə] + [n]	**the** new bed	[ðə] + [n]
a union	[ə] + [j]	**the** union	[ðə] + [j]
an apple	[ən] + [æ]	**the** apple	[ðɪ] + [æ]
an old tin	[ən] + [əʊ]	**the** old tin	[ðɪ] + [əʊ]
an hour	[ən] + [aʊ]	**the** hour	[ðɪ] + [aʊ]

We use *a* [ə] before a consonant sound and *an* [ən] before a vowel sound.

We use *the* [ðə] before a consonant sound and *the* [ðɪ] before a vowel sound.

19.2 **a/an** and **the**

1 There's **a man** and some girls in the water.
2a **The man** is swimming, but **the girls** aren't.
 b **The sun** is shining.
 c **The beach** is empty now.
   The water is nice and warm.
3 There's **a hotel** in the High Street where you can stay.
   There's only **one hotel** in this town.

1 We use *a/an* only with singular countable nouns. In the plural we use *some*. ▷ 19.3
   a/an = one. *a man* = one man (but we don't know *which* man), a man not mentioned before.
2 We use *the* with countable nouns (singular and plural) and with uncountable nouns.
   We use *the*
 a before nouns already mentioned. *The man* = the man I have just spoken about
 b before e.g. *sun* because there is only one sun
 c when it is clear that the speaker is talking about one special thing. *The beach* = this beach I am talking about (we know which beach).
3 We use *one*, not *a/an*, when we are interested in number, e.g. one hotel, not two or three.

19.3 **a/an** and **some**

Singular nouns
1a Look, there's **a horse** in the field.
 b It's **a pony**, not a horse.
 c **A horse** is bigger than a pony.

Plural nouns
2a I'm going to buy **some apples**.
 b No, let's get **oranges** today.
 c Well, **apples** are cheaper at the moment.

Uncountable nouns
3a Would you like **some tea**?
 b Is this **tea** or coffee?
 c I like **tea** best.

1a We use *a/an* only with singular countable nouns. *a/an* means one. ▷ 19.2
 b We use *a/an* when we are talking about what something is, e.g. *a pony*, not a horse.
 c We also use e.g. *a horse* to talk about all horses.
2a With plural nouns we use *some*. *some apples* = a number of apples.
 b We use a plural noun without *some* when we are talking about e.g. *oranges* (and not apples), and we are not interested in how many oranges.
 c We also use a plural noun without *some* to talk about e.g. all apples.
3a We can also use *some* with uncountable nouns.
 b We use an uncountable noun without *some* when we are talking about e.g. *tea* (and not coffee); and we are not interested in how much tea.
 c We also use an uncountable noun without *some* to talk about e.g. all tea.

▷ 18.8 countable and uncountable nouns;
   20.14 *some* and *any*

114 (19.1)

Can you say who these famous people were?
Write sentences from the table.

Example

Amundsen was a Norwegian explorer.

Amundsen			American	composer.
Cleopatra			Chinese	explorer.
Confucius		a	Egyptian	industrialist.
Nehru			English	painter.
Newton	was		German	philosopher.
Raphael			Indian	politician.
Rockefeller		an	Italian	queen.
Tolstoy			Norwegian	scientist.
Wagner			Russian	writer.

Activity

Ask the other students some quiz questions that they can answer using similar sentences. You can ask about living people, e.g. *Who is Rudolf Nureyev? Who is Jane Fonda?*

115 (19.2, 19.3)

Complete the instructions below on how to do an experiment. Decide if each word or phrase in brackets should have *a/an*, *the* or *some* in front of it, or if it should have none of these words.

  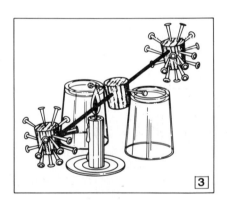

Experiment

Push (metal rod) through (cork) and then put two pins into (cork), as in Picture 1. Take two more corks and push (nails) into them. Put (pins) on two glasses and move (cork) to (right place) so that it balances, as in Picture 2. Then you need (candle) and (matches). Stand (candle) on (saucer) under one side of (rod) and light it. (Heat) that comes from (candle) will make (metal) expand (= grow bigger). This extra length will make (rod) fall, as in Picture 3. (Experiment) shows that (heat) makes (metal) expand.

Activity

Write about an experiment with a glass, some water, some salt and an egg. The experiment shows that an egg floats in salt water but not in water without salt.

19.4 **a/an** before jobs, nationalities and beliefs

1 Mr Malone is **a** writer and Mrs Stein is **an** artist.
2a He's **an** Englishman and she's **an** American.
b He's English and she's American.
3 He's **a** Catholic and she's **a** Protestant.

1 We use *a/an* before a noun saying what a person's job is. We cannot leave out *a/an*.
2a We use *a/an* before a noun of nationality.
b We can also use an adjective to give a person's nationality. ▷ 23.10
3 We use *a/an* before nouns which say what a person believes in.

19.5 **a/an** with **quite, such** and **rather**

1 The party was quite good.
We had **quite a good** time.
The story was so funny.
It was **such a funny** story.
2 The picture is rather nice.
It's **rather a nice** picture./**a rather nice** picture.

1 We can use *quite* and *such* before *a/an* but not after it.
2 We can use *rather* either before or after *a/an*. The meaning is the same.

▷ 24.8 adverbs of degree

19.6 **a/an** in phrases of price, speed etc.

These apples are forty pence **a** kilo.
You can only do thirty miles **an** hour on this road.

In these phrases *a/an* means *each* or *every*.

▷ 24.7 frequency

19.7   Uncountable nouns with and without **the**

1 **Meat** is expensive.
   Crime is increasing.
   We can learn a lot from **history**.
2 **The meat at our supermarket** costs a lot.
   The crime we read about in the papers is terrible.
   This book is about **the history of Europe**.

1 We do not use *the* before an uncountable noun with a general meaning. *Meat* = all meat.
2 But we use *the* before an uncountable noun with a limited meaning, e.g. *the meat at our supermarket*.

19.8   **school, prison** etc. with and without **the**

1 **School** is over at four o'clock.
   The man was sent to **prison** for stealing cars.
   Mrs Lee is in **hospital**. She's very ill.
2 **The school** cost a lot of money to build.
   The visitors came out of **the prison**.
   She's in **the new hospital**.
3 Judy's gone to **work**.
   She's gone to **the office**.

We sometimes leave out *the* before *school, prison, hospital, work, church, college, university, class, court, market, town, home, bed* and *sea*.

1 We leave out *the* when we are talking about school, prison etc. as an institution, and we are interested in what we use it for.
2 But we use *the* if we are talking about a school, prison etc. as a building. We must use *the* if there is a word or phrase describing the noun, e.g. *the new hospital*.
3 We leave out *the* before *work* (= place of work), but we use *the* before *office, factory* and *shop*.

19.9   Phrases of time without **the**

Years	in **1978**; after **1984**	But in **the** year 1978
Seasons	**Winter** begins next week. It's nice here in **summer**.	Or It's nice here in **the** summer.
Months	since **May**; **January** is often cold.	But **The** January of 1979 was very cold.
Special times of the year	**Easter** is in April this year. Are you going away at **Christmas**?	But Do you remember **the** first Christmas we spent together?
Days	on **Tuesday**; before **Friday**	But on **the** Tuesday before last
Parts of the day and night	at **midday**; at **night**	But in **the** morning; during **the** afternoon; in **the** evening; in **the** night
Meals	We had eggs for **breakfast.** **Dinner** is at half past seven.	But I didn't like **the** breakfast we had this morning.

▷   25.3 prepositions of time; 25.9 *by*

19.10   Names with and without **the**

1	*People*	This is **Mrs Orton**. **David**'s here.	But **the** Lawsons (= the Lawson family)
2	*Continents*	Have you been to **Africa**?	
3	*Countries*	**England** is a small country. I come from **Canada**.	But **the** West Indies from **the** United States to **the** Netherlands in **the** USSR
4	*Lakes and mountains*	Chicago is on **Lake Michigan**. Who first climbed **Mount Everest**?	But in **the** Highlands **the** Alps
5	*Rivers, canals and seas*		on **the** River Thames through **the** Suez Canal in **the** Atlantic Ocean
6	*Cities, towns and villages*	We stayed in **New York**.	But in **the** Hague
7	*Streets, parks and bridges*	in **Oxford Street** near **Piccadilly Circus** through **Hyde Park** **Tower Bridge**	But in **the** High Street **the** Strand, **the** Mall **the** Oxford road (= the road to Oxford) **the** Severn Bridge (= the bridge over the River Severn)
8	*Theatres, cinemas, hotels, museums and galleries*		**the** Shakespeare (Theatre) at **the** Classic (Cinema) **the** Hilton (Hotel) near **the** British Museum in **the** National Gallery **the** Empire State Building
9	*Other buildings*	to **Buckingham Palace** outside **Westminster Abbey** at **Shell-Mex House** near **Victoria Station** from **Heathrow Airport**	But at **the** White House
10	*Phrases with of* But at London University		in **the** House of Commons at **the** University of London **the** England of Shakespeare

	We do not use *the* before the names of		We use *the* before
1	people	1	plural names referring to a whole family ▷ 18.5
2	continents	3,4	plural place names and e.g. *USSR, UK*
3	countries	5	the names of rivers, canals and seas
4	lakes and mountains	8	the names of theatres, cinemas, hotels, museums and galleries
6	cities, towns and villages	10	phrases with *of*
7	streets, parks and bridges		
9	buildings other than hotels, museums etc.		

Complete this article about an (imaginary) explorer. Look at each noun or noun phrase in brackets and decide if it should have *the* in front of it.

Thomas French was one of the greatest explorers in (history). He travelled to (South America), (Greenland) and many other parts of (world). He was born in (1886), on (Christmas Day). His family lived near (Regent's Park). They were rich, and (money) was never a problem. Thomas left (school) because he wanted to go to (sea). He sailed across (Atlantic Ocean) with some friends. At twenty he joined an expedition to (Africa). Later he led expeditions to (Andes), to both Poles and even to parts of (USSR). He also climbed (Mount Everest) twice. (History) of all these journeys is in his diaries, which show us (life) of an explorer in the 1920's. (Breakfast) was French's favourite meal, and he always ate well. He went to (bed) early but often got up in (night) to write his diary. He also took hundreds of photos, which are now on show at (National Gallery).

Activity A

Try to find out proverbs or sayings starting with these words:
Time… Silence… Life… Practice… Honesty…

Activity B

Describe briefly the journeys you make every day between home and school or work. Say what time you leave and arrive.

Activity C

Make a list of all the places and sights you can think of in London. Tell the other students which sights you have seen or would like to see.

Complete the following by putting in *a, an* where necessary. In some places you don article at all.

Graham Mackay is … engineer. He works on … oil rig in … North Sea. He works on … rig for two weeks and then has two weeks at … home in Glasgow. … rig is 100 miles off … coast of Scotland. … oil company's helicopter flies him to and from … Aberdeen Airport. He does … important job, and he's paid over £350 … week.

Graham works twelve hours … day during his two weeks on … rig. His shift finishes at … midnight, when he goes to … bed. Although … work is important, it's rather … boring job. He shares … cabin with three other men. One of them is … friend of his, … American called Lee Driver, who comes from … New Mexico.

… men aren't allowed to drink … alcohol, so Graham has … milk or … tea with his meals. Most of the men smoke … cigarettes.

… weather can be pretty bad. Sometimes there are … storms. Everyone's always glad to get back to … mainland.

Activity

Ask a partner questions and find out the following information. Write down the information.

☐ where he/she lives
☐ his/her job, or whether he/she is a pupil at school, or a college or university student
☐ how many hours he/she works every day
☐ what he/she thinks of the job or school

20 Pronouns and quantifiers

20.1 Personal pronouns

Subject forms
1 **I**'ve got three bags.
2 **You** need some money.
3 What about Philip? Where is **he**?
4 Where's Jane? Is **she** coming?
5 What about the taxi? Where is **it**?
6 **We**'re late.
7 Where are the others? Are **they** coming?

Object forms
Help **me** with the bags, please.
I'll give **you** £5.
We're waiting for **him**.
This is **her** now.
I can't see **it**.
Can you take **us** with you?
Tell **them** to come now.

Form

	Singular		*Plural*	
	Subject	Object	Subject	Object
1st person	**I**	**me**	**we**	**us**
2nd person	**you**	**you**	**you**	**you**
3rd person	**he**	**him**	**they**	**them**
	she	**her**		
	it	**it**		

Use

We use pronouns to talk about the speaker (*I, we*) or the person we are speaking to (*you*). We also use them instead of a noun phrase when there is no need to say the full phrase (*he, she, it, they*).

We use the object form when the pronoun is
1 the direct object
2 the indirect object ▷ 18.3
3 after a preposition
4 the complement of the verb *be*

We use
1 *I/me* for the speaker
2 *you* for the person or the people spoken to
3 *he/him* to talk about a boy or man or a male animal, especially a pet animal
4 *she/her* to talk about a girl or woman or a female animal, especially a pet animal
5 *it* for a thing or an animal. And ▷ 20.2, 3
6 *we/us* for the speaker and another person or people
7 *they/them* for people or things. And ▷ 20.3, 4

20.2 Uses of **it**

1a Where's my watch? Have you seen **it**?
b There's someone at the door. ~ **It**'s Bob.
2 **It**'s getting late and **it**'s still raining.
3 **It** seems that no one is coming.
4a **It** would be silly to go out now.
   (= To go out now would be silly.)
b **It**'s strange that they haven't telephoned.
   (= That they haven't telephoned is strange.)
5 **It** was Pamela who wanted to go sailing.
   (= *Pamela* wanted to go sailing.)

We use *it*
1a to talk about a thing (e.g. *my watch*)
b to talk about a person when we are saying or asking who the person is. *It* = the person at the door.
2 as subject in sentences about time or the weather
3 as subject before *seem, appear* and *happen*
4 as subject when the subject clause (e.g. *to go out now, that they haven't telephoned*) comes later in the sentence
5 to emphasize a word or phrase, e.g. *Pamela* ▷ 28.4

▷ 5.3 *it/there* + *be*; 10.9 *it* + passive verb + clause

20.3 **it, one, them** and **some**

1a I've got the camera. **It**'s here.
 b I must buy a film. I'll get **one** today.
2a Have you seen these stamps? I like **them** better than the usual ones.
 b I need some stamps. I want **some** for these letters.
3a The coffee's nice. Where did you get **it**?
 b We need some coffee. I'll get **some** today.

1a *the, this, my* etc. + singular noun → *it*
 b *a/an* + singular noun → *one*
2a *the, these, my* etc. + plural noun → *they/them*
 b *some* + plural noun → *some*
3a *the, this, my* etc. + uncountable noun → *it*
 b *some* + uncountable noun → *some*

▷ 19.3 *a/an* and *some*; 20.21 quantifiers without a noun

Exercises

118 (20.1–20.3)

Some students are thinking of giving a party.
Complete the conversation by putting in *he, him, she, her, it, they, them, one* or *some*.

Don Trevor says we're giving a party on Saturday.
Lisa We're thinking of giving … . … was Alison who first thought of the idea.
Adam Gary won't be here. …'s going to London.
Melanie Gary won't mind if we go ahead without … .
Don Are we going to have food?
Lisa … would be expensive to buy food for all the guests. Let's just ask … to bring something to drink.
Melanie Have we got any glasses?
Adam There are … in the kitchen cupboard. …'ll be all right. We can use … .
Don There won't be enough, but we can borrow … .
Adam We can't use my record player. There's something wrong with … .
Melanie What about a cassette recorder? Hasn't Daniel got … ?
Adam He had …, but he's sold … .
Don Who are we going to invite?
Lisa Who was that girl who came here on Friday?
Adam Rosemary.
Lisa Well, don't invite … . … wasn't very nice. I don't like … at all.
Melanie We all went to Margaret and Angela's party, so we ought to invite … . But let's talk about it tomorrow. I'm too tired tonight. …'s getting late.

Activity A

Imagine your class are giving a party. Discuss what you will need and where you can get it.

Activity B

Say which famous person you would most like to invite to dinner. Give a reason for your choice.

20.4   A special use of **you, one, they** and **people**

1   **You** can't do much without money.

2   **One** can't do much without money.

3a   **They**'re building a new office block.

b   **They** ought to do something about all this pollution.

c   **They** say he's a good doctor.

4   **People** say he's a good doctor.

1   We sometimes use *you* to talk about people in general (= everyone), including the speaker.

2   We also use *one* to talk about people in general, including the speaker. *one* is more formal than *you*.

3a   We sometimes use *they* to talk about a group of people if it is not important to say who they are.

b   We sometimes use *they* to talk about the government or people in authority.

c   We use *they* for other people in general.

4   We use *people* for other people in general.

20.5   Possessive adjectives and pronouns

Possessive adjectives

That isn't **my** key.
Put **your** hands in **your** pockets.
Here's Jim's coat. Give him **his** coat.
Mary wants **her** bag.
The house lost **its** roof in the storm.
Can we have **our** records?
Where's the Arnolds' car? They can't find **their** car.

Form

my key	**mine**	**our** records	**ours**
your hands	**yours**		
his coat	**his**	**their** car	**theirs**
her hat	**hers**		
its roof			

We use possessive adjectives with a noun and possessive pronouns without a noun.

Possessive pronouns

Mine's here.
My hands are warm, but **yours** are cold.
It isn't **his**. It's Bill's.
This is **hers**.

We want **ours**, too.
Theirs is a blue Mini. That green car is the Grays'.

Use

We use possessive adjectives and pronouns to show that something belongs to somebody.

We use possessive adjectives and pronouns with parts of the body (e.g. *your hands*) and clothes (e.g. *your pockets*).

Note *its* is a possessive adjective. *it's* = it is.

▷   18.4 possessive form

20.6   Possessive adjective + **own**

Ben's got **his own** room now. He doesn't share with Dick any more.
Why don't you buy **your own** newspaper?

my own room = the room that belongs to me and not to anyone else

▷   20.11 *on my own*

20.7   **of** + possessive pronoun

Laura is a friend **of mine**.
I've got some records **of hers**.

a friend of mine = one of my friends

119 (20.1, 20.5, 20.7)

Some students are looking at an untidy pile of papers and other things. Complete what they say using these words: *me, you, him, her, us, them; my, your, his, her, our, their; mine, yours, his, hers, ours, theirs.*

1 **Sadie** This is Adam's ruler. It must be ... because it's got ... name on it.
  Gary I'll give it to ... .
2 **Trevor** Are these gloves ..., Rebecca?
  Rebecca Yes, they are. Thanks. They haven't got ... name in them, but they belong to ... .
3 **Alison** I think these notes belong to Lisa and Melanie. These pages are part of a project of ... .
  Daniel I can't see ... names on it, but I'll ask ... about it.
4 **Gary** Adam and I have been looking for these magazines. Someone took them from ... room. They belong to ... . We're using the pictures for a project of ... .
5 **Rebecca** Isn't this pen Emma's?
  Sadie I don't think it's one of ... . I know she's lost ... calculator, but I haven't heard ... say she's lost a pen.
6 **Daniel** Is that book ... ?
  Gary Yes, it's got ... name in it, so it must belong to ... . Here you are.
  Daniel Thanks, Gary.

Activity

Each of you puts one of your possessions on the teacher's desk. You then take it in turns to give one or two objects back to their owners. Ask e.g. *Whose is this? It is yours, Claudia? No, it doesn't belong to me. I think it's Bruno's.*

20.8 Reflexive pronouns

I'm teaching **myself** Italian.
Are you enjoying **yourself**?
Ernest Hemingway killed **himself**.
My sister can look after **herself**.
This kettle switches **itself** off.
We've found **ourselves** a nice place here.
Can you all help **yourselves** to sandwiches?
The children are behaving **themselves** today.

Form

myself	ourselves
yourself	yourselves
himself	themselves
herself	
itself	

The singular pronouns end in -*self*, e.g. *yourself*.
The plural pronouns end in -*selves*, e.g. *yourselves*.

Use

We use a reflexive pronoun to talk about the same person or thing that we mentioned in the subject of the sentence.

Note *enjoy yourself* = have a good time
help yourself to sandwiches = take some sandwiches
behave yourself = not be silly or naughty

20.9 Emphatic pronouns

We decorated this room **ourselves**.
The Queen **herself** visited the town last year.
I'll do it **myself**.

Form

The emphatic pronouns have the same form as the reflexive pronouns. ▷ 20.8
The emphatic pronoun has end position (*We . . . ourselves*), or it comes after the noun phrase it refers to (*The Queen herself . . .*).

Use

We use an emphatic pronoun to lay emphasis on a noun phrase, e.g. *we, the Queen. we ourselves* = we and no one else.

▷   20.11 *by myself*

20.10 **themselves** and **each other**

Both boys hurt **themselves** when they fell.
(= Each boy hurt himself.)
The two boxers hurt **each other**.
(= Each boxer hurt the other.)

20.11 **on my own** and **by myself**

The old man lives **on his own/by himself**.
I don't want to go out **on my own/by myself**.

on my own/by myself = alone, without anyone else

120 (20.8, 20.9)

Complete this advertisement by putting in the reflexive and emphatic pronouns.

THE BIG BOOK OF DO-IT-YOURSELF
by Bill Hawk

Lots of people have already bought Bill Hawk's super new book. They've saved ... a lot of money by doing jobs ... . Here are a few examples.

Mr Purlin of Hamleigh repaired the roof of his house ... .

'We decorated the whole house ... . This book made it easy,' say the Cleat family of Huxton.

The Spriggs of Granby put in central heating ... . 'I asked ... : why not?' said Mr Sprigg. 'With Bill Hawk's help it wasn't very difficult.'

'I put in a new bath ... ,' says Mr Hunter of Milchester.

Mrs Flashing of Wayford says 'We wanted a garage. A friend said "Why don't you build it ... ?" He showed us the book. So we did it ... . Now we feel really pleased with ... .'

Mrs Stiles of Backworth fitted a new front door all by ... . 'I couldn't imagine ... doing anything like that until I read this book.'

Activity

Have you ever done any of these jobs yourself? Is Do-it-yourself popular in your country? Do you think it is a good idea? Discuss these questions with the other students.

121 (20.8, 20.10)

Angela goes to a club called Weight Losers. It's for people who want to lose weight. Angela is talking to a friend about the club. Put in a reflexive pronoun or *each other*.

Angela I go to Weight Losers now, you know. I'm trying to lose weight. I have to force ... to eat the right food. My husband doesn't think I'm fat. 'You'll make ... ill,' he tells me. But it's doing me good. Lots of people go to the club. They're all trying to lose weight or keep ... slim. We all weigh ... on the scales and write down our weight. Then the members all tell ... their weight. Yesterday one man was one kilo heavier than the week before. He said he couldn't stop ... eating cakes. The teacher says, 'You must control ..., all of you.' Helen goes too, you know. She's losing weight. She's very pleased with ... . The Johnsons were there yesterday too. They're always arguing with ... . They've lost a lot of weight, so they must be really starving ... .

Activity A

Have you ever tried to teach yourself a language? Discuss the advantages and disadvantages of learning without a teacher.

Activity B

Think of contexts for these sentences. Write four short paragraphs, each containing one of the sentences.

They blamed themselves for the accident.
They blamed each other for the accident.
Everyone helped themselves.
Everyone helped each other.

20.12 Demonstrative adjectives and pronouns

Demonstrative adjectives
What about **this** tie here?
I like **that** dress there.
These shirts are nice, look.
Those coats are expensive.

Demonstrative pronouns
This is a nice colour.
That's cheap.
These are my size.
Do you like **those** over there?

Form

this   that
these   those

this and *that* are singular; *these* and *those* are plural.
For *this one* ▷ 20.13

Use

We use *this* and *these* to talk about things near the speaker.

We use *that* and *those* to talk about things that are further away from the speaker.

20.13 **one** and **ones**

1   *After an adjective*
Do you want a big bottle or a **small one**? The **big ones** cost £1.50.

2   *After* **the**
Our house is **the one** on the corner.
I don't like these plates as much as **the ones** we first looked at.

3   *After* **every**
We've seen plenty of coats. You've looked at **every one** in the shop.

4   *After* **each**
We've sixty tickets. **Each (one)** has a number.

5   *After a demonstrative adjective*
Which card do you want, **this (one)** or **that (one)**?
These (ones) are nicer than **those (ones)**.

6   *After* **which**
You've seen all the suits. **Which (one)** do you want?
You've seen all the shoes. **Which (ones)** do you want?

7   **one** *replacing a noun phrase*
We've got some biscuits. Would you like **one**?

We use *one* instead of a singular noun (a small bottle → a small one).
We use *ones* instead of a plural noun (the big bottles → the big ones).

We use *one/ones*

1   after an adjective in a noun phrase
2   after *the*
3   after *every* ▷ 20.15

We can use *one/ones* (but we can leave it out)

4   after *each* ▷ 20.15
5   after a demonstrative adjective, especially after *this* and *that* ▷ 20.12
6   after *which* ▷ 21.3
7   We can use *one* instead of a noun phrase with *a/an* (a biscuit →one). ▷ 20.3

20.14 **some** and **any**

1   I've got **some** money.
There are **some** oranges at the shop.

2   I haven't got **any** food.
Have you got **any** water?
There aren't **any** apples at the shop.
Are there **any** bananas?

3   Would you like **some** water? ~ Yes, please.
Can I have **some** bananas, please?

1   We use *some* in positive sentences.
2   We use *any* in negative sentences and in questions. But ▷ 20.15
3   We use *some* in questions when we think the answer will be *yes*, e.g. in offers and requests.

We use *some* and *any* with both uncountable nouns (e.g. *money*) and plural countable nouns (e.g. *oranges*).

▷   20.21 without a noun; 20.22 + *of*

122 (20.13)

Wendy and Diane are shopping together in London.
They're in a department store. Complete the
conversation. Use phrases with *one* or *ones* to
replace the phrases in brackets.

Wendy I need a new umbrella. I really must buy (an
umbrella) soon.
Diane I saw (some nice umbrellas) in Bymore's when
I was here last month.
Wendy I don't know the stores here very well.
(Which store) is Bymore's?
Diane It's (the new store), (the store) opposite
Harridge's.
Wendy Oh, yes, I know. Actually, Diane, I think your
umbrella is (a very nice umbrella). Where did you get
it?
Diane Oh, I've had (this umbrella) for a long time. I
don't think you'll find (an umbrella) like this now.
Wendy They must have umbrellas in this store. I
wonder which floor they're on.
Diane I think it's (this floor). Oh, yes, here they are.
Wendy I don't like (these brown umbrellas).
Diane (This umbrella) here is nice.
Wendy Well, I prefer (that umbrella) next to it, (the
red umbrella). But it's rather big. I like (the umbrellas)
that fold up very small.
Diane There's (an umbrella) here like that.
Wendy Yes, but I don't want (an umbrella) that
colour.
Diane (Which umbrella) do you like best?
Wendy I don't really like any of them.
Diane I think (the umbrellas) in Bymore's were
better. Shall we go there?
Wendy Yes, OK. Which way is the escalator?
Diane I think there's (an escalator) over there.

Activity A

Say which of these cars you would most like to have.
Discuss your choice with the other members of the
class.

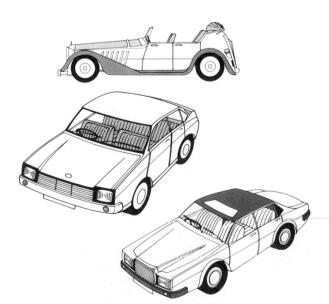

Activity B

Can you guess what *one/ones* refers to in these
phrases? For example, if someone says *A long one or
a short one?* They could be talking about a coat or a
dress.

☐ A single one or a double one?
☐ Brown ones or white ones?
☐ The red ones or the green ones?
☐ An electric one or a manual one?

123 (20.14)

Mrs Garland has bought a small house in the seaside
town where she lives. She's going to let the house to
tourists in summer. But first she needs to buy some
things for the house. Look at Mrs Garland's list and
say if the things she needs are in the sale.

Examples

There are some chairs in the sale.
There aren't any electric fires.

4 chairs	sofa
electric fire	shelves
2 beds	mirror
electric cooker	wallpaper
table	paint

BIG SALE

of furniture and household goods at the
Victoria Hall, Friday March 15th 7p.m.

Sofas, chairs, desks, cupboards, curtains,
carpets, mirrors, electric cookers, gas
heaters, kettles, wallpaper

Don't miss this wonderful chance to buy at
really low prices!

Activity

Does your classroom have everything you need to
learn English? Say what there is in your classroom or
in your school or college, e.g. *We've got some
pictures on the wall, and there's a map of the USA.
There aren't any travel posters*. What about a
cassette recorder, readers, and so on? Try to think
also of things you haven't got but think you ought to
have.

20.15 Quantifiers: **every, each** and **any**

1 There is a prize-giving **every** year.
   Every pupil has to be there.

2 One pupil from **each** class gets a prize.
   Each prize-winner can choose a book.

3 You can choose **any** book you like.
   Anyone can enter the competition.

1 We use *every* to talk about what the speaker sees as a large indefinite number of people or things. *Every pupil* = all the pupils.

2 We use *each* to talk about the individual people or things in a group. The group has a definite (and often small) number. ▷ 20.23

3 We use *any* to talk about one person or thing (but it doesn't matter which one) from a large indefinite number. *any book* = it doesn't matter which book; any book you like.
   When *any* has this meaning, it is stressed.
   Compounds with *any-* can also have the same meaning (*anyone* = it doesn't matter who).
   any is also the negative of *some*. ▷ 20.14

20.16 Compounds with **every-, some-, any-** and **no-**

1 **Everyone/Everybody** likes Alan.
   Someone/Somebody has left their bag here.
   Has **anyone/anybody** seen Dick?
   No one/Nobody told me.

2 Have you got **everything**?
   There's **something** in my shoe.
   Did you buy **anything**?
   We've got **nothing** to do.

3 I've looked **everywhere** for the key.
   It must be **somewhere**.
   I haven't seen it **anywhere**.
   It's **nowhere** here.

4 Dick isn't here, but **everyone else** is.
   (= all the other people)
   There's **something else** that I've forgotten.
   (= another thing)

5 Is there **anything interesting** on television?
   There's **nowhere nice** to go for a walk here.

1 We use *-one/-body* to talk about people.
2 We use *-thing* to talk about things.
3 We use *-where* to talk about place.
4 We can use *else* after these compounds.
5 We can use an adjective after these compounds.

We use *any-* in negative sentences and questions. ▷ 20.14 But ▷ 20.15

Note In informal speech Americans sometimes use *everyplace, someplace, anyplace* and *noplace* instead of *everywhere* etc.

124 (20.14, 20.15)

Teresa is on a week-long keep-fit and slimming course. She's writing to her friend Polly about it. Put in *every, each, any* or *some*. (Sometimes more than one answer is correct.)

Dear Polly,

It hasn't been easy to start this letter because I've been very busy with the course. We don't get ... time to ourselves.

The course is well organized. There are fifteen of us in three separate groups. ... group has its own tutor. ... of us also have our own individual timetable for part of the week. It's very hard work, but at least I've lost ... weight.

The worst thing is that we have to get up at six o'clock ... morning. I can't say I'm loving ... minute of it!

There simply isn't enough food. Lunch is different ... day, but yesterday it was a carrot and today a lettuce. Of course I was allowed ... water with it.

I've become friendly with ... other people on the course. We're getting to know ... other quite well.

I must stop now. My next training period begins at ... minute.

Love, Teresa

Activity A

Write some rules for people on the keep-fit and slimming course using *each* and *every*.

Activity B

Imagine you are on a slimming course. You are fed up with the diet. Say what food you would like and what you don't want.

125 (20.15, 20.16)

Two teachers are taking a group of pupils on an activity holiday. They're about to leave.
Complete the conversation using *every* (×2), *each* (×2), *any* and compounds with *every-*, *some-*, *any-*, and *no-*.

Mr Blake All the luggage goes in the back. Put ... in the back of the bus. And ... piece of luggage must have the owner's name on it.
Michelle I've got ... to eat here, look.
Mr Blake Yes, you can keep that with you.
Andrew Is it true we'll have to do written work ... evening?
Mrs Walters Yes, it is.
Sharon I can't find a seat. There's ... for me to sit.
Mr Blake Well, ... seat has a number. Yours is ten.
Sharon Neil is sitting there. He says we can have ... seat we like.
Mr Blake Well, he's wrong. He'll have to sit ... else.
Mrs Walters I think we're ready now. There's ... else to do before we go.
Simon There's ... missing. Nick isn't here. We've looked ... for him, but we can't find him ... .
Mrs Walters Has ... seen Nick?
Simon I've asked the others, but ... knows ... about him.
Mrs Walters Oh, it's all right. Here he is.
Mr Blake I hope ... has been to the toilet. We don't want to stop ... five minutes, do we?

Activity

Try to invent song titles using the words you put into the conversation, e.g. *Every time I look at you; I can't find her anywhere; Nothing will be the same again.*

20.17 Quantifiers: **a lot of/lots of, many, much, a few, a little**

Countable nouns

a lot of/lots of *(a large number)*

1   I've got **a lot of** records.
Lots of people came.

many *(a large number)*

2   How **many** books have you got?
Have you got **many** books?/a lot of books?

3   I haven't got **many** books./a lot of books.

4   I've got **too many** stamps.
I've got **as many** as I need.

a few *(a small number)*

5   I've only got **a few** tins.

Uncountable nouns

a lot of/lots of *(a large amount)*

There's **a lot of** bread here.
We've got **lots of** time.

much *(a large amount)*

How **much** beer is there?
Is there **much** beer?/a lot of beer?

There isn't **much** beer./a lot of beer.

That's **too much** wine for me.
I've got **as much** as you.

a little *(a small amount)*

There's only **a little** butter.

1   We use *a lot of* or *lots of* in positive sentences with both countable and uncountable nouns.

2   We usually use *many* and *much* in questions (but we sometimes use *a lot of* if we think the answer will be *yes*).
We use *many* with countable nouns and *much* with uncountable nouns.

3   We usually use *many* and *much* in negative sentences (but we sometimes use *a lot of* in informal English).

4   We use *many* and *much* after *too, as, so* and *very*.

5   We use *a few* with countable nouns and *a little* with uncountable nouns.

20.18 Quantifiers: **more, most; fewer, fewest; less, least**

Countable nouns

more *(a larger number)*
Our team has won **more** games than your team.

most *(the largest number)*
We've won the **most** games.
(= more games than anyone else)

fewer/less *(a smaller number)*
You've won **fewer** games/**less** games than we have.
(= You haven't won as many games as we have.)

fewest/least *(the smallest number)*
You've won the **fewest** games/the **least** games.
(= fewer/less games than anyone else)

Uncountable nouns

more *(a larger amount)*
You've got **more** money than I have.

most *(the largest amount)*
You've got the **most** money.
(= more money than anyone else)

less *(a smaller amount)*
I've got **less** money than you have.
(= I haven't got as much money as you have.)

least *(the smallest amount)*
I've got the **least** money.
(= less money than anyone else)

We use *more* and *most* with both countable and uncountable nouns.
With countable nouns we use *fewer/fewest* (or *less/least* in informal English).
With uncountable nouns we use *less/least*.

Exercises

126 **(20.17, 20.18)**

The table on the right shows the amount of exports from Malrovia this year. Write sentences with *a lot of, many* and *much*.

Examples

They've sold a lot of oil.
They haven't sold many motor cars.

Then compare the amounts for this year with those for last year.

Examples

They've sold less oil this year than last year.
They've sold more motor cars.

Activity A

Look at this information on kettles. Compare the five kettles, e.g. *The Heatmaster holds quite a lot of water. It holds more than the Superboil. The Aqualux takes less time to boil than the Hotflow, and it doesn't cost as much.* Decide which kettle is the best value.

Kettle	Holds (litres)	Time taken to boil 1.5 litres	Price
Heatmaster	1.75	4 min. 15 sec.	£19.95
Superboil	1.5	4 min.	£22.25
Pronto	2.0	3 min. 35 sec.	£27.50
Hotflow	1.4	4 min.	£24.75
Aqualux	1.5	3 min. 45 sec.	£19.50

Activity B

Discuss with the other students how much money people in these jobs earn in your country: doctor, garage mechanic, policeman, shop assistant, lorry driver, secretary, bank manager, pilot. Write the jobs in order starting with the one that earns the most and ending with the one that earns the least. If there are students in your class from more than one country, then discuss the jobs in groups, and compare your lists.

Exports

this year ■

last year □

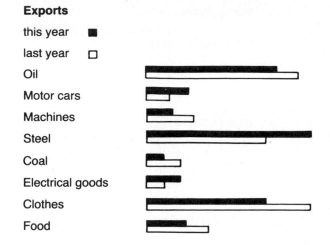

Oil
Motor cars
Machines
Steel
Coal
Electrical goods
Clothes
Food

20.19 **some more, another** and **other/others**

1 some more
Would you like **some more** sandwiches?
Have **some more** tea.

2 another
Would you like **another** sandwich?
Have you got these shoes in **another** colour?

3 other/others
They crossed to the **other** side of the road.
Kate's here, but where are the **others**?
I like this cheese better than the **other**.

1 *some more* = an extra quantity or amount
We use *some more* with both countable and uncountable nouns.

2 *another* = an extra one or a different one
We use *another* with countable nouns.

3 *other* = different
We use *other* with both countable and uncountable nouns.

20.20 **enough** and **plenty of**

Are there **enough** chairs for everyone?
I hope we've got **enough** petrol.
They took **plenty of** warm clothes.
Don't worry. We've got **plenty of** time.

We use *enough* and *plenty of* with both countable and uncountable nouns.
plenty of = more than enough

20.21 Quantifiers without a noun

With plural nouns
I need some potatoes. Can you lend me **some**?
We haven't got **any** in the house.
Have you got any old newspapers? ~
Well, not **a lot**, but I can give you **a few**. How **many** do you want?
I'm looking for some pins. There are **none** in the drawer.

With uncountable nouns
I need some sugar. Can you lend me **some**? We haven't got **any** in the house.
Can I borrow some ink? ~ I haven't got **a lot**, but I can give you **a little**. How **much** do you want?
I can't find any oil. There's **none** in the garage.

We can leave out a noun after a quantifier when the meaning is clear without it.
For *no* and *none* ▷ 20.23

20.22 Quantifiers + **of**

With plural nouns
We broke **some of** the eggs.
A few of my friends are coming round; you've met **two of** them before.
One of the windows was open.

With uncountable or singular nouns
Try **a little of** this cheese.
None of this wood is any use.
I saw **some of** the programme, but I missed **a lot of** it.

We use *of* when we talk about a quantity (e.g. *some*) which is part of a definite and limited quantity, e.g. *the eggs (in this box), my friends.*

▷   20.17 *a lot of*; 20.23

127 (20.17, 20.19, 20.20)

Betty Root is the leader of the Forwards Party. She doesn't agree with the Prime Minister George Wright and his Progressive Party. Betty is talking on television. Complete what she says using *too many, too much, some more, another* and *enough.*

Mrs Root George Wright and his party have made far … mistakes during their time as the government. Mr Wright doesn't really spend … time at his job, I'm afraid. Our Prime Minister spends … time playing golf. While he's doing that, our industry is dying. A lot of factories have closed in the last few years – … factories, in my opinion. And we've just learnt that … factories are going to close soon, thanks to George Wright again. The Progressives simply don't spend … money on the really important things, like helping industry. And of course they spend … on things that no one needs. We don't want … Progressive government after this one. Mr Wright would like to give us … of the same medicine. But the medicine is killing our country. You gave the Progressives a chance to put the country right, and you've seen the result. Don't give them … chance.

Activity

Mention some of the problems facing the world today, such as hunger or nuclear weapons. Use *too many, enough* etc in some of your sentences.

128 (20.21)

Robin and Kate are helping to serve food at a children's party. Complete what they say by putting in one of these quantifiers: *another, any, enough, a few, fewer, a little, a lot, many, much, none, some, some more.*

Robin I borrowed several chairs, but we still haven't got … for everyone.
Kate There are lots of children here. How … were invited?
Robin There's lots of room in here. Well, quite …, anyway.
Kate There's food over here, children. Would you like …?
Robin Wayne wants a drink of milk, but I can't find … .
Kate You've only had a biscuit, Natalie. You haven't eaten … .
Robin There aren't many clean plates. There are just … in the cupboard.
Kate You've finished your milk, Wayne. Let me pour you … .
Robin No, there's only one kettle here. I can't find … .
Kate And I can't find any clean cups. There are … in here.
Robin There weren't many cups. There were … than I thought.
Kate The children have drunk nearly all the orange juice. There's only … left.

Activity

Give your opinion on the subject of violence on television. Is there too much violence? Should there be less?

20.23 **all, most, both, either, neither, each, half** and **no/none**

1a **All** parties are exciting, I think.
b **All the** guests/**All of the** guests are here.
c Those magazines are **all** old. I've read them **all/all of** them.
d I've spent **all my** money/**all of my** money.
He's drunk **all this** bottle/**all of this** bottle.
e He's drunk **this whole** bottle/**the whole of this** bottle.

1a *all* = every ▷ 20.15
all + noun (without *the*) has a general meaning. *All parties* = every party in the world.
b *all the* + noun and *all of the* + noun have a more limited meaning. *All (of) the guests* = every guest at this party.
c We can use *all* in mid position or after an object pronoun.
d We can use *all* with uncountable and singular nouns as well as with plural nouns.
We can use it with *my, your* etc. and with *this, that* etc.
e We can use *whole* with a singular noun with the same meaning as *all*.

2a **Most** people like parties.
b **Most of the** guests were students.
c Bob spends **most of his** time here.

2a *most* = more than half
most + noun (without *the*) has a general meaning. *Most people* = most people in the world.
b *most of the* + noun has a more limited meaning. *Most of the guests* = most of the guests at this party.
c We can use *most* with uncountable nouns and singular nouns as well as with plural nouns.
We can use it with *my, your* etc. and with *this, that* etc. ▷ 24.11 *most/mostly*

3a **Both** windows/**Both the** windows/**Both of the** windows are open.
b The windows are **both** open. I left them **both/both of** them open.
c **Both these** plates are broken.

3a We use *both* to talk about two things or two people.
We can say *both* + noun, *both the* + noun or *both of the* + noun.
b We can use *both* in mid position or after an object pronoun.
c We can use *both* with *these* and *those*, and with *my, your* etc.

4a We can go **either** way, right or left.
b **Neither** box was big enough.
c I don't like **either of the** twins.
Neither of these boxes was/were big enough.

4a We use *either* and *neither* to talk about two things or two people. *either* = the one or the other.
b *neither* has a negative meaning. *Neither box was big enough* = both boxes were too small.
We can say *either/neither* + singular noun.
c We can also say *either of the/neither of the* + plural noun.
We can use *these* and *those* and *my, your* etc. ▷ 27.5 giving alternatives

5a **Each** child/**Each of the** children had a present.
b The children **each** had a present. We gave them **each/each of** them a present.
c These pens cost 60p **each**.

5a We use *each* to talk about the individual things or people in a group. ▷ 20.15
We can say *each* + singular noun or *each of the* + plural noun.
b We can use *each* in mid position or after an object pronoun.
c We can use *each* in end position.

6a **Half the** shops/**Half of the** shops were shut.
b I've read **half this** book/**half of this** book.
c **Half a** pound of butter, please.

7a We had **no** milk and **no** eggs.
b There's **no** telephone in here.
c I wanted some eggs, but there were **none** at the shops.
d I dropped the eggs, but luckily **none of** them broke.
e **None of my** friends live in London.

6a We ca
b We can u
   uncountable
   We can use it w
   etc.
c We can say half a/an +
   ▷ 24.8 half as an adverb

7a no has a negative meaning. W
   hadn't any milk. no is more empha
b We can use no with singular nouns a
   uncountable and plural nouns.
c We cannot use no without a noun. We use n
   instead.
d We cannot use no + of. We use none instead.
e We can use my, your etc. and this, that etc. after none of.

Exercises

129 (20.22, 20.23)

Can you answer the questions in this geography quiz?
Use *none, neither, one, two, three, both* or *all* in your
answers.

Example

How many of these are rivers?
the Amazon, the Mississippi, the Nile
All of them are rivers.

1 How many of these are islands?
   Cuba, Florida, Mexico
2 How many of these are in Spain?
   Casablanca, Lisbon
3 How many of these are in South America?
   Angola, Bolivia, Colombia, Peru
4 How many of these are oceans?
   the Atlantic, the Pacific
5 How many of these are in London?
   Central Park, Hyde Park, Regent's Park
6 How many of these are in the USA?
   Chicago, Los Angeles, Miami, Philadelphia
7 How many of these are in Europe?
   The Dead Sea, Mount Everest, Lake Ontario
8 How many of these are in Australia?
   Adelaide, Melbourne

Activity

Invent some similar quiz questions and give them to a
partner to answer. You could write questions about
English vocabulary, e.g. *How many of these are
food/clothes?* or about famous people, e.g. *How many
of these are film stars/politicians?*

...say half the + noun or half of the + noun.
...e half with singular nouns and
...nouns as well as with plural nouns.
...th this, that etc. and with my, your
...noun.

...e had no milk = we
...tic than not any.
...well as with
...one

...w and **whose**

1a *what* asks about actions or things.
 b *who* asks about people.
 c *where* asks about place.
 d *when* asks about time.
 e *why* asks about reason or purpose.
 f *how* asks about means, manner or degree. Also
    ▷ 29.2, 3 introductions, meeting someone
 g *whose* asks about possession.
2 We can use *else* after these question words.

s?)

...ubject and object

1 When *what* or *who* asks about the subject, the
   verb is the same as in a statement, e.g. *is making,
   knows, invited*.
2 When *what* or *who* asks about the object, an
   auxiliary or modal verb comes before the subject.
   We use a form of *do* in the simple present or
   simple past tense.

What's making that ...
The washing-machine.
Who knows the answer? ~ No one does.
Who invited you? ~ Ben invited me.

2 *Asking about the object*
What's David making? ~ A table.
Who do you know here? ~ Well, I know Nicola.
Who did you invite? ~ Oh, a few friends.

21.3 **who, what** and **which**

1 **Who**'s your favourite film star? ~ Paul Newman.
2a **What**'s your favourite sport? ~ Golf.
 b **What** sport do you like best? ~ I like golf.
 c **What** instruments do you play? ~
   I play the guitar and the violin.
3a **Which** do you play best, the guitar or the violin?
 b **Which** box are your photos in? ~ This one here.
 c **Which** photos/**Which** ones did you take in
   Germany? ~ The ones on this page.
   Which of these girls/**Which** one is your friend? ~
   The one on the left.

Form

1 *who* is always without a noun.
2 *what* can be
a without a noun
b with a singular noun
c with a plural noun
3 *which* can be
a without a noun
b with a singular noun
c with a plural noun, with *one/ones* (▷ 20.13) or with
   of (▷ 20.22)

Use

1 *who* asks about people.
2 *what* asks about things.
3 *which* asks about things or people.

We use *who*, *what* or *which* when there is a number
of possible answers to choose from.

We use *who* or *what* when there is an indefinite (and
often very large) number of possible answers, or
when the possible answers are unknown.

We use *which* when there is a limited (and often very
small) number of possible answers to choose from.

130 (21.2)

Author Brenda Bagg has written a story called 'Heartache'. It's about a Lord who loves a film star who loves a pop singer and so on. The diagram shows who loves who. Brenda is showing the story to the film director Max Finkel. Give Max's questions and Brenda's answers.

Examples

Mike Perry →
Who does Mike Perry love? ~ Princess Flora.

→ Mike Perry
And who loves Mike Perry? ~ Jackie Logan and Sophie Salinsky.

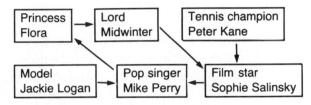

1 → Princess Flora   5 → Lord Midwinter
2 Princess Flora →   6 → Sophie Salinsky
3 Peter Kane →   7 Sophie Salinsky →
4 Lord Midwinter →   8 Jackie Logan →

Activity

For each of these events write two different quiz questions. Ask a partner about each event.

☐ David killing Goliath
☐ Galileo inventing the telescope
☐ Wellington defeating Napoleon
☐ Leonardo da Vinci painting the Last Supper and the Mona Lisa

Try to invent similar questions to ask a partner.

131 (21.3)

Complete these riddles using *who, what* or *which*. You may first need to find the correct answer in the box below.

1 ... goes up but never comes down?
2 ... is paid money for taking something away from you?
3 ... can go through a closed door?
4 ... of these words is longer: 'laughs' or 'smiles'?
5 ... has fingers but no arms?
6 ... sheep eat more grass, black ones or white ones?
7 ... invented the first pen?
8 ... has more tails, one cat or no cat?
9 ... is the difference between an African elephant and an Indian elephant?
10 ... king of England wore the biggest shoes?

A hairdresser.
About 3,000 miles.
A pair of gloves.
The one with the biggest feet.
Your age.
The Incas. (ink-ers!)
A noise.
No cat. (No cat has more than one tail.)
White ones. There are more of them.
'Smiles' because there's a 'mile' between the first and last letters.

Activity

Imagine that you have a friend who always stays at home in the evenings and never goes out. One day your friend tells you that he/she went out last night with someone to a cinema and then to a restaurant. What questions would you ask your friend?

21.4 Question phrases with **what** and **how**

What time did you leave? ~ Half past five.
What colour is the carpet? ~ Green.
What kind of/sort of shop is it? ~
It's a newsagent's.
I'm hungry. **What about** you? ~ Yes, me too.
How much is this table? ~ Sixty pounds.
How many children have they got? ~ Two, I think.
How old is Mr Hall? ~ Oh, about forty.
How often do you go out? ~ About once a week.

We use these question phrases to ask about the details of a person, a thing or an action.

▷ 20.17 *how much/how many*

21.5 Prepositions in questions

1 **Which** office is Pat working in now?
Pat is working in the small office now.

Who did you speak to ?
We spoke to the manager.

2 **In which** office is Pat working now?
3 **To whom** did you speak?
4 **What** did she want you for? ~
Oh, nothing important.
5 **What**'s she like? ~ She's very nice.

1 In a question we usually put a preposition in the same place as in a statement.
2 In more formal or written English we can put a preposition at the beginning of a question.
3 We use *whom* instead of *who* after a preposition. *whom* is formal and not often used in spoken English.
4 *What . . . for?* = Why?
5 *What . . . like?* asks a question that we can answer with an adjective.

132 **(21.1, 21.4)**

Martin's bicycle has been stolen. He's reporting it to the police. Complete the policeman's questions by putting in a question word or phrase.

Policeman	Martin
1 ...'s your name	Martin Wilkins.
2 ... do you live?	46 Elm Road, Granby.
3 And ... is the bicycle? ... owns it?	It's mine. I own it.
4 ... was it stolen?	This morning.
5 ... did you leave it?	Outside the town hall.
6 ... was this?	About eleven o'clock. When I came back at half past eleven, it wasn't there.
7 ... of bicycle is it?	It's a racing bike, a Silverman Special.
8 ... is it?	Blue.
9 ... is it?	It's two years old.
10 ... did it cost?	Oh, about £150.

Activity A

Act out the conversation with a partner, but invent some different answers. Imagine that your own bicycle, motor-bike or car has been stolen.

Activity B

Write a list of questions that the policeman might ask if someone reported that they had lost a lorry full of circus animals.

133 **(21.2, 21.5)**

Mr Pratt is telling his psychiatrist about his dreams. Put in the psychiatrist's questions.

Examples

Mr Pratt I dreamt I was looking for something.
Psychiatrist *What were you looking for?*
Mr Pratt I don't know. Someone laughed at me.
Psychiatrist *Who laughed at you?*
Mr Pratt I couldn't see his face.

Mr Pratt I was waiting for someone.
Psychiatrist ... ?
Mr Pratt I don't know. I was afraid of something.
Psychiatrist ... ?
Mr Pratt I'm not sure. Somebody ran towards me.
Psychiatrist ... ?
Mr Pratt A man I didn't know. Then I shouted at someone.
Psychiatrist ... ?
Mr Pratt I think it was my brother. But then I fell over something.
Psychiatrist ... ?
Mr Pratt Something lying in the road. Somebody was pointing at me.
Psychiatrist ... ?
Mr Pratt My father. He was talking to someone.
Psychiatrist ... ?
Mr Pratt I don't know. I woke up then.

Activity

A friend of yours has found a strange object in his garden. He thinks it is a space satellite. What questions might you ask him about it?

22 Relative clauses

22.1 Relative pronouns and relative clauses

1 The boy **who comes from Bristol** won the game.
   The sport **that I like watching** is tennis.

2 Peter Oates, **who comes from Bristol**, won the game.
   The first game, **which went on for a long time**, wasn't very exciting.

A relative clause (e.g. *who comes from Bristol*) begins with a relative pronoun (e.g. *who, that*). But ▷ 22.4, 10, 11
A relative clause comes after a noun phrase (e.g. *the boy, the sport*).

1 Most relative clauses are *defining clauses*, e.g. *who comes from Bristol* (without commas). ▷ 22.12. The relative clauses in 22.2–11 are defining clauses.

2 Some relative clauses are *non-defining clauses*, e.g. *who comes from Bristol* (with commas). ▷ 22.12–14

22.2 The relative pronouns **who** and **which**

1 The girl **who works at the café** is Martin's sister.
   Is that the café **which stays open till ten**?

2 Martin is the man **who we saw yesterday**.
   Did you see the motor-bike **which he bought for £20**?

who and *which* are relative pronouns. We use *who* with people and *which* with things.
who and *which* can be

1 the subject of a relative clause (*The girl* works at the café. *The café* stays open till ten.)

2 the object of the relative clause (We saw *the man* yesterday. He bought *the motor-bike* for £20.)

22.3 The relative pronoun **that**

1 Is this the train **that stops at Shenfield**?
   Here's the newspaper **that I found on the seat**.

2 Do you know the man **that sat next to us yesterday**?
   The woman **that you helped** is our neighbour.

We can use the relative pronoun *that* instead of *who* or *which*.

1 We mostly use *that* to talk about things.

2 We sometimes use *that* to talk about people, but we use *who* much more often. ▷ 22.2

22.4 Relative clauses without a pronoun: leaving out **who, which** or **that**

1 Martin is the man **who we saw yesterday**.
   Martin is the man **we saw yesterday**.
   Did you see the motor-bike **which he bought for £20**?
   Did you see the motor-bike **he bought for £20**?

2 His sister works in the café **that we went to**.
   His sister works in the café **we went to**.

We can leave out *who, which* or *that*

1 when it is the object of a relative clause (You saw *the man* yesterday. He bought *the motor-bike* for £20.)

2 when there is a preposition (We went *to the café*.) ▷ 22.5

We cannot leave out *who, which* or *that* when it is the subject of a relative clause.

134 (22.2)

'SF' is a radio programme about science fiction. The presenter is telling listeners about some new books. Look at the presenter's notes and give his sentences. Use a relative clause with *who* or *which*.

Examples

Tomorrow – A woman can see into the future.
'Tomorrow' is about a woman who can see into the future.

Into the Unknown – A spaceship loses its way.
'Into the Unknown' is about a spaceship which loses its way.

1 The Mind Machine – A computer controls people's thoughts.
2 Eureka! – A scientist discovers the secret of the universe.
3 Spaceville – Some people build a city in space.
4 Zero – An accident starts a nuclear war.
5 The President – A dictator rules the world.
6 Danger Hour – A cloud of gas pollutes the earth.
7 Starfight – A war breaks out in space.
8 Wait for Death – A man lives for a thousand years.

Activity

Do you like people who tell jokes all the time?
Do you like books which make you think? What about parties which go on all night? Write a few sentences about people and things you like or don't like. Then compare your sentences with a partner's.

---

135 (22.4)

Last summer Amanda went on holiday with some friends. After she got back, she showed people the photos they had taken. Look at the photos and give Amanda's words. Use relative clauses without a pronoun.

Examples

Amanda and her friends stayed at this hotel. *'That's the hotel we stayed at.'*

They hired a car. *'That's the car we hired.'*

1 Amanda went with these friends.

2 They swam in this pool.

3 Amanda bought this dress. 4 They met these people.

5 They went for a sail in this boat. 6 They visited this castle.

7 They liked this beach. 8 They walked round this lake.

Activity

Have you got any photos of yourself visiting places? If you can, bring some photos to the lesson. Show them to a group of other students and explain what is in the photos.

22.5 Prepositions in relative clauses

1 A girl **who** | I used to go out **with** | lives near here.
| I used to go out **with** | a girl.

2 Here's the map **that** | you were looking **for** |
| You were looking **for** | the map.

3 The article | you were talking **about** | earlier is in this magazine.
| You were talking **about** | the article.

In a relative clause we put a preposition in the same place as in a main clause. We do not usually put it before the relative pronoun. But ▷ 22.7

We can use a preposition in a relative clause

1 with *who* or *which*
2 with *that*
3 without a pronoun

▷   21.5 prepositions in questions

22.6 The relative pronoun **whom**

1 The woman **who they interviewed yesterday** has been given the job.
The woman **whom they interviewed yesterday** has been given the job.

2 The people **who we stayed with** are old friends.
The people **whom we stayed with** are old friends.

We use *who* and *whom* to talk about people.

We can use *whom* instead of *who*

1 when it is the object of the relative clause (They interviewed *the woman* yesterday.)

2 when there is a preposition (We stayed *with some old friends.*) ▷ 22.7

whom is more formal than *who* and is not often used in spoken English.

22.7 A preposition at the beginning of a relative clause

1 The person **who** I spoke **to** earlier isn't there now.
It's a problem **which** we can do very little **about**.

2 The person **to whom** I spoke earlier isn't there now.
It's a problem **about which** we can do very little.

1 In a relative clause we usually put a preposition in the same place as in a main clause. This is the normal order in informal spoken English. ▷ 22.5

2 In more formal or written English we can put a preposition at the beginning of a relative clause.
If we put a preposition at the beginning, we use *whom* or *which*. We cannot use the relative pronouns *who* or *that* after a preposition.

22.8 The relative pronoun **whose**

1 Workers **whose** wages are low should be paid more.

2 We are a nation **whose** wealth comes mainly from industry.

3 'Lively Lady' was the horse **whose** jockey fell.

4 That's the farm **whose** owner went to Australia.

We use *whose* to talk about possession.
whose can refer to

1 people
2 countries
3 animals
4 things

Note We also use *of which* to talk about things, e.g. *That's the farm the owner of which went to Australia.* In informal speech we often express the meaning in a different way, e.g. *The owner of that farm went to Australia.*

136 (22.2–22.5)

Find the right explanation for each of the twelve words below. Write a sentence with a relative clause to explain the meaning. Use *who, which* or *that*, or leave out the pronoun. (Sometimes there is more than one correct answer.)

Examples

A butcher is someone who sells meat.
A stamp is something you put on a letter.
Gloves are things that you wear on your hands.
A saucer is something you put a cup on.

1 socks	He/She sells fruit and vegetables.
2 a briefcase	You use them to row a boat.
3 a greengrocer	It heats water.
4 a present	You wear them on your feet.
5 a kettle	You try to hit it.
6 soap	You carry papers in it.
7 a target	It keeps the rain off you.
8 an artist	You give it to someone.
9 a seat	You can see yourself in it.
10 an umbrella	You sit on it.
11 oars	You wash with it.
12 a mirror	He/She paints pictures.

Activity A

Try to explain the meaning of these words: needle, mechanic, shampoo, sugar, brake, key.

Activity B

Ask the other students e.g. *What do you call a person who cuts your hair? What's a thing you cut wood with?* They have to find the answers.

137 (22.2–22.5, 22.8)

Complete the conversation. Put in the relative clauses using the information in brackets. (Sometimes there is more than one correct answer.)

Example

She's the woman … (She lives in West Street.)
She's the woman who lives in West Street.

Diane I saw Roger Cowley on Saturday.
Paul Roger Cowley?
Diane Yes, he's the man … (He works at Electrobrit.)
Jane It's Roger Cowley … (His wife owns the Top Shop.)
Mark What's the Top Shop?
Jane It's the shop … (It sells dresses.)
It's the one … (I went in it yesterday.)
Mark Oh, I know. It was Roger Cowley … (His car was stolen from outside his house.)
Paul That's right. It was the car … (He bought it from Richard Hunter.)
Jane And who's Richard Hunter?
Mark I don't think you've met him. He's the man … (I invited him to our party.) He didn't come, though.
Jane Is he the man … ? (His sister was on a TV quiz show.)
Paul No, that's Bob. Richard is the man … (David plays golf with him.)
Diane Yes, but I was talking about Roger Cowley.

Activity

Write similar sentences about people you know. Use *who, which, that, whose* and a sentence without a relative pronoun.

22.9 The relative pronoun **what**

We've found out **what** we need to know.
You never let me do **what** I want to do.

what we need to know = the thing that we need to know.

▷ 27.3 *what* in a clause used as subject or object; 28.5 *what* used for emphasis

22.10 Relative clauses without a pronoun: the infinitive

1 Gary was **the first** person **to arrive** and **the last to leave**.
(= . . . the first person who arrived and the last one who left.)

2 Jill was **the only** one **to remember** my birthday.
(= . . . the only one who remembered . . .)

3 Your party was **the most exciting** thing **to happen** here for months.
(= . . . the most exciting thing that's happened here . . .)

We can use the infinitive instead of a relative pronoun and a verb

1 after *the first, the second* etc. and *the next*
2 after *the only*
3 after superlatives

22.11 Relative clauses without a pronoun: the -ing form and the -ed form

1 People **wanting** to make an enquiry should go to the office.
(= People who want to make an enquiry . . .)

2 The men **building** the houses were well paid.
(= The men who were building the houses . . .)

3 New homes **offered** for sale today are sold very quickly.
(= New homes which are offered for sale . . .)

4 A house **bought** ten years ago is worth much more today.
(= A house which was bought ten years ago . . .)

1,2 We can use an -ing form instead of a relative pronoun and an active verb.

3,4 We can use an -ed form instead of a relative pronoun and a passive verb.

The -ing form or the -ed form can replace a verb

1,3 in a present tense or
2,4 in a past tense

138 (22.10, 22.11)

Rewrite the advertising slogans using the infinitive, the -ing form or the -ed form.

Examples

The Ramplus 64 is the first computer that will fit in your pocket.
The Ramplus 64 is the first computer to fit in your pocket.

The person who uses a Fotax camera takes the best photos.
The person using a Fotax camera takes the best photos.

Clothes that are washed in Whizz look extra white.
Clothes washed in Whizz look extra white.

1 Food that is bought at Brisco costs you less.
2 Someone who listens to a Meditone radio hears every word.
3 Cakes which are made with Bakewell flour taste wonderful.
4 Hed-Cure is the only thing that will make your headache really better.
5 A person who is sitting in a Super-Plush chair is sitting comfortably.
6 The most exciting toy you can give your child is a Playworld toy.
7 Everyone notices the man who wears a Windsor shirt.
8 A floor that is covered with a Wonderlay carpet looks ten times better.

Activity

Write similar advertisements for these:

22.12 Defining and non-defining relative clauses

1 *Defining relative clauses*
The man **who has worked here for 45 years** is retiring next month.
The company **he works for** is Wilson and Sons.

1 Most relative clauses are defining clauses. The clause *who has worked here for 45 years* defines the man (tells us *which* man).
The defining clause is necessary to understand the meaning of the main clause. There is no pause or comma before a defining relative clause.

2 *Non-defining relative clauses*
Mr Rose, **who has worked here for 45 years**, is retiring next month.
Wilson and Sons, **for whom he has worked since he was 20**, have been in existence since 1823.
The manager (**whose wife was also there**) handed a beautiful old clock to Mr Rose.
The clock—**which cost over £100**—was paid for by the people at the factory.

2 Some relative clauses are non-defining clauses. The clause *who has worked here for 45 years* adds extra information about Mr Rose. It does not define Mr Rose—we already know who he is.
We can leave out the non-defining clause and still have a sentence which means something.
There is a comma before and after a non-defining relative clause. The clause is sometimes in brackets or between dashes.
We form non-defining relative clauses with *who, whom, whose* or *which*. We do not use *that* in non-defining clauses.
Non-defining relative clauses are rather formal.

3 *Compare the use of two main clauses*
Mr Rose has worked here for 45 years, and he's retiring next month.

3 In informal spoken English we normally use two main clauses instead of a main clause and a non-defining relative clause.

22.13 **why, when** and **where**

1 I've forgotten the reason **why** we went to Bournemouth.
. . . the reason we went to Bournemouth.
I'll never forget the day **when** we arrived there.
. . . the day we arrived there.
Do you remember the hotel **where** we stayed?
. . . the hotel we stayed at?

1 We can use *why, when* and *where* in a defining relative clause. We can leave out *why* or *when*.
We can also leave out *where*, but then we must use a preposition, e.g. *the hotel we stayed at.*

2 We went in May, **when** it's normally quiet.
We stopped at Ashford, **where** there's that nice pub by the canal.

2 We can form non-defining relative clauses with *when* and *where*.
We cannot leave out *when* and *where* from a non-defining clause.

22.14 **which** referring to a whole clause

I was late again this morning, **which** made my boss angry.
The telephone wasn't working, **which** was an awful nuisance.

We can use *which* to talk about a whole clause, e.g. *I was late again this morning.*
These relative clauses with *which* are non-defining clauses.

139 (22.6, 22.7, 22.12)

'Jubilee Road' is a weekly television programme telling a story of the lives of ordinary people. Every week the programme starts with a summary of what has been happening. The writer of this week's summary has left out some important information, which the programme editor has noted below. Rewrite the summary and put in the missing information. Use non-defining relative clauses with *who, whom, whose* and *which*. (Sometimes more than one answer is correct.)

Example

Laura, who hasn't been feeling well lately, has gone to see the doctor.

Activity

Read these sentences from a guide book to London.

> Sir Christopher Wren, who built 52 London churches, is best known for St Paul's Cathedral.
>
> The Post Office Tower, which was completed in 1964, is 189 metres high.
>
> Charles Dickens, whose house in Bloomsbury you can visit, was a famous novelist.

Write similar sentences about your home town or about a town you know well. Use non-defining relative clauses.

Ex Laura has gone to see the doctor.	Laura hasn't been feeling well lately.
1 Len is giving a big party.	Len has finally found a new job.
2 Craig is hoping that Donna will be at the party.	Len has invited Craig.
3 Craig also wants to borrow some money from Gordon.	Gordon's cycle repair business is doing very well.
4 The new club in Jubilee Road is very popular with young people.	Everyone is talking about the new club.
5 A disco kept people awake half the night.	The disco took place at the club last weekend.
6 The new manager at the plastics factory wants Donna to work late.	No one likes the new manager.
7 He has arranged a staff meeting.	The meeting starts at ten o'clock tomorrow.
8 Donna is staying at number 33 with Teresa.	Teresa has given her the spare room.
9 The woman at number 35 is behaving rather strangely.	Donna spoke to the woman yesterday.
10 Meanwhile Robin is explaining his problems to Harriet.	Robin's wife has left him.

23 Adjectives

23.1 Introduction to adjectives

1 We've got an **old** house.
I like **old** houses.
2 This is a **nice** coat.
This coat is **nice**.
3 The boys are **afraid** of the dark.
The driver was still **alive**.

Form

1 An adjective has the same form in the singular and in the plural, e.g. *an old house, old houses*.
2 An adjective comes before a noun (*a nice coat*) or after *be* (*. . . is nice*). And ▷ 24.12
3 A few adjectives come after *be* but do not normally come before a noun. Examples: *afraid, alive, alone, asleep, awake, ill, well*.

Use

An adjective describes (tells us something about) a noun.

23.2 The regular comparison of adjectives

1 This radio's **cheap**. It's only £10.
This one's **cheaper** than that. It's only £7.50.
This must be **the cheapest** one. It's only £4.75.
2 This is an **expensive** coat. It's £80.
I can't afford a **more expensive** coat.
This one is the **most expensive** of all. It's £120.
3a You're taller **than Bob./than Bob is**.
b You're taller **than him./than he is**.
4a Which is the longest bridge **in the world**?
b It's the most exciting book **I've ever read**.

1 Short adjectives of one syllable (e.g. *cheap, tall, nice*) take *-er* in the comparative (*cheaper*) and *-est* in the superlative (*cheapest*). But ▷ 23.3
For spelling (e.g. *nicer, bigger, happier*) ▷38.3, 5, 6
2 Longer adjectives of three or more syllables (e.g. *expensive, interesting, dangerous*) take *more* in the comparative (*more expensive*) and *most* in the superlative (*most expensive*).
3a After the comparative form we can use *than*. After *than* we can put a noun phrase (*than Bob*) or a noun phrase + verb (*than Bob is*).
b A personal pronoun without a verb after *than* has the object form (*than him*).
4 After a superlative we often use
a a phrase with a preposition
b a relative clause without a pronoun ▷ 22.4

Note on adjectives of two syllables

These adjectives usually take **-er/-est** (but they can take **more/most**):

silly	sillier	the silliest
simple	simpler	the simplest
clever	cleverer	the cleverest
quiet	quieter	the quietest

Also: *funny, dirty* etc.; *gentle, feeble* etc.
Adjectives in *-ed* usually take *more/most*, even adjectives of one syllable. Some examples: *tired, bored, amused, annoyed, surprised*.

Most other two-syllable adjectives take **more/most**:

careful	more careful	the most careful
boring	more boring	the most boring
modern	more modern	the most modern
correct	more correct	the most correct
famous	more famous	the most famous

Also: *useful, hopeful* etc.; *tiring, willing* etc.
With these adjectives either *-er/-est* or *more/most* is used: *polite, stupid, narrow, pleasant, common, handsome*.

23.3 The irregular comparison of adjectives

1 Nottingham has some **good** shops.
Sheffield is **better** for shopping.
The shops in Manchester are **best**.

2 Thursday is market day. It's a **bad** day for parking.
The problem is **worse** in summer.
Saturday is the **worst** time of the week.

Form

1 **good**   **better**   **the best**
2 **bad**   **worse**   **the worst**

▷   24.14 irregular comparison of adverbs

Exercises

140 **(23.2, 23.3)**

Mike has the chance of a very good job in London. He and Wendy are discussing whether they should move from Milchester. Complete the conversation by putting in the comparative or superlative of each adjective in brackets.

Wendy I think we should go. You'll get a (high) salary with Multitech than you do now, and we'll have a (good) standard of living.
Mike Don't forget London is the (expensive) place we could possibly go to. For example, house prices are the (high) in the country. A house will be (difficult) to find there than in Milchester.
Wendy But it's probably the (big) chance you'll ever get. That's the (important) thing. And it'll be (easy) for me to find a good job than it was here.
Mike London is a (big) place than Milchester. Life won't be sc quiet.
Wendy Well, I'd like a (exciting) life. It is a bit boring here sometimes. And it'll be much (convenient) for shops and theatres, living in London. You've never really liked your job here. And things have got (bad) recently.
Mike Yes, they have. And Multitech is certainly one of the (good) companies in the business. But I don't want to go unless you really want to.

Activity A

Say in what way these things are record breakers: Everest, the Soviet Union, Antarctica, gold, football.

Activity B

Write a few sentences comparing town life and country life.

23.4 Comparison: **as . . . as** and **so . . . as**

1 The train is just **as** expensive **as** the plane. They both cost £85.
Unfortunately the news was **as** bad **as** we had expected.

2 Today isn't **as** cold **as** yesterday.
Today isn't **so** cold **as** yesterday.

3 Everything is just the same **as** before, really.

1 In positive sentences we use *as . . . as* to compare two things that are the same in some way.

2 In negative sentences we use either *as . . . as* or *so . . . as*.

3 We also use *as* after *the same*. Compare *different from* (▷ 25.12).

23.5 Comparison: **less, least**

These shoes are expensive. They're £30.
The black ones are **less** expensive. They're £20.
These here are the **least** expensive. They're £10.

less and *least* are the opposites of *more* and *most*.
▷ 23.2

23.6 Comparatives with **and**

The queue of people was getting **longer and longer**.
I began to feel **more and more nervous**.

We can repeat a comparative after *and* to talk about a change happening over a period of time.

23.7 Comparatives with **the**

The higher our wages, **the better** our standard of living.
The smaller a garden is, **the easier** it is to look after.

We use *the* + comparative to talk about a change in one thing which causes a change in something else.

23.8 **latest, last; nearest, next; further, farther**

1 The M7 is our **latest** motorway. It was opened only last week.
The M7 will be the **last** motorway. There's no money to build any more.

2 There are no garages here. The **nearest** one is 25 miles away.
You'd better get some petrol at this garage. The **next** one is 25 miles away.

3 How much **further/farther** is it to Glasgow?
Let's hope there are no **further** problems.

1 *latest* = newest
last = final (but *last week* = the week before this)

2 *nearest* = closest, least far
next = the one after this

3 *further/farther* = longer in distance
further = more

141 (23.2–23.5)

A motoring magazine has tested six new cars and given them marks for price, running costs, reliability, and so on. The cars get up to 5 marks in each category. For example, 5 means very cheap, very economical etc, and 0 means not at all cheap or economical etc. 5 is the best mark and 0 is the worst.

Compare the cars using the notes on the right.

Examples

Prince/easy to drive/Delta
The Prince is easier to drive than the Delta.

Sahara/comfortable/Superior
The Sahara is just as comfortable as the Superior.

Swift/reliable/Libretto
The Swift is less reliable than the Libretto OR
The Swift isn't as reliable as the Libretto.

1 Superior/comfortable/Libretto
2 Swift/spacious/Sahara
3 Delta/cheap/Prince
4 Sahara/reliable/Libretto
5 Prince/comfortable/Swift
6 Delta/fast/Sahara
7 Superior/economical/Delta
8 Swift/easy to drive/Superior
9 Sahara/good-looking/Prince
10 Swift/comfortable/Libretto

Then write six sentences (11–16) saying which car is the best in each category.

Examples

The Sahara is the cheapest.
The Prince is the most economical.

	cheap	economical	reliable	easy to drive	comfortable	spacious	fast	good-looking
Prince	3	5	5	4	3	2	3	1
Delta	4	4	4	2	1	0	3	3
Swift	3	2	2	5	5	4	3	4
Sahara	5	3	4	2	4	3	1	3
Superior	1	0	3	4	4	4	5	5
Libretto	2	3	4	3	4	5	4	4

Activity A

Talk to your partner about your own car (or the car you would like to have). Discuss the similarities and differences between the two cars.

Activity B

Discuss the advantages and disadvantages of travelling by public transport as against using your own car or bicycle.

142 (23.6, 23.7)

Samuel Tomani is a politician in Omagua. He's telling people how badly the government is doing. Look at his notes and give his sentences using the comparative patterns.

Examples

taxes high – hard to make a living
Taxes are getting higher and higher. The higher they become, the harder it is to make a living.

goverment corrupt – people bitter
The government is getting more and more corrupt.
The more corrupt it becomes, the more bitter people are.

1 food expensive – people hungry
2 industry weak – our problems great
3 things bad – important to do something
4 people poor – our chances of success small
5 situation hopeless – difficult to put it right
6 people desperate – necessary to act

Activity

Write a few sentences on present-day political, economic or scientific developments. For example, you could mention nuclear weapons, food or computers.

23.9 **the** + adjective

1   **The rich** are healthier than **the poor**.
2   You've got to take **the good** with **the bad**.

1   We use *the* + adjective to talk about a whole group of people, e.g. *the young, the old, the sick, the unemployed. The rich* = rich people.
2   We also use *the* + adjective to talk about abstract ideas, e.g. *the new, the unknown, the absurd*.

23.10 Nationality words

1a   I've bought some **Italian** shoes.
 b   Can you speak **Italian**?
 c   The owner is an **Italian**.
 d   **Italians/The Italians** are very artistic.
2a   It's a **Japanese** radio.
 b   I'm trying to learn **Japanese**.
 c   A lot of **Japanese** come here in summer.
 d   The **Japanese** sell lots of things to Europe.
3a   Was it an **English** film?
 b   My **English** is getting better.
 c   There was an **Englishman** opposite me.
 d   **Englishmen/The English** love dogs.

    We can use a nationality word
 a   as an adjective
 b   as the name of a language
 c   to talk about a person or a group of people
 d   to talk about a nation as a whole
1c   Some of the words for people are nouns with a singular and a plural form, e.g. *Italian(s), American(s), Brazilian(s), Swede(s)*.
2c   Some of the words for people are adjectives which we also use as nouns, e.g. *Japanese, Chinese, Portuguese, Swiss*. They can have a singular or a plural meaning.
3d   We can refer to some nations by using either a noun or an adjective, e.g. *Englishmen/the English, Irishmen/the Irish, Frenchmen/the French, Spaniards/the Spanish*.

    We can also use an adjective to refer to people, or nations, e.g. *They're Spanish. She's a French girl. English people love dogs*.

▷   19.4 *a/an*

24 Adverbs

24.1 Types of adverbs

1   *Adverbs of manner* ▷ 24.5
    The children walked home **quickly**.
    They ate their supper **hungrily**.

2   *Adverbs of place and time* ▷ 24.6
    Mr Barnes is going to have lunch **here**.
    You can speak to him **then**.

3   *Adverbs of frequency* ▷ 24.7
    The Smiths **often** visit us.
    They **usually** come on Sundays.

4   *Adverbs of degree* ▷ 24.8
    I'm **very** tired.
    I had to get up **really** early.
    I **almost** fell asleep this afternoon.

5   *Sentence adverbs* ▷ 24.9
    Maybe I'll come and see you.
    It'll **probably** be OK.
    I'm not very busy just now, **luckily**.

6   *Prepositional adverbs* ▷ 26.1
    The Browns weren't **in**.
    (=They weren't in the house.)
    The car stopped and a woman got **out**.
    (= A woman got out of the car.)

We use an adverb

1   to say *how* something happens
2   to say *where* or *when* something happens
3   to say *how often* something happens
4   to make the meaning of an adjective, adverb or verb *stronger* or *weaker*
5   to refer to a whole sentence and show what the speaker thinks about the sentence
6   Some adverbs are like prepositions without a noun phrase after them.

24.2 Adverb forms

1a It'll be eight o'clock **soon**.
b   Alan is **always** late.
c   He wasn't **so** late last week.
d   **Perhaps** he isn't coming.
2a We'll have to walk **fast**.
b   We had to leave **early** this morning.
3a We'll have to walk **quickly**.
b   It's been very warm **recently**.
c   I **usually** see her at lunch time.
d   We're **nearly** at the house now.
e   It's a bit further, **actually**.
4a The woman was friendly. She spoke **in a friendly way**.
b   Rain is likely. It's **probably** going to rain.

1   Some adverbs have no special form. These adverbs are
a   most adverbs of time and place ▷ 24.6
b   some adverbs of frequency ▷ 24.7
c   some adverbs of degree ▷ 24.8
d   some sentence adverbs ▷ 24.9
2   Some adverbs have the same form as adjectives. These adverbs are
a   some adverbs of manner
b   some adverbs of time
▷   24.10
3   We form some adverbs from an adjective + *-ly*. These adverbs are
a   most adverbs of manner ▷ 24.5
b   some adverbs of time ▷ 24.6
c   some adverbs of frequency ▷ 24.7
d   some adverbs of degree ▷ 24.8
e   most sentence adverbs ▷ 24.9
▷   38.3, 6 spelling
4   We cannot form an adverb from an adjective which ends in *-ly*. Instead we can use
a   the phrase *in a . . . way/manner* or
b   an adverb of similar meaning.
    But ▷ 24.10 *early*

24.3 Adverb phrases

She thanked us **with a smile**.
The game is **next Saturday**.
I see Alex **from time to time**.
We enjoyed the party **very much indeed**.
In actual fact, the story was untrue.

An adverb is sometimes a whole phrase, not just one word.

24.4 The position of adverbs

There are three places in the sentence where adverbs can come.

1 Front position

	Adverb	Subject + verb	
a	**Yesterday**	the team played	well.
b	**Usually**	I go	to the café.
c	**Perhaps**	I'll see	you later.

1 Front position is at the beginning of the sentence.
These kinds of adverbs go in front position:
a sometimes adverbs or adverb phrases of time and place ▷ 24.6
b sometimes adverbs of frequency ▷ 24.7
c sometimes sentence adverbs ▷ 24.9

▷ 28.3 front position for emphasis

2 Mid position

	Subject	(Auxiliary or modal verb)	Adverb	(Verb)	
a	He		**slowly**	opened	the door.
	I		**usually**	go	to the café.
b	I	don't	**really**	like	fish.
	We	've	**just**	finished	the painting.
c	The story	is	**certainly**		very exciting.

2 Mid position is
a before a verb in the simple present or simple past tense
b after the first auxiliary or modal verb in the verb phrase
c after be
These kinds of adverbs go in mid position:
a sometimes adverbs of manner ▷ 24.5 adverbs of frequency ▷ 24.7
b some adverbs of degree ▷ 24.8 sometimes a few adverbs of time ▷ 24.6
c sometimes sentence adverbs ▷ 24.9

3 End position

	Subject + verb	(Direct object)	
a	They talked		**quietly**.
b	He opened	the door	**slowly**.
c	City played		**well at York yesterday**.
d	Ben danced		**a lot with that tall girl**.
e	I go		**to the café usually**.
f	I'll see	you	**later, perhaps**.

3 End position is
a after the verb (if there is no direct object)
b after the verb + direct object
Sometimes there is more than one adverb or phrase in end position.
c The normal order is manner (well) + place (at York) + time (yesterday).
d We often put a short phrase (a lot) before a longer phrase (with that tall girl).
e In end position an adverb of frequency usually comes after an adverb or adverb phrase or place.
f A sentence adverb usually comes at the end of the sentence, sometimes after a comma.
In end position we put
a,b,c adverbs of manner 24.5
c sometimes adverbs or adverb phrases of time and place 24.6
d some adverbs of degree ▷ 24.8
e sometimes adverbs of frequency ▷ 24.7
f sometimes sentence adverbs ▷ 24.9

143 (24.4)

Maria is writing to her friend Helen in England. She's rather tired, and she's left some of the words out by mistake. Rewrite the letter putting in the adverbs and adverb phrases on the right.

Dear Helen,

Thank you for your letter. Is it four months since I last wrote? I'm   **really**

sorry, but I've been very busy.   **lately**

I'm working for my exams   **already**

I've planned my revision. I work   **carefully**

until about ten o'clock in the   **usually**

evening. I've finished for today.   **just**

I don't keep to my plan. I   **of course,**
always
Saw a marvellous film. It was   **yesterday**

called 'The Secret Game'. Have you seen it?

I don't go out. Suzanne   **actually, often**

comes about once a week. We   **here**

talk.   **a lot**

I hope to visit England again.   **next year**

I had a lovely time last year.   **there**

It would be great to see you.   **again**

I'm trying to save some money.   **hard**

How are you? Is your new flat all right? Please write.   **soon**

love,
Maria

Activity

The class divides into two teams. A student from Team 1 finds a sentence in an English book or newspaper. He/She writes the sentence on the board, leaving out one adverb or adverb phrase. He/She then writes the adverb on the board, under the sentence. Team 2 have to say where the adverb was in the sentence. They score two points if they guess exactly where it was, and they score one point for a correct position which is different from the original sentence. Then it's Team 2's turn to choose a sentence.

If this is too easy, find sentences with two adverbs or adverb phrases.

24.5   Adverbs of manner

1 *Adjective*   The journey was very **slow**.
   Adverb   We travelled **slowly**.
2 *Adjective*   Mr Harris is a **careful** driver.
   Adverb   He drives his car very **carefully**.
3 *Adjective*   The climb up the hill was **easy**.
   Adverb   We **easily** climbed the hill.
4 *Adjective*   The singing was **loud**.
   Adverb   They sang **loudly/loud**.

1 An adjective (e.g. *slow*) describes a noun (e.g. *journey*). An adverb of manner (e.g. *slowly*) describes a verb (e.g. *travelled*).
   An adverb of manner ends in *-ly*. ▷ 38.3, 6 spelling. But the adverb of *good* is *well*. And ▷ 24.11 *high*, *near* etc.
2 An adverb of manner usually comes at the end of a sentence. Do not put it between the verb and the direct object.
3 An adverb of manner sometimes has mid position.
4 In informal English and in American English an adjective is sometimes used instead of an adverb. In British English this happens especially with *loud*, *cheap*, *slow* and *quick*.

24.6   Place and time

1 **At the disco** they played my favourite records.
   Yesterday they played my favourite records.
   They played my favourite records **at the disco**.
   They played my favourite records **yesterday**.
2 They played my favourite records **at the disco yesterday**.
   We went **there on Saturday evening**.
3 Bob will **soon** be here.
   He's **just** arrived.

1 An adverb or adverb phrase of place or of time can usually come at the beginning or end of a sentence. Some more examples: *here, at home, in the street, over there; afterwards, again, tomorrow, last week.*
2 Place normally comes before time in end position.
3 A few adverbs of time can have mid position, e.g. *soon, just, already, now, then.*

▷   24.16 *yet*, *still* and *already*

24.7   Adverbs of frequency

1 She **always** stays in bed on Sunday morning.
   Have you **ever** been to Greece?
   I **sometimes** listen to the news.
2 **Sometimes** I listen to the news.
   I listen to the news **sometimes**.
   Do you come here **often**?
3 **Every August** they went on holiday.
   You have to pay the rent **every week**.
   I go to the dentist **twice a year**.

Adverbs of frequency say how often something happens. Some examples: *always, often, usually, normally, sometimes, occasionally, ever, never.*
1 Adverbs of frequency usually have mid position.
2 *sometimes, usually, normally* and *occasionally* can also have front or end position. *often* can have end position.
3 Adverb phrases of frequency with *every* and with *a/an* usually have front or end position.
   For *daily, hourly* etc. ▷ 24.10

▷   19.6 *a/an* in phrases of price, speed etc.; 36.4 *once, twice* etc.

144 (24.7)

Amanda is looking for a boy-friend. The Find-a-Friend Club wants to help her. She's doing a personality test for them. Look at Amanda's answers and write sentences about her.

Examples

Amanda doesn't often lie awake at night.
She's sometimes angry.

Activity A

Say how often you do the things in the personality test.

Activity B

Discuss with a group of other students which television programmes you like. Say how often you and members of your family watch them.

How often do you do these things?	always	usually	often	sometimes	not often	never
lie awake at night					✓	
be angry				✓		
argue with people					✓	
worry			✓			
take risks						✓
be late for work	✓					
tell jokes					✓	
laugh at comedy shows		✓				
wish things were different			✓			
be sad					✓	

24.8 Adverbs of degree

With adjectives and adverbs

1 The music was **very** loud.
Why did it take **so** long?
The shelf is **too** high.

2 I'm not tall **enough**.

3 £25 is **very/extremely** expensive for a meal.
£15 is **rather/pretty/fairly/quite** expensive.
£10 is **a bit/a little** expensive.

4 The food was **quite/absolutely** excellent.
This book is **completely/totally** useless.

5 The stadium was **half** empty.
I'm **ninety-nine per cent** certain.

With comparatives

6 You need something **a bit/a little** bigger than that.
I did it **much/a lot** more easily the second time.
Is your mother **any** better today?

With verbs

7 I **just** love this record.
We **almost** had an accident.
I **completely** forgot about it.

8 I didn't like her first book very **much**, but I like this one **a lot**.

An adverb or adverb phrase of degree makes the meaning of an adjective, adverb or verb stronger or weaker.

1 An adverb of degree comes before the adjective or adverb it describes.

2 But *enough* comes after the adjective or adverb it describes.

3 *very* and *extremely* make the meaning of an adjective or adverb stronger; *rather, pretty, fairly* and *quite* make the meaning a little stronger; *a bit* and *a little* make the meaning weaker. *pretty* and *a bit* are rather informal.

4 We also use *quite* (and e.g. *absolutely, completely, totally*) to give emphasis to the meaning when the adjective or adverb already has a very strong meaning, e.g. *excellent* (= very good), *useless, awful, marvellous, perfect, right, wrong, correct, sure, impossible.*

5 We sometimes use a fraction or a percentage as an adverb of degree.

6 These adverbs can come before a comparative: *much, a lot, rather, a bit, a little, any, no.*

7 An adverb of degree that describes a verb has mid position, e.g. *just, almost, completely, quite, rather.*

8 But *much, a lot, a bit* and *a little* have end position when they describe a verb.

24.9 Sentence adverbs

Fortunately the weather was good.
Of course you can come.
We **certainly** need some help.
David will **probably** be there.
He won't be there, **actually**.
He isn't very well, **unfortunately**.

Sentence adverbs show what the speaker thinks about the sentence. *fortunately* means that the speaker is pleased about the weather.

Sentence adverbs can have front position, mid position or end position.

Some more examples: *in fact, really, surely, possibly, maybe, perhaps, naturally, (un)luckily.*

24.10 Adverbs with the same form as adjectives

1 *Adjective* Mrs Wells is a **hard** worker.
  Adverb She works very **hard**.
  Adjective We were **early**.
  Adverb We arrived **early**.

2 *Adjective* The **daily** newspaper arrives at seven o'clock.
  Adverb The newspaper arrives **daily** at seven o'clock.

1 *hard* and *early* are both adjectives and adverbs. Other adverbs with the same form as adjectives are *fast, high, low, deep, near, late* and *long*. But ▷ 24.11

2 *daily, hourly, weekly, monthly* and *yearly* are both adjectives and adverbs. We form them from the nouns *day, hour* etc.

145 (24.8)

Robert Gorman is writing a guide to hotels in England. Here are his notes on the two main hotels in Milchester. Say how good the two hotels are.

		Grand Hotel	Castle Hotel
	comfortable?	+	0
	pleasant views?	0	+ +
1	good service?	+	+ +
2	good food?	0	+ +
3	clean?	+ +	0
4	quiet?	+	+ +
5	convenient?	+ +	+
6	reasonable prices?	0	+ +

+ + = very good
+ = fairly good   0 = not very good

Examples

The Grand is fairly comfortable.
It's a bit more comfortable than the Castle.
The Castle isn't very comfortable.

The views at the Grand aren't very pleasant.
They're a lot less pleasant than at the Castle.
The views at the Castle are very pleasant.

Activity A

Is there a system of school and college marks or grades in your country? Do teachers give marks from 1 to 5 or a percentage mark? Explain the meaning of the different grades.

Activity B

Describe your country's climate. Say how hot or cold and how wet or dry it is, and so on, at different times of the year.

146 (24.5, 24.10)

Mrs Lake is a teacher of English. She is making notes on her students. Say how well each student is doing at English. Use an adverb of manner in each sentence. (Most but not all of these adverbs end in -*ly*.)

Example

Ahmed: Bad spelling. Careless written work.
Ahmed spells badly. He does his written work carelessly.

1 Stella: Satisfactory progress. Good homework.
  Stella is progressing … . She does … .
2 Emil: Fluent speaker of English. Wide reading.
3 Milena: Hard worker. Fast learner.
4 Victor: Slow speech. Incorrect pronunciation of some common words.

Activity A

Invent sentences which would be spoken in a certain manner, e.g. *We mustn't make a noise* or *Hurry up!* Your partner has to say how they are spoken, e.g. *quietly, impatiently.*

Activity B

One student thinks of an adverb (e.g. *quickly*) which he/she does not tell anyone. Ask the student to do different actions, e.g. *Clean the board. Walk across the room.* The student does these actions quickly (or happily, or carefully etc), and you guess the adverb by asking e.g. *Are you doing it quickly?*

24.11   high, highly; near, nearly; hard, hardly; late, lately; most, mostly

1 The balloon didn't go very **high**.
  I'm reading a **highly** amusing book.
2 The fish came quite **near**.
  I **nearly** caught one.
3 They worked very **hard**.
  They **hardly** had any time for lunch.
4 We arrived **late** because of bad weather.
  There have been a lot of storms **lately**.
5 What I hate **most** about air travel is waiting at airports.
  On long journeys I **mostly** travel by plane.

high, near, hard and *late* are adverbs with the same form as adjectives. ▷ 24.10

most is an adverb with the same form as a quantifier. ▷ 20.18

highly, nearly, hardly, lately and *mostly* are also adverbs, but they have different meanings from *high, near* etc.

1 *highly* = very
2 *nearly* = almost
3 *hardly any time* = almost no time
4 *lately* = recently, in the last few days/weeks
5 *mostly* = mainly, usually

24.12   Adjectives instead of adverbs after **feel, look** etc.

I feel **hungry**.
The garden looked very **nice**.
This pudding tastes **delicious**.

We use an adjective (not an adverb) when we can use *be* instead of the verb. *I feel hungry* means that I *am* hungry.

We use an adjective after *feel, look, taste, smell, sound, seem, appear, become, get* (= become) and *stay*.

24.13   The regular comparison of adverbs

1 Could you say that **more slowly**, please?
  Tom can shoot the **most accurately**.
2 You'll just have to get up **earlier**.
  Sarah ran the **fastest**.
3 Shout a bit **louder/more loudly**.
  You can buy them **cheapest/most cheaply** at Scott's.

1 Adverbs in *-ly* form their comparative and superlative with *more* and *most*. (But note *earlier* in 2.)
2 Adverbs with the same form as adjectives form their comparative and superlative with *-er* and *-est*.
3 Some adjectives can be used instead of adverbs in informal English, e.g. *loud, cheap, slow, quick*. ▷ 24.5

24.14   The irregular comparison of adverbs

1 Adrian can draw very **well**.
  He can draw **better** than I can.
  He can draw animals **best**.
2 The team played **badly**.
  They played **worse** than last week.
  Jones played the **worst**.
3 Martin can't swim very **far**.
  You can swim **further/farther** than Martin.
  Sarah can swim the **furthest**/the **farthest**.

Form

1	**well**	better	best
2	**badly**	worse	worst
3	**far**	further/farther	furthest/farthest

▷ 23.3 irregular comparison of adjectives; 23.8 *further/farther*

24.15   Comparison: **as . . . as, less** etc.

I can't do crosswords **as quickly as** you.
The old man's son visits him **less often** nowadays.
They went **faster and faster** down the hill.
The more you practise, **the better** you'll play.

We use *as . . . as, less* etc. with adverbs as well as with adjectives. ▷ 23.4–7

147 (24.12)

Tom and Angela are at Lynn's party. Complete their conversation by choosing the correct adjective or adverb in the brackets.

Tom Well, the party is going very (nice/nicely), isn't it? Have one of these sausages. They taste (good/well).
Angela No, thanks.
Tom You don't sound very (happy/happily), Angela. And you look (pale/palely). Are you all right?
Angela I feel rather (tired/tiredly). And I'm (hot/hotly).
Tom It is getting a bit (warm/warmly) in here, isn't it? Well I can (easy/easily) open this window.
Angela Thanks. Actually, my head aches quite (bad/badly) too. I think it's (slow/slowly) getting worse.
Tom I'm (sure/surely) the music isn't helping. It seems rather (loud/loudly), doesn't it? Look, would you like me to take you home?
Angela No, it's all right, thanks. But if I could sit (quiet/quietly) somewhere for a few minutes, I might be OK.
Tom I'll ask Lynn if there's somewhere you can go.

Activity

Complete the sentences in your own words to form a paragraph. Use an adjective or adverb in each sentence.

Harry got up … . He felt … . His face in the mirror … . His voice … . His breakfast tasted … . He ate … . Everything seemed … .

148 (24.13, 24.14)

The Drama Club are rehearsing a new play. Jane is telling the actors what to do. They aren't doing things right yet. Complete what Jane says using the comparative of an adverb.

Examples

You didn't go out quietly enough, Mark. Can you go out *more quietly* next time?

You aren't near enough, Tom. Come *nearer* to her.

1 You have to speak really clearly. Can you speak … , please, Helen?
2 You didn't wait long enough, Lynn. Can you stay a little … in the doorway?
3 You haven't learnt your words very well, Peter. I hope you know them … next time.
4 You aren't angry enough, Sarah. Can you shout rather … ?
5 Angela, that isn't far enough. Walk … to the left.
6 And you're supposed to be nervous. Can you look round a bit … ?
7 I want you to hit the table hard. You can hit it … than that, Bob.
8 Be careful when you lay the table, Sue. Try to do it … next time.

Activity

Explain what these evening courses at Milchester College will teach you to do.

☐ Map-reading Made Easy
☐ Faster Typing
☐ More Fluent French
☐ Improve Your Cooking

24.16 yet, still, already and no longer

1 Has the letter come **yet**? ~ No, not **yet**.
We haven't seen our new neighbours **yet**.

2a Are you **still** waiting?
She's fifteen, but she **still** takes a teddy bear to bed with her.

b The letter **still** hasn't come.

3a I've **already** done that exercise.
Have you **already** had lunch?

b I've done that exercise **already**. It was easy.
Have you had lunch **already**? It's only quarter past twelve.

4a Mr Baker **no longer** lives here.

b He doesn't live here **any longer/any more**.

1 We use *yet* to talk about something we are expecting.
We use *yet* in questions and in negative statements.
yet comes at the end of a sentence.

2 We use *still* to talk about something going on longer than we expected.
still comes

a in mid position in questions and positive statements

b after the subject in negative statements

3 We use *already* to talk about something happening sooner than we expected.
We use *already* mainly in positive statements and in questions.
already comes

a in mid position

b at the end of the sentence if we want to give it more emphasis

4 We use *no longer* and *any longer/any more* to talk about something that has come to an end.

a *no longer* has a negative meaning. It comes in mid position.

b We use *any longer/any more* in negative statements. It comes at the end of a sentence.

24.17 only and even

1 The couple **only** stayed one night at the hotel.
We could **only** get a cheese sandwich.

2 He's very active for an 80-year-old. He **even** plays golf.
I can't **even** remember my own telephone number.

3 Some houses haven't got electricity **even** today.

4 **Only** tourists buy these things.
Even the stupidest person could understand it.

5 The **only** food we could get was a cheese sandwich.

6 The couple stayed **only** one night at the hotel.

7 This car park is for customers **only**.

1 In informal English, *only* has mid position. It need not come next to the word that it refers to, e.g. *one*.

2 *even* also has mid position.

3 *even* can come before the word it refers to.

4 When *only* and *even* refer to the subject, they come before it.

5 We can also use *only* as an adjective.

6 In rather formal or careful English, *only* can come before the word or phrase that it refers to, e.g. *one*.

7 In official written English, e.g. on notices, *only* comes after the word or phrase that it refers to, e.g. *customers*.

24.18 long and far

1 Have you been here **long**?
How **far** is it to Cambridge?
I won't stay **long**.
We didn't go **far**.

2 I've been waiting **a long time**.
It's **a long way** to the park.

3 The meeting went on so **long** I missed my bus.
It's too **far** to walk.

1 We normally use the adverbs *long* and *far* only in questions and negative statements.

2 We normally use *a long time* and *a long way* in positive statements.

3 But we use *long* and *far* after *too, so* and *as*, even in positive statements.

25 Prepositions

25.1 Prepositions of place and movement

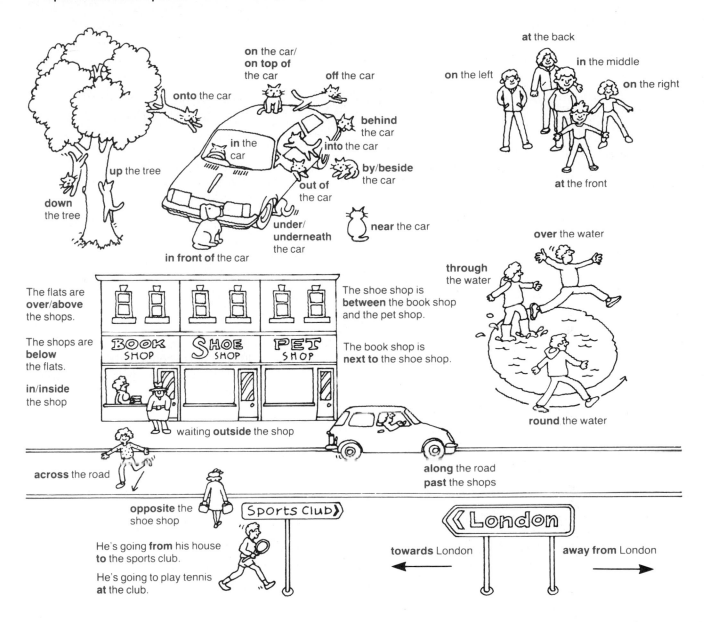

on the car/
on top of
the car

off the car

onto the car

behind
the car

into the car

in the
car

by/beside
the car

up the tree

out of
the car

down
the tree

under/
underneath
the car

near the car

in front of the car

at the back

in the middle

on the left

on the right

at the front

over the water

through
the water

round the water

The flats are
over/above
the shops.

The shops are
below
the flats.

in/inside
the shop

The shoe shop is
between the book shop
and the pet shop.

The book shop is
next to the shoe shop.

BOOK
SHOP

SHOE
SHOP

PET
SHOP

waiting **outside** the shop

across the road

along the road
past the shops

opposite the
shoe shop

Sports Club

London

He's going **from** his house
to the sports club.

He's going to play tennis
at the club.

towards London

away from London

25.2 Prepositions of place: **at** and **in**

1 Simon was **at** the bus stop.
2 We live **at** 23 Bolton Road.
3 We were **at** the theatre.
  (= . . . watching a play.)
  The boys are **at** the swimming-pool.
  (= . . . swimming or watching the swimmers.)
4 We stopped **at** a village near Coventry.
5 The Jamesons live **at** Oxford.

1 Susan was **in** the garden.
2 We live **in** Bolton Road.
3 It was dark **in** the theatre.
  (= . . . inside the theatre.)
  It was cold **in** the swimming-pool.
  (= . . . in the water.)
4 There were two shops **in** the village.
5 The Jamesons live **in** Oxford.
6 They're on holiday **in** Spain.

We use *at* with
1 a position
2 a house or an address
3 a building (e.g. *theatre*), when we are thinking of the activity that takes place there
4 a village or town on a journey
5 a village or town (but *in* is more usual)

We use *in* (= inside) with
1 something big enough to be all around a person
2 a road or street
3 a building or other large space
4 a village
5 a town or city
6 a country

25.3 Prepositions of time: **at, on** and **in**

at
at four o'clock
at breakfast
at night
at Christmas
at the weekend
at that time

on
on Friday(s)
on Tuesday morning
on May 21st
on the next day

in
in the morning
in June
in summer
in 1985

No preposition
Is there a meeting this week?
I'll see you next Tuesday.
We went there last year.

In informal American English the preposition is also left out in e.g. *He'll be back Saturday.*

▷ 19.9 phrases of time without *the*

25.4 Prepositions of time: **before, during** and **after**

The post office is very busy **before** Christmas.
I'm always out at work **during** the day.
We had to take a taxi home **after** the party.

We can also use *before* and *after* as conjunctions.
▷ 15.2; 27.2
during is a preposition; *while* is a conjunction with the same meaning. ▷ 15.2; 27.2

25.5 Prepositions of time: **till/until** and **by**

1 My mother's staying with us **till** Friday/**until** Friday.
2 Can you give me the money **by** the weekend?

1 *till Friday/until Friday* = from now to Friday.
  till is more informal than *until*.
2 *by the weekend* = not later than the weekend.

▷ 27.2 *till/until* as a conjunction

149 (25.1, 25.2)

One of Brenda Bagg's stories is going to be made into a film. It's a romantic comedy about a girl who works in a baker's shop. The picture shows how Brenda imagines the scene at the start of the film. Complete her description of the scene for the film director. Put in some of these prepositions: *above, across, along, at, behind, between, by, from, in, inside, near, off, on, opposite, out of, outside, round, through, to, towards, under, up*. (Sometimes more than one answer is correct.)

Street scene. There are three shops. … the middle there is a baker's, which is … an antique shop and a toy shop. The toy shop is … the right. There is a phone box … the left … the corner of the street. A car is coming … the corner. There is a man on a bike … the car. There is also a car parked … the baker's. This car has a suitcase … its roof. A woman is just stepping … the pavement to walk … the road. She has come … the baker's. Two girls are standing … the baker's. A window cleaner is climbing … a ladder … the window … the toy shop. He has got a bucket … his hand. A woman is looking … the window. A boy is walking … the pavement … the ladder … the street corner. There is a man … the antique shop looking … an old telescope. There is a young man … the phone box, and three people are standing … the pavement waiting – a woman, a man and a boy. The boy is … the back of the queue.

Activity A

Describe your daily journey to school or work, giving full details of your route.

Activity B

Find a photo of an outdoor scene. (If possible, use a photo of your own.) Describe the photo using *on the right/left, in the foreground/background, next to* and other prepositions.

Activity C

Discuss possible methods of escaping from prison. These words may be useful: *cell, bars, rope, wall, ladder, tunnel, hide, gate, guard, disguise.*

25.6 Prepositions of time: **from . . . to/till/until**

The sale was **from** December 28th **to** January 3rd.
The shop is open **from** nine **till** five thirty.
It will be closed **from** tomorrow **until** next Tuesday.

We use *from . . . to/till/until* to talk about the beginning and end of a period of time.
Americans use *from . . . through*, e.g. *It will be closed from tomorrow through next Tuesday.*

25.7 Prepositions of time: **for, since** and **in**; the adverb **ago**

1 I've only had this watch (**for**) six months.
  Dick's going to France **for** a year.

2 I've only had this watch **since** March.
  I haven't seen Julia **since** Christmas.

3 I bought this watch six months **ago**.
  Shakespeare was born over four hundred years **ago**.

4a Dick will be leaving for France **in** two days.
 b He ran the mile **in** 3 minutes 55 seconds.

1 We use *for* with a period of time, e.g. *six months*. We can sometimes leave out *for*.

2 We use *since* with a point of time, e.g. *March*. *since March* = from March to now.

3 We use *ago* for past time measured from the present. *six months ago* = six months before now.

4 We use *in* to talk about
a a point of future time measured from the present. *in two days* = two days from now.
b a period of time needed to do something.

▷ 15.2; 27.2 *since* as a conjunction

25.8 Means: **with** and **by**

1 The thief opened the door **with** a key.
2 He got in **by** using a key.

1 We use *with* + noun phrase to talk about means. But ▷ 25.9
2 We use *by* + -ing form.

25.9 Means of transport and communication: **by**

1a Did you go **by** train or **by** air?
 b We went on foot./We walked.
2 We can let them know **by** telegram.

1a We use *by* + noun (without *the*) to talk about means of transport, e.g. *by train, by air, by bus, by car, by sea, by boat*. (We can also say *on the train, on the plane, on the bus, on my bike* and *in the car*.)
 b But we say *on foot* or we use the verb *walk*.
2 We also use *by* for means of communication, e.g. *by telegram, by letter, by telephone*.

25.10 Describing: **with** and **in**

1 Police are looking for a tall man **with** fair hair.
  It's the house **with** the green door.
2 Who's that woman **in** the red dress?
  She had a red dress on/was wearing a red dress.

1 In descriptions *with* means having. *a man with fair hair* = a man who has fair hair.
2 We can use *in* or *have (got) . . . on* to talk about clothes.

25.11 **as** and **like**

1   Trevor is working **as** a disc jockey.
    I use this room **as** my office.

2   He talks **like** a disc jockey.
    She's just **like** her mother.

1   We use *as* to say what someone's job is or what something is used for.

2   We use *like* to compare two things that are the same or similar in some way.

▷   23.4 *as . . . as*

25.12 Adjective + preposition

I'm **afraid of** the dog.
He's very **different from** his brother.
Are you **ready for** a walk?

Some more examples of adjective + preposition:
bored with, fed up with, fond of, good at, interested in, keen on, tired of, worried about.

Exercises

150 (25.3–25.7)

Complete the news item about the British runner Stan Crowe. Put in the missing prepositions.

CROWE TO RUN AGAINST BOTO

Stan Crowe hopes to run against James Boto of Kenya in a 1500 metres race in Paris … June 16th. Both men will want to break Cliff Holding's world record. Holding ran the 1500 metres … 3 minutes 28 seconds last year. Holding will also be running in Seattle … June 14th, two days … the Paris meeting.

British fans have been hoping … several months to see Crowe win back his record. He last ran against Boto … April, when he fell and hurt himself … the race. He was just behind Boto … the time. The two men had not met … the last Olympic Games in Peking. Crowe has had to rest … his accident, but he was back in action … seven o'clock … Saturday evening when he won a rather slow race in Edinburgh. He hopes to be fully fit … the end of this month at the latest. If he is not fit for Paris, he will have to wait … the Commonwealth Games. These games take place in Ottawa … August 14th … the 20th.

Activity A

Explain when school holidays and public holidays occur in your country.

Activity B

Explain what the dates in brackets mean.

☐ William Shakespeare (1564–1616)
☐ Richard Nixon, US President (1969–73)
☐ The Bicentenary of American Independence (1976)

Activity C

Say what you do and how you feel before, during and after an important exam.

151 (25)

Complete this story of an (imaginary) person who spent three years alone on an island. Put in the missing prepositions.

… a Thursday evening … October 1931, … about eight o'clock, the ship 'Voyager' sank. The ship had been sailing … the end of September, when she left London, and was on her way … England … Australia. The only survivor was an Englishman called Wilfred Batty, who saved himself … swimming two miles. He spent three years … an island … the middle of the Indian Ocean.

The island was quite small, and he could walk … the whole of it … an hour. He climbed … the one hill and put a flag … it … a signal. … night Batty slept … a cave, where he felt quite … home. … the day, he often fished … a home-made net. He cooked the fish … a wood fire.

Batty stayed … the island … almost three years, … August 1934. A ship was sailing … the island, and the captain saw Batty's signal. The sailors found a man … a long blue coat … dark hair and a beard, looking rather … a gorilla. Batty was soon home, and a few years later he finally arrived in Australia … air.

Activity

Look at an English story and choose a paragraph with some prepositions in it. Copy the paragraph, leaving a blank instead of the prepositions. Then ask your partner to put in the prepositions.

26 Verbs with adverbs and prepositions

26.1 Verbs with adverbs (phrasal verbs)

1 We **went away** for two weeks. We only **came back** yesterday.

2 I'm sure I **wrote down** the address, but I think I **threw away** the piece of paper.

3 The plan didn't **come off**—I'm afraid it **fell through**.

4 Mr Gray doesn't want to **give up** smoking, but he's **cutting down** the number of cigarettes he smokes.

1 A phrasal verb is a verb + adverb, e.g. *go away*.

1,2 Sometimes the meaning of a phrasal verb is clear from the meaning of the verb and adverb, e.g. *go away, come back, write down, throw away*.

3,4 Sometimes the verb + adverb has a special meaning, e.g. here *come off* (= succeed), *fall through* (= not succeed), *give up* (= stop), *cut down* (= reduce).

1,3 These phrasal verbs have no object.

2,4 These phrasal verbs have an object, e.g. *wrote down the address*.

Some other examples of phrasal verbs: *blow up, call off, carry on, fall down, find out, get up, go away, make up, pick up, put down, put up, set off, sit down, take off, wash up, work out*.

26.2 Phrasal verbs with an object

The young people **picked up** the litter.
A lorry **took away** all the bottles.

The young people **picked** the litter **up**.
A lorry **took** all the bottles **away**.

The young people **picked up** the litter left by the crowd.
A lorry **took away** all the bottles they found.

What about the litter? ~
The young people **picked** it **up**.
Who took the bottles? ~ A lorry **took** them **away**.

If the object of a phrasal verb is a noun, the adverb can come

1 before the object or

2 after it.

3 If the object is very long (e.g. *the litter left by the crowd*), then the adverb comes in front of it.

4 If the object is a pronoun, the adverb always comes after it.

26.3 Prepositional verbs

We finally **decided on** a holiday in Morocco.
We had to **wait for** the plane.
Can I **look at** your photos?

A prepositional verb is a verb + preposition, e.g. *decide on*.

Some other examples of prepositional verbs: *agree with, arrive at, ask for, believe in, belong to, deal with, depend on, hope for, insist on, laugh at, listen to, look after, look for, pay for, send for, talk about*.

Exercises

152 (26.1, 26.2)

Anthony Knight appears on the television programme 'Newswatch'. He asks important questions about people and things in the news. Complete his questions using these phrasal verbs:

blow up	(= explode)	*go up*	(= rise)
bring up	(= raise)	*knock down*	(= demolish)
come off	(= succeed)	*put off*	(= postpone)
find out	(= discover)	*put up*	(= increase)
get away	(= escape)	*work out*	(= calculate)

Examples

We've heard the government have postponed the decision. *Why have they put it off?*

The prisoners escaped, yes, but *how did they get away?*

1 Prices will rise. The question is, how much ... ?
2 Someone calculated these figures, but the government won't say who ... .
3 The Prime Minister says he's going to raise the question in Brussels, but when ... ?
4 We know the petrol tank exploded. Why ... ?
5 So the government are going to increase taxes. Well, how much ... ?
6 The Council say they're going to demolish the building, but why ... ?
7 The government say they discovered the mistake, but when ... ?
8 The plan succeeded. Why ... ?

Activity

Write a short news report about a meeting between the management and the trade union at the Electrobrit factory. Use these notes: ask/put up/wages–prices/ go up–turn down/request–threaten/strike–go on/talk/ all day–agree/put off/strike–both sides/think over.

153 (26.2, 26.3)

Betty Root is talking on television. She doesn't agree with Prime Minister George Wright and his Progressive Party. Add a sentence about what happened when Betty was Prime Minister. Use *it* or *them* in the sentence.

Examples

Mr Wright hasn't carried out the national plan.
But we carried it out.

The Progressives haven't looked after old people.
We looked after them.

1 This government has closed down the universities. We didn't ... .
2 George Wright's government has put up income tax. We didn't ... .
3 The Progressives haven't listened to ordinary people. But we listened ... .
4 They've let down the country. We ... .
5 The Prime Minister has to look for excuses. But we didn't have to ... .
6 The Progressive government hasn't dealt with the unemployment problem. We ... .
7 They haven't kept down the cost of living. We ... .
8 They don't care about the people of this country. But we care ... .

Activity

Talk about your country's present government, what its ideas are and what it has done.

26.4 Phrasal verbs and prepositional verbs

1 *Phrasal verb*
We **paid back** the money.
We **paid** the money **back**.
The money was **paid back**.

2 *Prepositional verb*
We **paid for** the flat.
The flat was **paid for**.

1 If a phrasal verb has an object, the adverb can come before or after it. ▷ 26.2
We normally stress the adverb.
Some examples of adverbs in phrasal verbs: *about, away, back, by, down, in, off, on, out, over, past, round, through, to, under, up.*

2 A prepositional verb always has an object. The object comes after the preposition. ▷ 26.3
We do not normally stress the preposition.
Some examples of prepositions in prepositional verbs: *about, after, at, for, from, in, into, like, of, off, on, to, with.*

26.5 Phrasal-prepositional verbs

I say we should **do away with** this unfair tax.
Let's hurry up and **get on with** the job.
I hope you won't **go back on** your promise now.
Don't **let** Mr Barnes **in on** our secret!
I'm really **looking forward to** our holiday.
Why do you **put up with** all this noise?
Watch out for cows in the road along here!

A phrasal-prepositional verb is a verb + adverb + preposition, e.g. *do away with.*

27 Conjunctions and other linking words

27.1 Main clauses and sub clauses

Two main clauses
1 I've got a headache, and I feel sick.

*Sub clauses (with **if, when** etc.)*
2 We can go if you like.
   If you like, we can go.
   We'll go when this film's over.
   When this film's over, we'll go.

Reported clauses
3 It said in the paper (that) it finishes at ten.
   It finishes at ten, it said in the paper.

Relative clauses
4 The film that came first was awful.
   'Love in the East', which came first, was awful.

Conjunctions

1 We join two main clauses together with the conjunctions *and, but* and *or.*
2 A sub clause can begin with a conjunction, e.g. *if, when, because, so that.*
3 A reported clause begins with *that* or has no conjunction. ▷ 12.1. For reported questions ▷ 12.5
4 A relative clause begins with a relative pronoun. ▷ 22.1. But ▷ 22.4

Order of clauses

2 A sub clause with *if, when* etc. can come before or after the main clause.
3 A reported clause usually comes after the main clause.
4 A relative clause comes after the noun it tells us about.

Punctuation

For the use of commas with main clauses and sub clauses ▷ 39.3

▷   13.2 sub clauses of future time

27.2 Clauses of time

When/While/As I was eating my lunch, the fire alarm rang suddenly.
He wanted to have everything ready **before the guests arrived**.
After/When she had wrapped up the parcel, she took it to the post office.
I came **as soon as I heard the news**.
We can wait here **till/until the rain stops**.
We haven't seen Sue **since she came back from her holiday**.

Clauses of time can come either before or after the main clause.

▷   13.2 sub clauses of future time; 15.2; 17.2 the -ing form

27.3 Sub clauses with **that** and with question words

1 *With* **that**
The problem is (**that**) **we haven't got a key**.
I forgot (**that**) **he was coming today**.
I'm worried (**that**) **you might hurt yourself**.
It seems unlikely (**that**) **the experiment will succeed**.
That the experiment will succeed seems unlikely.

2 *With question words*
I'm trying to find out **when the concert is**.
No one can understand **how the accident happened**.
Sarah wasn't sure **where she'd put the letter**.
What we're going to do about it is the important question.

We can use these sub clauses as subject or object of a sentence, after *be*, or after an adjective.

1 We can leave out *that* in informal English except at the beginning of a sentence.
▷ 12.1 reporting verbs; 20.2 uses of *it*

2 The word order after a question word is the same as in a statement (not a question).
▷ 12.5 reported questions; 28.5 *what* used for emphasis

27.4 Clauses with **and, too, as well** etc.

1 Stephen rides a motor-bike, and he can drive a car (**too/as well**).
Stephen rides a motor-bike. He can drive a car **too/as well**.

2 Jenny can't sing, and she can't dance **either**.
Jenny can't sing. She can't dance **either**.

3 The old man couldn't read **or** write.

4 Stephen rides a motor-bike. He can **also** drive a car.

5 David likes modern jazz **as well as** pop music.
He likes **both** pop music **and** modern jazz.
Jean is **not only** a good singer **but also** a first-class guitarist.

1 *too* and *as well* usually come at the end of a clause.

2 We use *either* instead of *too* in a negative sentence.

3 We normally use *or* instead of *and* to link two words or phrases after a negative.

4 *also* usually has mid position.

5 *as well as, both . . . and* and *not only . . . but also* are more emphatic.

▷ 9.1 short additions to statements

27.5 Giving alternatives

1 We can buy a colour television **or** a black and white one.

2 We can buy **either** a colour television **or** a black and white one.
We can **either** buy a television **or** hire one.
There isn't any sport today on BBC **or** on ITV/**either** on BBC **or** on ITV.

3 **Neither** BBC **nor** ITV is/are showing any sport.

1 We use *or* to talk about an alternative.

2 We can use *either* and *or* in a positive or a negative sentence.

3 *neither* and *nor* have a negative meaning.

We use *either* and *neither* to talk about *two* things.
▷ 20.23

▷ 8.2 alternative questions

154 (27.2)

Ten detectives work for Bymore's department store. Their job is to stop customers stealing things. Look at this note from the store manager and put in these conjunctions: *after, as, as soon as, before, since, until.*

To: All store detectives   **From**: Manager

Please remember these points.

1 It is important to act quickly. ... you see a customer behaving suspiciously, inform the control team by radio.
2 Follow the customer ... he moves around the store.
3 Do not speak to the customer inside the store. Wait ... he has left the store.
4 ... you have informed the control team, a second detective will join you to help with the arrest.
5 Arrest the customer outside and bring him to the control room for questioning. Do not question him ... you get to the control room.
6 Remember that the control team have been filming the customer ... you first informed them about him.

Activity

Frank Simlein is a writer of science fiction. He's writing a story about an American family called Mitchell who have survived a nuclear explosion and are living in an underground shelter. Suggest a few sentences with clauses of time that Frank might use.

155 (27.3)

A man walked into a London hospital yesterday not knowing his own name. He'd lost his memory. Rewrite the man's words putting the main clause first and the sub clause second. Use a question word or *that.* (You can leave out *that* if you like.)

Examples

Who am I? No one knows.
No one knows who I am.

I'll get my memory back soon, I hope.
I hope that I'll get my memory back soon.

1 What's my name? I've no idea.
2 Where do I live? I don't know.
3 I'm a long way from home, I've got a feeling.
4 Why do I think so? I'm not sure.
5 Something strange has happened to me, I know.
6 How did it happen? I can't understand.
7 I just walked into the hospital, I've heard.
8 When did I come here? I can't remember.

Activity

Complete these sentences in your own words using sub clauses.

☐ I hope ...
☐ I can never understand ...
☐ I believe ...
☐ I don't know ...

27.6 Clauses of contrast: **whereas, while** and **on the other hand**

America is a rich country, **whereas/while** India is a poor country.
America is an industrial country. India, **on the other hand**, is an agricultural country.

on the other hand often has mid position or comes after the subject. It can also have front or end position.

27.7 Clauses of contrast: **but, though, however** etc.

1 Thousands of pupils are leaving school, **but** there are no jobs for them.
There are no jobs for them, **though**.
There are, **however**, no jobs for them.

2 **Although/Though/Even though** Ann did well at school, she can't find a job.
Ann can't find a job **in spite of** doing well at school.

1 As an adverb, *though* usually comes at the end of a sentence. *though* is rather informal.
however often has mid position or comes after the subject. It can also have front or end position.

2 Clauses with *although, though* and *even though* and with *in spite of* + -ing form can come either before or after the main clause.
We can also use *in spite of* + noun phrase, e.g. *She can't find a job in spite of her exam results.*

▷ 15.2 the -ing form

27.8 Clauses of reason

They didn't go **because** it was snowing.
As/Since we were late, we didn't get any food.

We can express reason with *because, as* or *since*.
We can sometimes use *because of* + noun phrase instead of a clause, e.g. *They didn't go because of the snow.*

▷ 17.4 the -ing form and the -ed form

27.9 Clauses of purpose

1 The government puts up taxes **to** get more money from us.
We need more money **in order to** build more hospitals.
They called a meeting **so as to** hear everyone's opinion.

2 I wrote down the address **so that** I wouldn't forget it.

3 Schools are **for** learning.

4 What's the meeting **for**? ~
It's **to** discuss the new plan.

We can express purpose by using

1 an infinitive after *to, in order to* or *so as to. in order to* and *so as to* are rather formal.

2 a clause with *so that*. We often use *can, could, will, would* or *needn't*.

3 *for* + -ing form.

4 We often answer the question *What . . . for?* in a sentence with *to* and the infinitive.

156   (27.6, 27.7)

The management of Albion Motor Cycles are discussing the company's problems. Rewrite each sentence beginning with the linking word in brackets.

Examples

We borrowed money, but we couldn't really afford to. (although)
Although we borrowed money, we couldn't really afford to.

We enjoy a good reputation, but we have financial problems. (in spite of)
In spite of enjoying a good reputation, we have financial problems.

1 We brought out two new models, but sales didn't increase. (even though)
2 We made a big effort, but we failed to sell enough bikes. (even though)
3 They're good bikes, but they're expensive. (although)
4 People want quality, but they don't want to pay for it. (although)
5 Sales are going down, but costs are increasing. (while)
6 We've reduced our work-force, but we've still got a high wages bill. (in spite of)
7 We bought some new equipment, but we've still had production problems. (even though)
8 Other companies are moving ahead, but we're standing still. (whereas)

Activity

Think of sentences that might be said by someone who has failed a driving test for the tenth time. Use linking words of contrast.

157   (27.8, 27.9)

Some people are saying why they are learning English. Give each person's reason.

Examples

Marcel I need it in my job.
Marcel is learning English because he needs it in his job.

Astrid I wanted to give myself a new interest.
Astrid is learning it to give herself a new interest.

Bruno I can use it when I travel.
Bruno is learning it so that he can use it when he travels.

1 **Ingrid** I like learning languages.
2 **Anita** I can help my daughter with her homework.
3 **Martin** I might need it some time.
4 **Claudia** I want to get a better job.
5 **Gaston** I'll be able to understand American films better.
6 **Andrea** I have to do it at school.
7 **Sven** I'll be able to read engineering textbooks in English.
8 **Jan** I want to impress my girl-friend.

Activity A

Make a list of things you would need in order to survive comfortably on a desert island. Say why you would need each one.

Activity B

Give as many reasons as you can think of why people want jobs.

27.10   Clauses of result: **so, therefore** etc.

1   The party wasn't very good, **so** I left early.
2   The management refused to increase wages, and the workers **therefore** went on strike.
3   The club bought two new players, and **as a result** they began to win more games.
     This year's harvest was very poor. **Consequently** the price of wheat has gone up dramatically.

1   (*and*) *so* always comes at the beginning of a clause, but it does not normally start a new sentence.
2   *therefore* often has mid position, but it can have front or end position.
3   *as a result* and *consequently* often have front position but they can have mid or end position.

We can use *therefore, as a result* and *consequently* in a clause with *and* (e.g. *and as a result . . .*) or in a new sentence (e.g. *Consequently . . .*).

27.11   Clauses of result: **so/such . . . (that) . . .**

We laughed **so** much (**that**) it hurt.
I was **so** tired (**that**) I fell asleep in the taxi.
It was **such** a lovely day (**that**) we simply had to go out somewhere.
Tom talks **such** nonsense (**that**) no one listens to him any more.

We can leave out *that* in informal speech.

27.12   Conditional clauses

We can stop **if** you want.
Even if Marcia leaves now, she'll still be late.
You can't go in **unless** you've got a ticket.
We have to do the job **whether** we like it or not.
You can borrow it **as long as** you give it back.
I don't mind working overtime **provided** (**that**) I'm paid for it.
Take an umbrella **in case** it rains.

These clauses can come before or after the main clause.
unless = if . . . not

▷   11 if-clauses

158 (27.10, 27.11)

Last year the Cross family had a very disappointing holiday. Join each pair of sentences using *so* or *so/such … that …*. (You can leave out *that* if you like.)

Examples

They wanted a holiday. They looked at a Suntime brochure.
They wanted a holiday, so they looked at a Suntime brochure.

The holidays were very cheap. They booked one immediately.
The holidays were so cheap that they booked one immediately.

Alporta looked a very nice place. They decided to go there.
Alporta looked such a nice place that they decided to go there.

1 There was fog. Their flight was delayed.
2 The plane was very late. They got to bed at three in the morning.
3 It was a very long way to the beach. It took an hour from the hotel.
4 It was a very crowded beach. There was hardly room to sit down.
5 The hotel was very noisy. They couldn't sleep.
6 Their room had a very unpleasant view. It made them feel quite miserable.
7 They weren't enjoying themselves. They went home.
8 The holiday was very disappointing. They decided to ask for their money back.

Activity

Write similar sentences about an unsuccessful walk in the country.

---

159 (27)

Complete the short article on the bicycle as a form of transport. Put in these words or phrases: *after, also, although, because, but, but also, either, if, not only, on the other hand, or, so, that, when, whereas.* (Some of the words or phrases may be used more than once.)

The bicycle

Driving a car can be expensive. The bicycle, … , is a cheap form of transport. A bicycle … costs very little … lasts much longer than a car. It is … very cheap to use … of course it doesn't need any fuel. In fact, it costs practically nothing … you've bought it. It … helps keep you fit … you get exercise … you ride it. Another good thing about a bicycle is … it doesn't pollute the air. … everyone rode bicycles instead of driving cars, we wouldn't be using up the world's oil so quickly.

… the bicycle has these advantages, it has some disadvantages too. It is convenient only for relatively short journeys, … by car you can travel quite a long way in comfort. Another problem is … the cyclist is not protected from the weather and gets wet … it rains. Cycling isn't very nice in heavy traffic …. In Britain there are very few cycle paths, … bicycles have to share the road with cars and lorries. The best place for a bike ride is a quiet country lane. Main roads and city streets are often … busy … it needs some courage to take a bike on them. The cyclist has no protection, and … he is more likely than a motorist to be seriously hurt … killed … he does have an accident. Cycling keeps you healthy, … the cars may kill you!

Activity

Write a similar short article discussing the advantages and disadvantages of another form of transport such as the car, the train or the aeroplane.

28 Emphasis

28.1 Emphatic stress

The party isn't on Saturday—it's on **Friday**.
Will your German friend be there? ~
He's **Dutch** not German.

When we want to give emphasis to a word or phrase (make it more important), we can speak it with extra stress.

In writing we can underline the word to give it emphasis. In a book the word can be printed differently, as in the examples.

28.2 The emphatic form of the verb

1 These motorways aren't necessary. ~
I think they **are** necessary.
They shouldn't build them. ~
I think they **should** build them.

2 People don't use them. ~
But people **do** use them.
You didn't come on the motorway. ~
I **did** come on the motorway.

We use the emphatic form of the verb to give emphasis to the meaning of a whole sentence.

1 Auxiliary and modal verbs are stressed in the emphatic form.

2 The simple present and simple past tenses have an emphatic form with *do*. The form of *do* is stressed. ▷ 5.1

28.3 Emphatic word order

1 '**Eatwell**' the restaurant was called.
2 The steak was nice, but **this pudding** I don't like at all.
3 **Slowly** the restaurant began to fill up.

If we want to give emphasis to a word or phrase, we can put it at the beginning of the clause or sentence. We can do this with

1 a complement
2 an object
3 an adverb

28.4 *it* + *be* used for emphasis

1 **It was your wife** who told us the news.
2 **It was in 1979** that we went to Yugoslavia.
3 **It's Bob** I'm looking for, not Mike.
4 **It wasn't me** that broke the window.

1 We can use *it* + *be* and a relative clause to give emphasis to a noun phrase, e.g. *your wife*.

2 We can also use *it* + *be* to give emphasis to an adverb or adverb phrase, e.g. *in 1979*.

3 We can leave out *who* or *that* when it is the object of the relative clause or when there is a preposition. ▷ 22.4

4 If we use a pronoun after *it* + *be*, we use the object form, e.g. *me*. ▷ 20.1

160 (28.2)

There were lots of things wrong with David's car, so he took it to Crook's Garage for repairs. But the garage didn't do the work properly, so David went back next day. Put in Mr Crook's sentences, using the emphatic form.

Examples

David You haven't done the work.
Mr Crook *We have done it. We did everything.*

David You didn't check the brakes.
Mr Crook *We did check them, you know.*

David The car doesn't feel safe.
Mr Crook It .... There's nothing wrong with it.
David The lights don't work.
Mr Crook .... We mended them.
David You didn't replace the front tyres.
Mr Crook .... I remember doing it.
David The back doors won't open.
Mr Crook ..., you know.
David And the heater doesn't work.
Mr Crook .... We checked it.
David But you didn't check the battery.
Mr Crook Yes, ... The battery is OK.
David Anyway, the bill isn't correct.
Mr Crook .... I wrote it myself.
David You don't know what you're talking about.
Mr Crook .... Repairing cars is our business.

Activity

Agree or disagree with these statements:

☐ Smoking doesn't do you any harm.
☐ Women can't do important jobs.
☐ Exams don't matter – learning is the important thing.

161 (28.4)

Police have arrested bank robber Hank Williams. They've promised to let him go if he gives them some information. He's telling them about the gang he belongs to. Look at the detective's notes and give Hank's words. Use *it* and *who/that*.

Examples

Williams joined the gang last March.
'*It was last March that I joined the gang.*'

Grabski organizes the bank raids.
'*It's Grabski who organizes the bank raids.*'

1 Bozo shot the policeman in Marseilles.
2 He went into hiding in Monaco.
3 Ross bought the guns.
4 They're planning to rob the Standard Bank next.
5 Gregory finds out all the inside information.
6 They're going to meet on Long Island next week.
7 Grabski intends to go to Morocco afterwards.
8 He's afraid of the Mafia.

Activity

Use the information below to write sentences about 'firsts'. Use *it* and *who/that*.

Example

It was in California that the first supermarket opened.

The first supermarket opened.	in 1914
the first President of the USA	Yuri Gagarin
The First World War began.	George Washington
the first person in space	in Greece
The first Olympic Games took place.	in California

28.5 **what** used for emphasis

I need a good sleep.
What I need is a good sleep.
I'm going to go to bed.
What I'm going to do is go to bed.

We can use *what* + clause + *be* to give emphasis to a word or phrase, e.g. *a good sleep*.

what = the thing that

▷ 22.9 *what* in relative clauses; 27.3 *what* in other sub clauses

28.6 Emphatic use of **here** and **there**

The bus is late. ~ **Here it comes** now, look.
Here comes the bus.
Where are the books? ~ **There they are**.
There are the books, over there.

Form

We can use *here* or *there* to begin a sentence.

The verb is the present tense of *be* or a verb in the simple present tense (usually *come* or *go*).

If the subject is a pronoun, it comes before the verb (e.g. *Here it comes*). If the subject is a phrase with a noun, it comes after the verb (*Here comes the bus*).

Use

We use *here* and *there* at the beginning of a sentence to draw someone's attention to (= make someone look at) something that we can see.

162 (28.2, 28.4, 28.5)

Charlotte is writing a publicity brochure for a car called the Atlas. Here are her notes. Rewrite each sentence in the way suggested in brackets, so that the underlined part has more emphasis.

Examples

An Atlas looks stylish. (do)
An Atlas does look stylish.

The Atlas gives you the best of modern technology. (it)
It's the Atlas that gives you the best of modern technology.

The Atlas is famous for its economy. (what)
What the Atlas is famous for is its economy.

1 The Atlas won the 'Road' magazine prize. (it)
2 It won the Monte Carlo rally last year. (do)
3 The Atlas gives you reliability. (what)
4 You have lots of room in an Atlas. (do)
5 The expert design makes you feel so comfortable. (it)
6 You'll never believe how much luggage it holds. (what)
7 The low price will really surprise you. (it)
8 The Atlas costs less than £7,000. (do)
9 You'll never want to let anyone else drive your Atlas. (what)
10 You ought to be driving an Atlas now. (what)

Activity

Write advertising slogans for these things. Give emphasis to your statements using *do, it* etc.

163 (28.5)

Gordon has strong views on how the country should be run. Whenever he goes to the pub, he tells everyone his opinions and often repeats things several times. Repeat each sentence using *what* for emphasis.

Examples

We should change our attitudes, in my opinion. *What we should change are our attitudes.*

I feel strongly that something should be done, you know. *What I feel strongly is that something should be done.*

1 This country needs a sense of purpose, I tell you. *What this country …*
2 People want strong government, don't they?
3 I think that we too often take the easy way out, without a doubt.
4 You don't realize how bad thing are, I'm afraid.
5 I say that we're going downhill, no doubt about it.
6 I'd like to see some action, I would indeed.
7 I believe that our problems can be solved, you know.
8 I'm looking for some positive thinking, don't you know?
9 You don't understand how much things have changed. No, indeed.
10 We're all hoping for a better world, aren't we?

Activity

Complete these sentences in your own words.

What always makes me nervous is …
What I like/don't like about the English …
What I'd really like to do if I had enough money …

29 Communication:
Starting and finishing a conversation; being friendly

29.1 Starting a conversation with a stranger

Excuse me, could you tell me the time?
I beg your pardon, do you have the time? (*USA*)

29.2 Introductions

Introducing people
Tony, **this is** Elaine.
Pamela, **meet** Andy./**have you met** Andy?/**do you know** Andy?
Mrs Green, **I'd like you to meet/let me introduce you to** Mr Bridges. (*rather formal*)

Meeting someone for the first time
Hello, Andy. ~ **Hello**, Pamela. (*informal*)
Hi, Elaine. ~ **Hi**, Tony. (*informal, and especially USA*)
How do you do? ~ **How do you do?** Pleased to meet you. (*rather formal*)
How are you? ~ **How are you?** (*USA*)

29.3 Meeting someone you already know

Greeting someone
Hello, Paul.
Hi, Sue. (*informal and especially USA*)
Good morning./Good afternoon./Good evening.
(*a little more formal than* hello)
Morning./Afternoon./Evening.
(*leaving out* good *is less formal*)

Being polite
Nice to see you. **How are you?** ~
Very well, thank you./ Fine, thanks. And how are you?/And you? ~ **OK, thanks./Not too bad, thanks.**
How's life?/How are things? (*informal*)

We use *how* for a polite enquiry but *What . . . like?* for a question about the special qualities of someone or something, e.g. *What's her husband like?* ~ *Well, he's a rather quiet person.*

29.4 Starting a telephone conversation

Saying who you are and who you are calling
Hello. This is Carl./ Carl **here**./Carl **speaking**.
Can I speak to Maria?/**Is** Maria **there**, please?

Asking who the other person is
Is that Mr Tucker? **Is that** Ashford 73780?
Is this Elaine? (*USA*)
Who's speaking?/Who am I speaking to, please?

When you think you have been cut off
Hello? Are you there?

29.5   Saying goodbye

Well, I must be going now./I have to go now. **Goodbye**, Phil.
(I'll) see you (**later**).
Bye!/Bye-bye! (*informal*)
Cheerio!/So long! (*informal*)
Good night. (*at the end of the day*)

29.6   Starting and finishing a letter

Starting a letter		*Finishing a letter*	
Informal	*Formal*	*Informal*	*Formal*
Dear Brian, **Dear** Mrs Moody,	**Dear Sir,** **Dear Madam,**	**Yours sincerely,** **Sincerely yours,** (*USA*) **Yours (ever),** **Love (from),**	**Yours faithfully,**

29.7   Good wishes

Good wishes for success

All the best. Good luck in your new job.
I hope everything goes all right/ goes well for you.
I'd like to wish you every success. (*more formal*)

Good wishes to a third person

Remember me to Chris./ **Regards to** Chris./
Love to Chris.

Good wishes for a holiday etc.

Enjoy yourself/yourselves.
Have a good time/holiday/trip/journey.
Look after yourself. Take care on the roads.

Good wishes at special times of the year

Merry Christmas./Happy Christmas. And a
Happy New Year.
Have a nice Easter.
Happy birthday./Many happy returns (of the day).

Before drinking

Cheers! (To your very) good health./Here's to
the two of you.
There is no special phrase spoken before a meal.

29.8   Compliments

Clothes

I like your coat./**That's a lovely** coat./**You look nice in** that coat. ~
Thank you. It's nice of you to say so.

Cooking

That was **a nice/lovely meal**. The steak was **delicious**. ~
I'm glad you enjoyed it.

29.9   Congratulations and sympathy

Congratulations

I hear you've passed your exam. **Well done!**
Congratulations on passing the exam. ~ Thank you.

When someone has been unsuccessful

Bad luck./Hard luck. Never mind. Better luck next time.

Sympathy

My father died last week. ~ Oh, **I am sorry**.
I was very sorry to hear about your father.

30 Communication: Information, opinions and ideas

30.1 Asking for information

Excuse me. **Can you tell me** the way to Oxford Street?
Could you tell me what time the next train to Bristol is, please?
Do you know if there are any seats left?
Could you give me some information about things to do here?

30.2 Agreeing with or correcting a statement

Statement	Agreeing	Correcting
It's the fifth of May today (, isn't it?) ~	**Yes**, it is.	**No**, it isn't; it's the sixth.
	That's right.	It's the sixth **actually**.

30.3 Asking about language

When you don't hear what someone says
Pardon? Could you repeat that, please?
I beg your pardon?
I'm sorry, I didn't catch what you said.

When you don't understand
I'm sorry, **I don't understand**.
What do you mean?
I'm not with you. (*informal*)

Asking the meaning of a word
What's 'cider'? ~ It's a drink made from apples.
What does 'annually' **mean**? ~ It means 'every year'.
What's the meaning of the word 'library'? ~
A library is a place you can borrow books from.

Asking for a word
What do you call it when water becomes ice? ~
We say it 'freezes'.
What's the word for the thing you put a letter in? ~
Oh, you mean an 'envelope'.

Asking about pronunciation and spelling
How do you pronounce this word?
How do you say that?
How do you spell 'sincerely'?
How is it spelt?

30.4 Explanations

Asking for an explanation
Why won't they serve me?
Could you explain why they won't give me a drink?
Could someone **please tell me** what's happening?
I don't understand why we have to go.
I just **don't see** why the pub has to close now.

Giving an explanation
The reason is that it's eleven o'clock.
Well, **the thing is**, pubs can only open till eleven.
It's like this, you see. There's a law which says . . .

Saying that you understand
Oh, I see.
I understand now, thank you.

30.5 Being sure and unsure

Being sure
I'm sure/I'm certain/I know there's a bank in this street.
There**'ll** be one here./ There **must** be one here. ▷ 7.10
There's **certainly/definitely** one in the next street.

Being less sure

It's **probably** that way.
I think/I should think/I believe we have to turn right here.
I don't think/I doubt if we should go left.
I suppose/I expect that's the road to the village.

Being unsure

Maybe/Perhaps we can go straight on.
That **may/might/could** be the road to the village. ▷ 7.7, 8

Not knowing

I don't know/I'm not sure/I've no idea/I wouldn't like to say how far it is to the village.

30.6 Predictions

Brazil **will** win the World Cup. ▷ 4.1
West Germany have a good team. I think they**'re going to** win. ▷ 4.3
I bet/I expect it'll be exciting.
I guess a South American country will win. (*USA*)
The Italians **are sure to** do well/**are bound to** do well.
I'm sure the Italians are going to do well.

30.7 Opinions

Asking for an opinion

What do you think about the strike?
What's your opinion of the workers' action?
Do you agree with/Are you in favour of the
workers getting more money?

▷ 35.1 approving and disapproving

Giving an opinion

Well, personally, **I think/I believe/I('d) say/I feel**
they should go back to work.
I don't think they should be on strike.
**As far as I can see,/As far as I'm concerned,/It
seems to me/In my opinion**, the workers are badly paid.
I'm convinced the workers are right. (*emphatic*)

Agreeing with an opinion

I (quite) agree./That's right./Quite./Exactly./Of course.

Disagreeing with an opinion

I don't agree/I disagree.
I wouldn't say that./I'm not so sure./I wonder./
Do you really think so? (*more polite*)
But **don't you think** . . .?/Well, **I think** . . ./But **on
the other hand** . . ./**Yes, but** . . .

30.8 Having ideas

Just **imagine** if there was life on Mars.
What if the people there could build spaceships?
Supposing they visited the earth?
I wonder what I'd say to a person from Mars.

▷ 7.9 *would*; 13.3 the unreal present

31 Communication: Telling and asking people to do things

31.1 Orders

Open your mouth, please. **Don't** talk. ▷ 6.1
You **must** sleep now. You **mustn't** talk. ▷ 7.4
You**'re to** drink this. You**'re not to** leave any.
I want you to drink it all. ▷ 14.6
Fasten seat belts. **No** smoking. (*written*)
Ball games are **prohibited**. (*written*)
Nurses **will** wear uniform at all times. (*a strict order*)

Ordering food and drink
I'll have the chicken.
A coke **for me**, please.

Sometimes we put an order in the form of a request
(▷ 31.2) to make it more polite,
e.g. *Could you open your mouth, please?*

31.2 Requests

Making a request
Would you mind taking me to the station?
Would you like to wash up?
Would you pass the butter, please?
Will you wait a moment, please?
Could you tell me when the next train is?
Can I have some water, please?
Open the window, **would you?/will you?/could you?/can you?** (*informal*)
Passengers **are requested to** remain in their seats. (*formal*)

would you mind + *-ing* form is a polite request.
would and *could* are rather more polite than
will and *can*.

▷ 11.2 if-clauses

Asking someone to move out of the way
Excuse me. Can I get past?

Agreeing to a request
**OK./All right./Yes, of course./Sure.
Certainly.**

Refusing a request
Unfortunately I haven't time.
I have to go now, **actually**.
I'm sorry, but I'm just going out.
I'm afraid I can't just at the moment.

31.3 Permission

Asking permission
Can I use your pen?
May I borrow this book, please?
(*more formal than* Can I . . .?)
Do you mind if I open the window?
Is it all right if we sit here?

Giving permission
Yes, **of course.** Go ahead.
Of course **you can/you may**.
Yes, **all right**.
Certainly. (*more formal*)

Refusing permission
No, **I'm afraid** that's not possible.
I'm sorry, I'm reading it myself at
the moment.

▷ 7.3 *can, may, be allowed to*

31.4 Suggestions

Asking for a suggestion
What **shall/can** we do?
Have you got any ideas/suggestions?

Agreeing with a suggestion
Good idea./OK./Fine./Yes, let's do that./Yes, why not?

Making a suggestion
Shall we go for a swim?
What about/How about playing cards/ a game of cards?
Why don't we/**Why not** lie in the sun?
Let's go for a walk (, **shall we**?) ▷ 6.2
We **could** go to the park. ▷ 7.8

Disagreeing with a suggestion
Well, **I was just going to** make some coffee.
I don't feel like cards/don't want to play cards, **actually**.
I'm sorry, it's too hot for me. Let's go to the club **instead**.
That would be nice, but I have to meet someone.

31.5 Advice

Asking for advice
What **shall** I do?
What **should** I do/**ought** I **to** do about a job? ▷ 7.6
What **would** you do **in my position?**/ **if you were me?** ▷ 7.9
Could you advise me what to do?
I'd like to ask your advice about a job.

Giving advice
I think you **ought to/should/had better** talk to your parents.
If I were you,/If you ask me, I wouldn't leave school yet.
Well, **I'd advise you to** stay at school.
If you want/ask/take my advice, you won't decide in a hurry.
The best thing for you to do is talk to your head teacher.

31.6 Telling someone how to do something

Turn left and then **take** the first turning on the right.
Don't touch it until it's dry.
First you beat the eggs, **and then** you have to add some sugar.

When you've done that, you . . .
Make sure it's clean.
You **must** pull hard.
This is how you do it./You do it like this.

31.7 Warnings

Look out!/Watch out! (*warning of immediate danger*)
If you take all those glasses, you**'ll** drop them. ▷ 11.1
They're heavy, **I'm warning you./I warn you./ let me warn you.**

Mind those glasses.
Be careful, or there'll be an accident.

31.8 Reminders

Don't forget your money./**Don't forget to** take your money.
Remember to post the letter.
Make sure you lock the door.

31.9 Threats

Don't move **or I'll** shoot!
If you do anything stupid **you'll** be sorry.

Any trouble from you **and I'll** call the police.

31.10 Insisting

I really must have the money today.
I'm sorry to insist, but I need it today.
I'm afraid I **simply can't** wait any longer.

It's absolutely essential you pay me today.
I insist on having it now. (*formal*)

31.11 Persuading

Why don't you join the club? ~ I don't want to.
Why not? All your friends go there.
Go on./Come on. You could try it. You might enjoy it. ~ Well, I don't know. I'll think about it.

Look, it would be better than doing nothing, wouldn't it? You **really must** get out sometimes. ~ Oh, all right then. I'll go next week.

32 Communication: Decisions and intentions

32.1 Decisions

Asking someone to decide
What **are you going to** do?
Have you decided/Have you made up your mind where you'd like to go this evening?

Making a decision
Yes, **I'll** buy it.
I think I'll go home now.

Changing a decision
I've changed my mind. I want this one instead.

32.2 Intentions

I'm going to visit the USA next year. ▷ 4.3
I've decided to go there/**I've decided on** the USA.
I intend to see as much as I can.

I may go/**I might** go/**I'm thinking of** going to Los Angeles. (*less sure*) ▷ 7.7

32.3 Willingness

Asking if someone is willing
Are you willing to/prepared to work on Sundays?
Would you be willing to/prepared to organize the competition?
Do you mind/Would you mind sleeping on the sofa?

Saying you are willing
I'm perfectly **willing** to help.
I'd be prepared to wait a day or two.
I don't mind/I wouldn't mind walking.

Saying you are unwilling
I'm not prepared to go to so much trouble.
I wouldn't be willing to do anything dangerous.

32.4 Refusing

I won't put up with rudeness.
I'm not going to pay £1 to go in.

I refuse to wait any longer.
I'm afraid **it's quite out of the question**. (*formal*)

No way! (*informal*)

32.5 Promises

You**'ll**/ You **will**/You **shall** get your money back.
I'll/I **will**/I **shall** give it you back by the weekend.

I promise I'll do it/**I promise to** do it tomorrow.
I won't be long, **I promise.**

33 Communication: Offers and invitations

33.1 Offers

Offering to help

Let me help you.
Can I carry that suitcase?
I'll take this bag, (**shall I?**)
Shall I do it for you?
Would you like me to get you a taxi?

Offering e.g. food or drink

Would you like/Will you have/Won't you have something to eat?
(Do) have some tea. (*informal*)

Accepting an offer

Yes, please. **Thank you** very much. That's very kind of you.

Refusing an offer

(*of help*) **No, thank you**. It's all right. I can manage.
(*of food or drink*) **No, thank you./Not just now, thank you**.

33.2 Invitations

Giving an invitation

Would you like to have dinner with us?
Will you have/**Won't you** have dinner with us?
(Do) come and see us tomorrow.(*informal*)
What about coming/**How about** coming to our house?(*informal*)
Do you feel like coming/**Do you want to** come to a party?(*informal*)

Accepting an invitation

That's very nice of you. **Thank you./Yes, fine**. I'll look forward to it.
Yes, **that'd be nice/lovely**. I'd be delighted to come.

Refusing an invitation

Well, **that's very kind of you, but** I won't be here tomorrow.
I'd love to, but I'm afraid I have some work to do.
Well, **thank you very much, but** I'm afraid I can't.
I'm afraid I won't be here, **but thank you all the same**.

33.3 Thanks

Thanking someone

Thanks./Thanks a lot./Thanks very much.(*informal*)
Thank you./Thank you very much.
That's very good/kind/nice of you. **Thank you very much indeed**. I'm very grateful to you.(*emphatic*)

Answering someone who thanks you

That's all right/OK.
It's a pleasure./Not at all./Don't mention it.
You're welcome.(*mostly USA*)

There is often no answer after *thank you* etc.
in British English.

34 Communication: Feelings

34.1 Exclamations

how + *adjective*

Someone broke into the house while we were away. ~
Oh, **how** awful!
How funny that programme was!

what + *noun phrase*

What a lovely view you've got from your house!
What nonsense!
Oh, **what** beautiful flowers!

Negative question forms

Isn't it lovely!
Wasn't that fun!

Other types of exclamation

Help!
Hey, you!
Oh, well done!

34.2 Being pleased and annoyed

Being pleased

I've won £1000. ~ That's **good/great**.
That's **wonderful/marvellous/terrific**. (*more emphatic*)

Being annoyed

The train is half an hour late. ~
Oh, no!/Oh, dear. What a nuisance!
Oh, hell!/Damn! (*swear words*)

34.3 Likes and dislikes

Asking about likes

Do you like that colour?
How do you like this picture?
What did you think of the film?

Expressing likes

This place is **nice/great/lovely**, isn't it?
I like/I love/I enjoy/I'm fond of the seaside.
I like/I love/I enjoy/I'm fond of going to parties.
It's my **favourite** drink.

Expressing dislikes

This programme's **not very good/not very interesting.**
It's **terrible/awful.**(*more emphatic*)
I don't like/I dislike/I hate pop music.
I don't like/I dislike/I hate doing the cleaning.
I can't bear/I can't stand that man. (*more emphatic*)
I can't bear to sit and do nothing.
I'm fed up with this programme/with watching
this rubbish.

▷ 16.2 the infinitive and the -ing form

34.4 Looking forward to something

With pleasure

I'm really **looking forward to** my holiday./**to** going away.
I can't wait to get on the plane.

Without pleasure

I'm not looking forward to the exam at all.
I'm dreading next Thursday.

34.5 Wishing and hoping

Wishing

I wish the weather was nicer./it would stop raining.
If only something exciting would happen.
Why can't/won't these flies go away?
I'd like to/I'd love to/I want to have a holiday right now.
I'm dying to sit down. **I'm dying for** a drink. (*more emphatic*)

Hoping

I hope the parcel comes soon.
Let's hope it hasn't got lost.

▷ 13.3 the unreal present

34.6 Preferences

Asking about preferences
Would you prefer/Do you prefer tea or coffee?
Would you rather have milk or cream?
Which would you like?

Expressing preference
I'd prefer to go out rather than sit here.
I usually **prefer** walking **to** doing nothing./**like** walking **better than** doing nothing.
I'd rather do something **than** just sit. **I'd rather not** stay here.
I'd rather you came with me. ▷ 13.3

Having no preference
I don't mind/I don't care what we do. It's all the same to me.
It doesn't matter to me where we go.

34.7 Showing surprise and interest

Surprise
I'm going to give up my job. ~ You're not, are you? ▷ 8.5
Are you **really**? ▷ 9.1
Really? Well, **that *is* a surprise.**
Good heavens./Good Lord.
You aren't going to sell the house, are you? ▷ 8.5
Aren't you going to work here any more? ▷ 8.3

Interest
I'm going to buy a farm. ~ Oh, are you? ▷ 9.1
Oh, **really?** **That *is* interesting.**
So you're going to buy a farm, are you? ▷ 8.5

34.8 Regret

Unfortunately/I'm afraid the car won't start.
What a pity!/shame!
It's a pity/shame it happened today.
I'm sorry to say/**I regret** to say we're going to miss the show.
I'm sorry not to have seen/**I regret** not having seen the show.
(regret *is more formal*)

34.9 Worry

Asking someone what the matter is
What's the matter?/What's wrong?/What's up?
(Is) anything wrong/the matter?

Being worried
I'm worried about the money.

Telling someone not to worry
Don't worry./There's nothing to worry about.
It's all right./It's OK./It doesn't matter.

Expressing relief
I've found the passport. ~ Oh, **thank goodness** for that. That's a relief.
Thank goodness we caught the train.

35 Communication: Right and wrong

35.1 Approving and disapproving

Approving

I'm glad/I'm pleased the government are increasing the tax on petrol.
The government are **right**/It's **right** to do it.
They're **doing the right thing. It's a good idea.**
I approve of them making petrol more expensive.
I'm in favour of it. **I'm all for it.** (*informal*)

Disapproving

People **oughtn't to** drive/**shouldn't** drive big cars. ▷ 7.6
It's **wrong/not right** to use so much petrol.
I don't approve of/**I disapprove** of people using up so much energy.
I'm against people driving big cars.

▷ 30.7 opinions

35.2 Blaming someone

The accident was the lorry driver**'s fault**.
I blame the lorry driver. The lorry driver was **to blame**.
He **ought to have/should have** stopped. ▷ 7.6, 15

35.3 Complaining

I'm afraid I have a complaint to make about the food.
I'm sorry to have to say this, but the service isn't very good.
Look, **I really must protest** about the condition of my room.
Can't something be done to stop the noise?

35.4 Apologies

Making an apology

I'm sorry I've damaged your car.
I'm very/extremely/awfully/terribly sorry.
I beg your pardon.
I apologize/I do apologize. ▷ 28.2
Please accept my apologies. (*formal*)
Excuse me./Pardon me. (*starting or interrupting a conversation; after sneezing, coughing etc.*)

Accepting an apology

That's all right/OK, as long as you pay for the damage.
It doesn't matter.
Don't worry. Forget it. (*informal*)

36 Numbers, money etc.

36.1 Cardinal numbers

0	nought/zero/oh				

1	one	11	**eleven**	21	twenty-one
2	two	12	**twelve**	22	twenty-two
3	three	13	**thir**teen	30	**thir**ty
4	four	14	fourteen	40	**for**ty
5	five	15	**fif**teen	50	**fif**ty
6	six	16	sixteen	60	sixty
7	seven	17	seventeen	70	seventy
8	eight	18	eighteen	80	eighty
9	nine	19	nineteen	90	ninety
10	ten	20	**twen**ty	100	a/one hundred

101	a/one hundred and one
138	a/one hundred and thirty-eight
572	five hundred and seventy-two
1,000	a/one thousand
36,429	thirty-six thousand four hundred and twenty-nine
1,000,000	a/one million

In British English *and* comes between the hundreds and the rest of the number e.g. *five hundred and seventy-two*. But Americans say *five hundred seventy-two* without *and*.

In informal English we can say *a hundred* or *a thousand* etc. instead of *one hundred* or *one thousand*, but only at the beginning of a number.

hundred, thousand. million etc. do not have *-s* except in indefinite numbers, e.g. *There were thousands of people in the stadium.*

one thousand is written 1,000 or 1000.

In British English *a billion* usually means one thousand million, but it can mean one million million.

We usually speak the number 0 as *nought* (mainly GB) or *zero* (mainly USA). ▷ 36.6

In telephone numbers we say *oh*. ▷ 36.9

For *a/an* and *one* ▷ 19.2

36.2 **exactly, about, over** etc.

I've got **exactly** £12.69 on me.
(= £12.69, no more and no less)

I've read **about** fifty pages of the book.
(= not exactly fifty, perhaps between forty and sixty)

We've had this washing-machine **over** ten years/**more than** ten years now.
(= perhaps eleven or twelve years)

The job will take **at least** five days.
(= five days or more)

He earns **under** £100/**less than** £100 a week.
(= perhaps £90 or £95)

There are **almost/nearly** 4 million people without a job in this country.
(= only a few less than 4 million, perhaps 3,900,000)

36.3 Ordinal numbers

1st	**first**	11th	eleventh
2nd	**second**	12th	**twelf**th
3rd	**third**	13th	thirteenth
		20th	twent**ieth**
4th	fourth	40th	fort**ieth**
5th	**fif**th	50th	fift**ieth**
8th	eigh**th**	86th	eighty-sixth
9th	**nin**th	90th	ninet**ieth**
10th	**tenth**	100th	hundredth/one hundredth

101st	(one) hundred and **first**
133rd	(one) hundred and thirty-**third**
157th	(one) hundred and fifty-seventh
1,000th	(one) thousandth

The British runner David Barton came **tenth** in the race.

They've already got five children, and she's expecting a **sixth**.

The washing-machine has broken down for the **third** time this year.

Today's programme is the (**one**) **hundred and seventy-eighth** in the series.

Elizabeth II ('Elizabeth the second').

▷ 36.5 fractions; 36.11 dates

36.4 **once, twice** etc.

I clean my teeth **once** a day/**twice** a day/**three times** a day/**four times** a day.

We use *once, twice* etc. to express frequency.
▷ 24.7
We use *times* with numbers above *two*.

36.5 Fractions

½	a/one **half**	half an hour ▷ 20.23
⅓	a/one **third**	a third of a mile
¾	three **quarters**	three quarters of a pound
⅝	five **eighths**	five eighths of an inch
1½	one and a half	one and a half days/ a day and a half

3⅔	three and two thirds	three and two third metres
5¼	five and a quarter	five and a quarter hours
33/76	thirty-three over seventy-six *or* thirty-three seventy sixths	

36.6 Decimals

0·5 point five/nought point five
zero point five (*USA*) (= ½)
2·33 two point three three (= 2⅓)

5·75 five point seven five (= 5¾)
6·08 six point oh eight

36.7 Percentages

50% fifty **per cent** [pə'sent]   2½% two and a half **per cent**   6·25% six point two five **per cent**

36.8 Sums

16 + 7 = 23   Sixteen **and** seven **is** twenty-three.
Sixteen **plus** seven **equals** twenty-three.
18 − 5 = 13   Eighteen **take away** five **is** thirteen.
Eighteen **minus** five **equals** thirteen.
4 × 9 = 36   Four nines **are** thirty-six.
Four **times** nine **is** thirty-six.
Four **multiplied by** nine **equals** thirty-six.
27 ÷ 3 = 9   Twenty-seven **divided by** three **is/equals** nine.

36.9 Telephone numbers

Telephone 0270 53399   oh two seven oh, five three three nine nine
oh two seven oh, five double three double nine

36.10 Money

1p	a **penny**/one **p** [piː]
10p	ten **pence**/ ten **p**
£1	a **pound**/one **pound**
£3−75 or £3·75	three **pound(s)** seventy-five **pence** three **pounds(s)** seventy-five three seventy-five

1¢	a/one **cent**
$1	a/one **dollar**
$3·75	three (**dollars**) seventy-five (**cents**)

36.11 Dates

23 June/23rd June	the twenty-third of June twenty-third June (*USA*)
June 23rd/June 23	June the twenty-third June twenty-third (*USA*)
1983	nineteen eighty-three

In Britain 1.4.83 = 1st April 1983.
In America 1.4.83 = 4th January 1983.

36.12 The time of day

1 7.00 seven o'clock
         seven (*informal*)

2 8.00 a.m. eight a.m. [eɪ'em]/eight o'clock in the
              morning
   10.00 p.m. ten p.m. [piː'em]/ten o'clock in the
              evening

3 7.30 half past seven/seven thirty
         half seven (*informal*)
   7.15 (a) quarter past seven/seven fifteen
   7.45 (a) quarter to eight/seven forty-five
   9.20 twenty (minutes) past nine/nine twenty
   9.55 five (minutes) to ten/nine fifty-five
   10.23 twenty-three minutes past ten/ten
         twenty-three
   10.46 fourteen minutes to eleven/ten forty-six

4 16.08 sixteen oh eight
   21.00 twenty-one (hundred) hours

1 We only use *o'clock* on the hour. We can leave it out in informal speech, e.g. *I'll see you at seven.*

2 We use *a.m.* (= before noon) and *p.m.* (= after noon) or *in the morning/in the afternoon/in the evening/at night* to make clear which part of the day we mean.

3 We normally use *half past seven, five to ten* etc. in informal English. We use *seven thirty, nine fifty-five* etc. to talk about a timetable.

   We can leave out *minutes* only after 5, 10, 20 and 25, e.g. *twenty past nine* but *twenty-one minutes past nine.*

   after and *of* are also used in American English instead of *past* and *to,* e.g. *twenty after nine, a quarter of eight.*

4 The 24-hour clock is used in timetables. For times on the hour we sometimes say *hundred hours.*

36.13 Measurements

I need a piece of wood about an eighth of an **inch** (⅛″)/three **millimetres** (3 mm) thick.
Kay is five **feet** six **inches** (5 ft 6 ins/5′6″)/a hundred and sixty-eight **centimetres** (168 cm) tall.
A **metre** (1 m) is longer than a **yard** (1 yd).
It's five **miles**/eight **kilometres** (8 km) to Bath.
I need four **ounces** (4 oz)/a hundred **grams** (100 gm) of flour.
Four **pounds** (4 lbs)/two **kilos** (2 kg) of potatoes.
I weigh ten **stone** three (10 st 3 lbs)/a hundred forty-three **pounds** (*USA*)/sixty-five **kilos**.
Ben drank a **pint**/half a **litre** of beer with the meal.
We bought five **gallons**/twenty **litres** of petrol.
The temperature is fifty **degrees Fahrenheit** (50°F)/ten **degrees Celsius/Centigrade** (10°C).

1 inch = 25·4 mm
1 inch = 2·54 cm
12 inches = 1 foot = 30·48 cm
3 feet = 1 yard = 91·44 cm
1760 yards = 1 mile = 1·61 km
1 ounce = 28·35 gm
16 ounces = 1 pound = 0·454 kg
14 lbs = 1 stone = 6·356 kg
1 pint = 0·57 litres = 1·20 pints (*USA*)
8 pints = 1 gallon = 4·54 litres = 1·20 gallons (*USA*)

37 Word-building

37.1 Nouns for jobs and other activities

-er/-or

teach**er**, build**er**, wait**er**, manag**er**, driv**er**
doct**or**, edit**or**, act**or**

-ist

art**ist**, chem**ist**, journal**ist**, tour**ist**

-ant/-ent

shop assist**ant**, civil serv**ant**, account**ant**
travel ag**ent**, stud**ent**, presid**ent**

-man/-woman/-person

police**man**, post**man**, milk**man**, sales**man**,
chair**man**
police**woman**, post**woman**
sales**person** (= salesman/saleswoman)
chair**person**

-ess

act**ress**, wait**ress**, princ**ess**

There are no rules to say which words have *-er* or
-or or *-ist* etc. You have to look in a dictionary.

Words in *-man* refer to men; words in *-woman* or
-ess refer to women; other words refer to both men
and women, e.g. *teacher, doctor, student.* But we
can say, e.g. *a woman teacher, women doctors, a
male nurse, a female student.*

37.2 Using two nouns together

a **shoe shop**	= a shop that sells shoes
a **bus-driver**	= a person who drives a bus
a **London theatre**	= a theatre in London
a **bedroom**	= a room with a bed
a **stone wall**	= a wall made of stone
an **egg sandwich**	= a sandwich with egg in it
the **river bank**	= the bank of the river

We often use a noun like an adjective by putting it
in front of another noun.

Sometimes the two nouns are written as one
compound word or with a hyphen. ▷ 39.7

The first noun is nearly always singular, e.g.
a shoe shop (a shop that sells shoes).

Some more examples: *police-car, bicycle factory,
youth club, pocket-money, school bus, bank
robber, film star, Christmas present, January
sales, evening meal, housework, paper bag, gold
watch, orange juice, garden gate, table leg,
kitchen door, girl-friend.*

For e.g. *the bank of the river* ▷ 18.7

37.3 Compound nouns with adjective and -ing form

I grow tomatoes in the **greenhouse**.
We sat in the **waiting room**.

greenhouse and *waiting room* are compound
nouns. The stress is on the first part of the
compound ('greenhouse, 'waiting room).

Some other examples: *high school, grandfather,
shorthand, hot dog, drinking water, riding lesson,
playing-field, washing-machine, shopping bag.*

For e.g. *the waiting 'car* ▷ 17.1

37.4 Nouns formed from verbs

1 *give* → **giving**, *make* → **making** *etc.*
The **building** of the new university will begin next month.

2 *Same word for verb and noun* (**attack, change** *etc.*)
The **promise** of more money for schools has pleased teachers.

3 *communicate* → **communication,** *suggest* → **suggestion,** *produce* → **production** *etc.*
The **discussion** of our economic problems was very interesting.

4 *move* → **movement,** *develop* → **development** *etc.*
The **employment** of 3,000 people will be a great help to the area.

Most nouns formed from verbs have *of* before the object (e.g. *the building of the new university*), but some nouns have other prepositions after them, e.g. *an attack on the government, a change in/of policy.*

37.5 Compound verbal nouns

One of his hobbies is **stamp-collecting.**
Letter-writing is a job I don't enjoy.
I like **sunbathing.**
Is **water-skiing** difficult?

The noun in the compound is always singular, e.g. *stamp-collecting* (= collecting stamps).
We use a hyphen in most of these compounds.

▷ 15.1 the -ing form; 37.6 compound adjectives

37.6 Compound adjectives with **-ing** and **-ed**

Noun/adverb + -ing form
Britain is an **oil-producing** country.
Reducing taxes is a **vote-winning** policy.
Are the British **hard-working** enough?

Adverb/adjective + -ed form
Mrs Johnson always looks **well dressed.**
She's the **fair-haired** woman, isn't she?
You've got a very **badly paid** job.

The noun in the compound is always singular, e.g. *a vote-winning policy* (= a policy that wins votes).
We normally use a hyphen in a compound adjective, especially when it comes before a noun.

▷ 17.1 the -ing form and the -ed form used as adjectives

37.7 Compound adjectives with numbers

Number + noun
They're a **two-car** family.
It's a **fifteen-minute** drive to Glasgow.

Number + noun + adjective
Mr Gould is a **forty-year-old** businessman.
There was a **three-foot-deep** hole in the road.

The noun in the compound is always singular, e.g. *a two-car family* (= a family with two cars).
We normally use a hyphen (-) in compound adjectives.
We can only use a compound adjective with a number before a noun. Compare *Mr Gould is forty years old.*
For *fifteen minutes' drive* ▷ 18.6

37.8 Prefixes

1 The story is **untrue**.
  It was a very **informal** meeting.
  I **disagree** with you.
  Let's find a **non-smoker**.

2 Most workers here are **underpaid**.
  You can **re-use** these envelopes.
  I must have **miscounted** the money.
  Those were **pre-war** days.
  These shoes are **substandard**.
  The government is **pro-Catholic**.
  Try the **multi-storey** car park.
  We all sat in a **semi-circle**.

We use a prefix to change or add to the meaning of a word. Here are a few examples.

1 We can sometimes use *un-, in-, im-, ir-, il-, dis-* or *non-* to make an opposite. You have to look in a dictionary to find the correct prefix.

2 *under* = not enough   *sub* = below
  re = again   *pro* = on the side of
  mis = wrongly   *multi* = many
  pre = before   *semi* = half

38 The pronunciation and spelling of endings

38.1 The pronunciation of -s/-es

1 shops [ps]   2 sees [iːz]   3 prices [sɪz]
  writes [ts]   eyes [aɪz]   loses [zɪz]
  Mick's [ks]   jobs [bz]   watches [tʃɪz]
  cliffs [fs]   beds [dz]   Mr Blish's [ʃɪz]

1 -s is [s] after voiceless sounds (but see note 3).

2 -s is [z] after voiced sounds (but see note 3).

3 -s/-es is [ɪz] after the sounds [s], [z], [ʃ], [ʒ], [tʃ] and [dʒ].

▷ 2.4 the simple present; 18.1, 2 plurals of nouns; 18.4 the possessive form

38.2 Putting in e before -s

1 dish → dishes   2 price → prices
  box → boxes   lose → loses
  watch → watches   realize → realizes

1 After the sounds [s], [z], [ʃ], [ʒ], [tʃ] and [dʒ] the ending is -es.

2 If the word ends in e, the ending is -s.

38.3 Leaving out e

1 writ**e** → writing   3 make → makes
  lik**e** → liked   nice → nicely
  nic**e** → nicer
  fin**e** → finest   4 true → truly
                            whole → wholly
2 agr**ee** → agreeing/   5 possibl**e** → possibly
         agreed   probabl**e** → probably

1 We leave out e before an ending with a vowel, e.g. -ing, -ed, -er, -est.

2 If the e is part of a vowel sound (e.g. agree), we do not leave it out before -ing.

3 We do not leave out e before an ending with a consonant, e.g. -s, -ly.

4 But we leave out e from true and whole before -ly.

5 When an adjective ending in -le becomes an adverb, e changes to y.

38.4 The pronunciation of -ed

1 stopped [pt] 2 showed [əʊd] 3 waited [tɪd]
looked [kt]   played [eɪd]   ended [dɪd]
passed [st]   cleaned [nd]
laughed [ft]   used [zd]

1 -ed is [t] after voiceless sounds (but see note 3).
2 -ed is [d] after voiced sounds (but see note 3).
3 -ed is [ɪd] after [t] and [d].

38.5 The doubling of consonants

1 plan   planning
stop   stopped
big   bigger
fat   fattest
2 play   playing
show   showed
clean   cleaner
short   shortest
3 be'gin beginning
4 'visit visiting
5 travel travelling

1 In short words with one written vowel (a, e, i, o, u) + one written consonant (n, p, g, t etc.), we double the consonant (nn, pp, gg, tt) before an ending with a vowel, e.g. -ing, -ed, -er, or -est.
2 We do not double the consonant if it is y or w (e.g. play, show).
We do not double it if we write the vowel with two letters (e.g. clean).
We do not double it if the word ends in two written consonants (e.g. short) or in x.
3 In longer words we double the consonant if the last part of the word is stressed (e.g. be'gin).
4 We do not double the consonant if the last part of the word is unstressed (e.g. 'visit).
5 But we double l in British English (e.g. GB travelled, USA traveled).

38.6 Consonant + y

1 lady → ladies
fly → flies
carry → carried
funny → funnier
silly → silliest
happy→ happily.
2 the secretary's desk
the secretaries' desks
3 play → played
4 fly → flying
5 lie → lying

1 In words ending in a consonant (d, l, r, n, p etc.) + y, the y changes to ie before -s and to i before -ed, -er, -est and -ly.
2 In the possessive form we use an apostrophe + s with a singular noun and an apostrophe with a plural noun. ▷ 18.4
3 y does not change after a vowel.
4 y does not change before -ing.
5 ie changes to y before -ing.

39 Punctuation

39.1 The sentence

1 **W**e'll go for a walk now.
But bring your coat.

2 **D**o you want to go to **H**yde **P**ark?
Shall we look at the shops first?
Are they open on **S**aturdays?

3 **L**ook what **I**'ve got!
What a fantastic dress!

At the end of a sentence we put

1 a full stop (.) after a statement or imperative

2 a question mark (?) after a question

3 an exclamation mark (!) after an exclamation

We write a capital letter (a big letter)

1 at the beginning of a sentence (e.g. *We . . .* or *But . . .*)

2 at the beginning of each word in a name (e.g. *Hyde Park*) and days and months (e.g. *Saturday*), but not in other nouns (e.g. *shops*)

3 for the word *I*

39.2 The semi-colon

The farmer and his sons start work at six o'clock every morning; they have to get up early because there is always so much to do.

We use a semi-colon (;) between two main clauses when the second main clause is not linked grammatically to the first.

39.3 The comma

We put a comma

1 He looked for the key, but he couldn't find it.
He looked for the key but couldn't find it.

1 usually between two main clauses before *but*, *and* or *or*, but only if the second clause has a subject (e.g. *he*)

2a When I saw the photo, I laughed.

2a after a sub clause

b The questions were easy, Alan said.

b after a reported clause

c Mr Sims, who lives opposite, is ninety-six.

c around a non-defining relative clause ▷ 22.12

d I laughed when I saw the photo.

d not usually before a sub clause

e Alan said (that) the questions were easy.

e not before a reported clause

f We all saw what happened.

f not before a question word or *that* ▷ 27.3

g The man who lives opposite is ninety-six.

g not with a defining relative clause ▷ 22.12

3 The police came to the house to ask him some questions.

3 not before an infinitive

4 On Thursday afternoon, they all went out together.
They all went out together on Thursday afternoon.

4 sometimes after an adverb phrase but not usually before it

5 Mr Reid, the owner of the company, lives near Southport.

5 usually around a phrase in apposition ▷ 18.16

6a The food, however, was good.

6a usually around a linking word

b On the other hand, we need a quick decision.
We could go to Tunisia, for example.
Actually, I'm a Liberal.
It won't be easy, of course.

b usually after or before a linking word or sentence adverb

c Have you got the number, please? ~ Yes, I have.

c usually before *please* and after *yes* or *no*

7 before or after the name of a person we are speaking or writing to ▷ 29.6

8 in a list of more than two things

7 Have you seen this, Pat?
  Dear Mr Bright,
    Thank you for your letter . . .
8 Inside the room there was a table, two chairs, a
  lamp and a television set.

39.4 Quotation marks

David said, **'**It's time to go now.**'**
'It's time to go now,**'** David said./said David.

We use quotation marks ('. . .') before and after direct speech. We usually put a comma before or after the direct speech.

39.5 The apostrophe

1 These are my girl-friend**'s** records.
2 Chris isn**'t** thirty. He**'s** only twenty-five.

We use the apostrophe
1 in the possessive form of nouns ▷ 18.4
2 in short forms ▷ 39.6

39.6 Short forms

1 We**'ve** had nice weather.
2 This salad**'s** nice.
3 What**'ll** you do?
4 There**'d** be plenty.
5 Here**'s** Sarah now.
6 They are**n't** ready.

Form

When we use the short form, we leave out part of the word we are writing. We put an apostrophe (') instead of the missing part and we write the two words together as one.

Short forms

'm = am	**'ve** = have	**won't** = will not
're = are	**'d** = had/would	**n't** = not
's = is/has	**'ll** = will/shall	

Sometimes there are alternative short forms, e.g.
it is not → it isn't/it's not
they will not → they won't/they'll not

Use

We can use a short form only if the word is unstressed. We do not use short forms in short answers with *yes* (*Yes, we have*) or when a word is stressed (*We really 'have had nice weather*).

We can use short forms
1 after a pronoun
2 sometimes after a noun
3 sometimes after a question word
4 after *there* and *that*
5 for *is* after *here*
6 for *not* after an auxiliary or modal verb

We use short forms when we write down an informal conversation or in informal writing, e.g. in a letter or a postcard to a friend.

39.7 The hyphen

1a That's a **police dog**.
 b I've rung the **police-station**.
 c Here's a **policeman**.
2 There's a **three-mile-long** tunnel.
3 Don't **over-fill** the tank.
  We can **re-use** these bottles.

1 The rules about hyphens aren't very definite. We write some compound nouns as two words (a), some with a hyphen (b) and some as one word (c).
2 We normally use a hyphen in compound adjectives. ▷ 37.6, 7
3 We often use a hyphen after a prefix. ▷ 37.8

40 List of common irregular verbs

Base form*	Past tense	Past participle	Base form*	Past tense	Past participle	Base form*	Past tense	Past participle
awake	awoke	awaked/awoke	forgive	forgave	forgiven	set	set	set
be (am, is, are)	was, were	been	freeze	froze	frozen	shake	shook	shaken
beat	beat	beaten	get	got	got/gotten (USA)	shine [aɪ]	shone [ɒ]	shone [ɒ]
become	became	become	give	gave	given	shoot	shot	shot
begin	began	begun	go (goes)	went	gone ▷ 5.4	show	showed	shown/showed
bend	bent	bent	grow	grew	grown	shut	shut	shut
bet	bet/betted	bet	hang	hung	hung	sing	sang	sung
bite	bit	bitten/bit	have (has)	had	had	sink	sank	sunk
blow	blew	blown	hear [ɪə]	heard [ɜ:]	heard [ɜ:]	sit	sat	sat
break	broke	broken	hide	hid	hidden	sleep	slept	slept
bring	brought	brought	hit	hit	hit	smell	smelt	smelt
build	built	built	hold	held	held		smelled†	smelled
burn	burnt	burnt	hurt	hurt	hurt	speak	spoke	spoken
	burned†	burned	keep	kept	kept	spell	spelt	spelt
burst	burst	burst	know	knew	known		spelled†	spelled
buy	bought	bought	lay	laid	laid	spend	spent	spent
catch	caught	caught	lead	led	led	spoil	spoilt	spoilt
choose	chose	chosen	learn	learnt	learnt		spoiled†	spoiled
come	came	come		learned†	learned	spread	spread	spread
cost	cost	cost	leave	left	left	spring	sprang	sprung
cut	cut	cut	lend	lent	lent	stand	stood	stood
deal [i:]	dealt [e]	dealt [e]	let	let	let	steal	stole	stolen
dig	dug	dug	lie	lay	lain	stick	stuck	stuck
do (does [ʌ])	did	done	light	lighted/lit	lighted/lit	sting	stung	stung
draw	drew	drawn	lose	lost	lost	stink	stank/stunk	stunk
dream [i:]	dreamed [i:]	dreamed [i:]	make	made	made	strike	struck	struck
	dreamt [e]	dreamt [e]	mean [i:]	meant [e]	meant [e]	sweep	swept	swept
drink	drank	drunk	meet	met	met	swim	swam	swum
drive	drove	driven	pay	paid	paid	swing	swung	swung
eat [i:]	ate [et]	eaten [i:]	put	put	put	take	took	taken
	[eɪt] (USA)		read [i:]	read [e]	read [e]	teach	taught	taught
fall	fell	fallen	ride	rode	ridden	tear	tore	torn
feed	fed	fed	ring	rang	rung	tell	told	told
feel	felt	felt	rise	rose	risen	think	thought	thought
fight	fought	fought	run	ran	run	throw	threw	thrown
find	found	found	say [eɪ]	said [e]	said [e]	understand	understood	understood
flee	fled	fled	(says [e])			wake	woke	woken
fly	flew	flown	see	saw	seen		waked	waked
forbid	forbade [æ]	forbidden	seek	sought	sought	wear	wore	worn
	forbad		sell	sold	sold	win	won	won
forget	forgot	forgotten	send	sent	sent	write	wrote	written

* and irregular simple present forms

† Some verbs have two past forms, e.g. *learnt/learned*. The form with *-t* is more usual in British English and the form with *-ed* in American English. *burned, learned, smelled, spelled* and *spoiled* can be pronounced with [t] or [d].

Index

Key

Key

An oblique stroke is used to indicate alternatives, and brackets indicate words which may be left out. For example, *He's washing the car/his car* means that *He's washing the car* and *He's washing his car* are both correct. *She's riding (a horse)* means that *She's riding* and *She's riding a horse* are both correct.

1

1 You must pay us £250,000.
2 The boy is safe.
3 He can go when we've got the money./When we've got the money, he can go.
4 He will be all right.
5 The money must be in £10 notes.
6 Bring the money to the car park.
7 Don't show this to the police.
8 If you talk to the police, you'll be sorry./You'll be sorry if you talk to the police.

2

Are we all here now?
Where*'s* Tom?
He *isn't* here.
Oh, he *isn't* very well.
He*'s* in bed.
And Sarah *isn't* here.
Oh, yes, I *am*.
Oh, there you *are*, over in the corner.
Angela*'s* late.
Or *is* she ill, too?
No, she *isn't* ill.
Peter and Sue *aren't* here.
Yes, they *are*.
They*'re* in the kitchen.
Am I late?
Yes, you *are*.
Oh, I*'m* sorry.
It*'s* all right.
Here we *are*.
Now we*'re* ready to start.

3

1 The garden is lovely.
2 The views to the north and east are beautiful.
3 The house has six bedrooms.
4 The rooms are large.
5 The downstairs rooms have carpets.
6 The sitting room has a lovely old fireplace.
7 The kitchen has plenty of cupboards.
8 The garage is big enough for three cars.

4

1 He's got a watch.
2 She's got a coat.
3 They've got a table.
4 He's got a (toy) car.
5 She's got some books.
6 They've got a television.

5

1 He's combing his hair.
2 She's reading the newspaper.
3 He's climbing a ladder.
4 They're carrying something.
5 She's washing her hands.
6 He's brushing his teeth.
7 They're playing cards.
8 She's eating an apple.

6

He *lives* in Belgravia in London's West End. He's very rich, and he *owns* the company Office Blocks International. Every morning the young Lord *has* breakfast in bed and *reads* the newspapers. He *gets* up at ten o'clock and usually *goes* for a walk in Hyde Park. He *has* lunch at his club. He sometimes *meets* the Directors of OBI, and they *talk* about the company's plans. In the afternoon Lord Stonebury and his friends sometimes *play* golf. Then they *have* a few drinks. Or sometimes he and a girl-friend *go* for a drive in his sports car. After dinner Lord Stonebury *goes* to a night club or a casino with one of his girl-friends. They *get* home at about two o'clock.

7

She doesn't play computer games.
She likes music.
She often visits people.
She doesn't like sport.
She doesn't go swimming.
She doesn't like animals.
She goes for walks.
She doesn't often go out in the evenings.

8

Brenda, where *do you get* your ideas for all your stories?
Does it take a long time to write a book?
Do you write every day?
And *where do you work*?
Do you type your stories?
Does your husband *like/read* your stories?
Where does your husband *work*,/*What does* your husband *do*, Brenda?
Why do so many people *read* your books, Brenda?

9

Milchester *is* a lovely old town on the River Swenley. The famous castle *brings* lots of tourists to the town. The old streets near the castle *have* many interesting little shops, and there *is* a very good museum. The town also *has* a theatre and a cinema. 27,000 people *live* in Milchester, and quite a few of them *work* at the new computer factory. Other industries *are* paper-making and chocolate.

10

1 Brian builds houses. He's washing the car/his car at the moment.
2 Alice teaches music. She's swimming at the moment.
3 Maureen and Jackie make dresses. They're playing tennis at the moment.
4 Alan drives a lorry/drives lorries. He's eating a banana at the moment.
5 Stephen plays golf. He's watching television/TV at the moment.
6 Jessica reads the news. She's reading a book at the moment.
7 Tony and Roger sell cars. They're jogging at the moment.
8 Miranda takes photos/photographs. She's riding (a horse) at the moment.

11

Greetings from Wales! Ben and I *are doing* something different this year. We're at the North Wales Activity Centre. People *come* here every summer to learn more about their hobbies and interests. I*'m doing* photography and tennis this week and Ben *is learning* about computers. We *get* up at half past eight every morning and *do* lessons from ten to half past twelve. We *have* lunch at one, and then there are more lessons. So it's hard work. But I *like* it here. We*'re having* a super time. It's half past seven in the evening now, and we*'re sitting* out on the grass in front of the Centre. The weather is good. See you soon. Love, Kate.

12

I hear there *was* a barbecue at the college last Saturday. *Were* you there?
Yes, I *was*. Where *were* you?
Oh, I *wasn't* here on Saturday. I *was* in London.
That's a pity. It *was* a very good barbecue. The food *was* great.
What *was* the weather like here?
Oh, we *were* very lucky with the weather. It *was* nice and warm.
Were there a lot of people there?
Yes, lots. Lynn *wasn't* there, though. She *wasn't* very well.
What about Mark and Jane?
Oh, they *were* still on holiday last Saturday, so they *weren't* at the barbecue. But all the others *were* there.

13

What happened? Where *were* you? And where *was* the monster?
I *was* here on the beach. I saw the monster in the water. Then it swam out to sea. It *was* a great shock. It *wasn't* very nice, I can tell you.
What *was* the monster like?
Big. It *was* a very large animal. It *had* a large body, but it *had* a small head. Its eyes *were* blue and round. It *had* teeth, but they *weren't* very big. It *didn't have* any ears.
Did you take a photo of it?
I *didn't have/hadn't got* my camera with me, I'm afraid. And it *was* very quick. It all happened in a moment.

14

Picasso painted pictures.
Billie-Jean King played tennis.
Neil Armstrong went to the moon.
Marco Polo travelled to China.
Martin Luther King worked for Black people's rights.
Christian Dior made clothes.
Columbus sailed to America.
Edison invented the electric light.

15

1 Why did you disappear?
2 Did you leave the country?
3 How did you travel?
4 Did your friends hide you?
5 What did you do in all that time?
6 Did you read the stories about you in the newspapers?
7 Why did you come home?
8 Did your husband find you?

16

He didn't repair the broken window.
He didn't book a holiday/his holiday.
He wrote to the bank/his bank.
He didn't phone the sports club.
He paid the electricity bill/his electricity bill.
He tidied the garage.
He didn't paint the gate.
He didn't clean the windows.

17

1 Bob has repaired the fence.
2 Philip and Mark have decorated the club room.
3 Angela has bought some new curtains.
4 David has polished the cups.
5 Martin has serviced the minibus.
6 Paul and Sarah have laid a new carpet in the bar.
7 Mike and Helen have cleaned out the kitchen/have cleaned the kitchen out.
8 Tom has put up some more shelves/has put some more shelves up.

18

He's made a pop record. He made one in 1965.
He's walked to the South Pole. He walked to it/walked there in 1952.
He's climbed Everest. He climbed it in 1959.
He's run a marathon. He ran one in 1955.
He's won the Monte Carlo rally. He won it in 1962.
He's swum the English Channel. He swam it in 1950.
He's flown an aeroplane. He flew one in 1974.
He's met the Queen. He met her in 1980.

19

Hello, Bob.
Hello. I *haven't seen* you for a long time.
I *saw* you in town two or three weeks ago, but you *didn't see* me. I *was* on a bus.
Well, how are things? Are you still living over the shop?
No, I*'ve moved* now. I *found* a super flat just before I went on holiday. I*'ve been* there three months.
Have you *passed* your driving test yet?
Yes, I have. I *passed* in October. I *haven't bought* a car yet, though. But what about you, Bob? *Has* anything exciting *happened* to you lately?
No, not really. My mother *hasn't been* very well for a few months now.
Oh, dear. I'm sorry to hear that.
And my brother's out of work.
Did he *leave* school in the summer, then?
Yes. He *didn't do* very well in his exams and he *hasn't found* a job yet.
Are you still working at Scott's?
Yes. They*'ve* just *given* me a pay rise.
Well, that's one piece of good news.

20

1 After the bank clerk had looked at my cheque, she counted out the money.
   After she had counted out the money, she gave it to me.
2 After the tourists had got out of the coach, they took photos.
   After they had taken photos, they got back in the coach.
3 After the reporter had gone to the scene of the accident, she interviewed the people there.
   After she had interviewed the people there, she wrote a report on the accident.
4 After the mechanic had taken the wheel off the car, he put a new tyre on.
   After he had put a new tyre on, he put the wheel back on.

21

David Williams of Milchester *has had* such a terrible time this year that he ought to be in *The Guinness Book of Records*. The trouble *started* one morning last January when David *found* that his car *had gone* from outside his house. He *hasn't seen* it since.

In February David's joy at winning £200,000 on the football pools *didn't last* long — he *had forgotten* to post the letter. In March he *bought* a new car, but he *hadn't had* it more than a week when someone *crashed* into the back of it. These disasters *have continued* right up to the present time. Two days ago David *sat* on a seat that someone *had finished* painting only minutes before. He *had on* a new suit that he *had bought* only the previous week.

August *has been* the worst month so far this year. David *spent* three days of his holiday at airports because of strikes. When he *arrived* home, he *discovered* that someone *had broken* into his house. His video-recorder and television *had disappeared*.

David doesn't know what he *has done* to deserve all this bad luck. He just hopes his luck will change soon.

22

1 I was walking across a bridge when I met a tiger.
2 The roof fell in when we were watching television.
3 I was climbing the stairs when I saw a ghost.
4 I was looking into the mirror/a mirror when it broke.
5 The wind blew me over the cliff/a cliff when I was walking along a path.
6 We were lying on the beach when an elephant came out of the sea.
7 I was digging the garden when I found a dead body.

23

Melanie has been washing up for half an hour.
Sadie and Adam have been tidying up for an hour and a half/for one and a half hours.
Lisa has been looking for a bucket for ten minutes.
Alison and Jason have been working in the garden for three hours.
Don has been cleaning the stairs for half an hour.
Emma has been repairing the toaster for an hour.
Trevor has been mending the door bell for twenty minutes.
Daniel and Rebecca have been brushing carpets for two hours.

24

Manchester United manager Brian Price *has gone* to Turin for talks with the Juventus club about Wayne Simmonds. Simmonds *joined* Juventus a year ago, and he *has scored* 18 goals for them. Last autumn he *was scoring*/he *scored* almost every week, but he *has not been playing*/he *has not played* well recently. English fans would welcome his return, and yesterday everyone at United *was talking* about Simmonds. In fact, the club *has been waiting* for some time now for a chance to talk to the player.

At the moment Simmonds is England's greatest footballer, although he *has been* in the game for only two years. He *was playing* amateur football for Mendip Athletic when Bristol City *invited* him to join them. When Arsenal *bought* Simmonds for £750,000, he *had spent* only six months with the Bristol club, but he *had already played* twice for England Under-21s. Simmonds quickly *became* a big star, and he *has now played* five games for the full England team, although he *has played* only one game since he *left* Arsenal for Juventus.

25

1 The accident *happened* at 10.47 pm on October 23rd at the corner of Compton St and Brooks Rd, Milchester.
2 Mr and Mrs Johnson *were* on their way home. Mr Johnson *was driving*.
3 The couple *had been visiting* friends. They *had been drinking*, but Mr Johnson *had had*/Mr Johnson *had* only one small whisky. He *had finished*/He *finished* this drink at 10.15 pm.
4 It *was not raining* at the time, but it *had been raining*/it *had rained* shortly before, and the roads *were* wet.
5 At 10.47 pm Mr Richard Hunter *was cycling* north along Brooks Rd. He *had* his lights on.
6 Mr Johnson *did not stop* at the 'Stop' sign. As he *was turning*/he *turned* into Brooks Rd, he *hit* Mr Hunter and *knocked* him off his bike.
7 Mr Hunter *was* not badly hurt, but his bike *was* damaged. Mr Johnson *stopped* and *reported* the accident.
8 Mr Johnson *has been driving* for twenty years now. He *has not had* an accident before.

26

How long *have* you *been living/have* you *lived* in this house, Mrs Vincent?
I*'ve been living*/I*'ve lived* here for seventy-five years now.
And how long is it since your husband *died*?
Oh, he*'s been* dead for forty years. Yes, he *died* a long time ago. I*'ve been* alone since then. It*'s been* a long time.

And where *did* you *live/did* you *use to live* before you *came* here?
Well, before we *got* married I *lived*/I *used to live* with my parents in William Street. They*'ve knocked* the house down now. I*'ve* only *lived* in two houses all my life.
I expect you*'ve seen* a lot of changes in all that time.
Oh, yes. Milchester *was/used to be* very quiet in my young days. And it *wasn't*/it *didn't use to be* as big as it is today. I *used to go* for picnics on Long Hill with my brothers and sisters. Now they*'ve built* houses there.
Did you *enjoy/Did* you *use to enjoy* life in those days?
Oh, yes. We *had/*We *used to have* a wonderful time. People *were/*People *used to be* a lot friendlier in those days. We *did/*We *used to do* things together. Nowadays people just sit at home and watch television, don't they?

27

Robots will do all the hard work.
There won't be/There will not be so many jobs.
People will have more free time.
The weather will be colder.
There won't be/There will not be very much oil.
There will be fish farms under the sea.
People will fly to other planets.
People won't be/will not be very happy.

28

1 Neil is going to look for an outdoor job.
2 Michelle and Kevin are going to do electronics.
3 Sharon is going to become a taxi driver.
4 Simon is going to take a course in banking.
5 Nick and Julie are going to stay at school another year.
6 Adrian is going to work for the family business.
7 Tina is going to train to be a social worker.
8 Ian and Jeremy are going to hitch-hike round the world.

29

1 We're going to put in new escalators. They'll move people around more quickly.
2 We're going to employ more assistants. They'll help our customers.
3 We're going to put in cameras. They'll stop people stealing things.
4 We're going to play music. It'll produce the right atmosphere.
5 We're going to have televisions. They'll inform customers about things in the store.
6 We're going to have a children's room. Parents will be able to leave their children there.

30

Someone told me you and the family *are going to* go and live in Alaska. Is it true?
Yes, it is. I*'m going to* work for a building company.
That*'ll* be interesting.
I hope so. It*'ll* be something different. It*'ll* certainly be/It*'s* certainly *going to* be a lot colder than London.
When *are* you *going to* leave?
On the tenth of next month. We*'ll* be/We *shall* be there in three weeks.
Oh, so it *won't* be long now. Jerry and I *will* be sad to see you go.
Oh, we*'ll* be/we *shall* be back some time. We *won't* be/We *shan't* be/We *aren't going to* be there for ever. And you can always come to Alaska and see us.
Well, that isn't a bad idea. We*'re going to* visit my sister in Vancouver next summer.
Oh, that's great. We*'ll* see/We *shall* see you next summer then.

31

On Tuesday he leaves Madrid at 7.40 and arrives in Athens at 13.55. He is visiting the Ramplus offices.

On Wednesday he leaves Athens at 8.15 and arrives in Milan at 12.35. He is opening a/the new Ramplus factory.
On Thursday he leaves Milan at 10.10 and arrives in Strasbourg at 11.15. He is meeting the President of the Common Market.
On Friday he leaves Strasbourg at 10.45 and arrives in the Hague at 11.40. He is having discussions with the Dutch Minister of Technology.
On Saturday he leaves the Hague at 9.30 and arrives in Stockholm at 12.25. He is going to the Computer Show.

32

Where *are* you and Ben *going* for your holidays/*are* you and Ben *going to go* for your holidays, Kate?
Morocco. We're *spending*/We're *going to spend* ten days in Agadir.
Oh, that'll *be*/that *will be* nice. When *are* you *going*?/When *do* you *go*?
On Friday night. Our plane *leaves* at seven, and we *arrive*/we'll *be arriving* at four in the morning.
You'll *need*/You're *going to need* a holiday after that.
Oh, I don't mind night flights. Anyway, we'll *be enjoying* the sunshine this time next week.
Are you *staying*/*Will* you *be staying* in a hotel?
Yes, a big hotel not far from the beach.
Our holiday *isn't* until next month. Jerry and I *are going to tour* Scotland in the car, we've decided. We're *going to do*/We'll *be doing* some walking, too. The weather *won't be* like/*isn't going to be* like Agadir, of course.
How long *are* you *going* for?
Two weeks. We haven't been to Scotland before, so it'll *be*/it *will be* something different.
Are you *going to take*/*Are* you *taking*/*Will* you *be taking*/*Will* you *take* your caravan?
No, we don't want to take the caravan. We'll *have to*/We *shall have to* find hotels to stay in as we go.
Well, we'll *be*/we *shall be* back from Morocco before you go.
Have a nice time, Kate.

33

1 World leaders are to meet next month.
2 A dock strike is starting tomorrow.
3 The Prime Minister is to visit Greece in August.
4 The Queen is leaving for Australia tomorrow.
5 Some Chinese tourists are arriving in Britain next Saturday.
6 A shoe factory is to close.
7 The European Games are to take place next year.
8 Three new players are joining Liverpool.

34

1 You *will be* on holiday soon. In two weeks from now you *will be lying* on a beach.
2 You *will have* a good life, and you *will live* a long time.
3 Your personality is changing all the time. In ten years time you *will have changed* completely.
4 At some time in your life you *will have* a bad accident, but you *will not die*.
5 You *will marry* when you are twenty-three.
6 In twenty years from now you *will be living* on the other side of the world. By that time you *will have left* your husband.
7 You *will be* rich. When you are thirty-five, you *will already have made*/will already be making a lot of money.
8 At this time of your life you *will be working* very hard. Your life *will be* very exciting.

35

Mr and Mrs Stokes *were* sitting in the garden of their Bristol home when I arrived to interview them and their fourteen-year-old son Carl. But Carl *was* working upstairs. 'He *doesn't* often leave his room,' his mother explained.

At the moment Carl *is* working on a programme for a new computer game. Computers *have* become his whole life. In the last year Carl *has* earned over £25,000 from writing

programmes. A lot of other people *are* trying to do the same nowadays, but not many of them *have* done as well as Carl.

'When *did* he buy the computer?' I wondered. 'We bought it for him eighteen months ago for his birthday,' said Mr Stokes. 'We *didn't* know what we *were* doing. Our son *has* changed. Eighteen months ago he *hadn't* seen a computer. Now he *doesn't* talk about anything else. And we *don't* understand a thing about computers.' 'And *do* you think it's good for him?' was my next question. 'No, we *don't*. We worry about him,' said Mrs Stokes. 'He *doesn't* have any other interests now. And he *hasn't* done any work for his school exams. It's often quite a job to make him go to school at all.'

Carl's parents *don't* understand computers, but Carl certainly *does*. 'I love computers,' he said. 'I soon got tired of playing games, though. I like writing programmes much better. I've got three computers now. I bought two more. I *didn't* earn much at first, but now I *do*. My parents make me put most of it in the bank.'

36

There has been heavy rain in the North today. There will be more rain tomorrow.
There have been strong winds in Wales today. It will be less windy tomorrow.
It has been cool in the Midlands today. There will be some sunshine tomorrow and it will be warmer.
It has been dry in the South today. It will be wet in places tomorrow but there will be sunny periods.

37

Hello, Mike. *Did* you *have* a nice time in France?
Hello, Paul. Yes, we did, thanks. We *didn't have* very good weather, but we still *had* a good time.
Have you already *had* your lunch?
Yes, I was early today. And I only *had* a sandwich.
You can *have* one of my sausages if you like.
No, thanks. I'm only *having* light lunches this week. I'm trying to lose weight.
You haven't got anything to worry about.
You're going camping in Wales next week, aren't you?
That's right.
I hope you *have* nice weather.
So do I. Did you know Mark and Jane are in Benidorm at the moment? We *had* a postcard from them on Friday. They say they're *having* a marvellous time.
I took some photos in France. You can *have* a look at them some time if you like.
OK.
Come round to our house tonight, and we can *have* a talk.

38

Let's go this way past the sports centre.
Oh, I *didn't* know there was a sports centre here. It looks new. When *did* it open?
A few months ago. Since your last visit, anyway. It's very good. You can *do* all kinds of sport.
Do you use the centre a lot?
Quite a lot, yes. There are courses in different sports. I'm *doing* a tennis course this term. I *did* judo last term.
Judo? That's for boys, isn't it?
Don't be silly. Lots of girls *do* it as well as boys. I've *done* it for ages.
How much *does* it cost to go in?
You have to pay every year to be a member. But it *doesn't* cost very much, luckily. You can go in as my guest if you want to.
Oh, good.
What about a game of badminton some time?
I *don't* like badminton much. *Do* they have table tennis?
Yes, of course. We can have a game this evening.

39

Friday
We couldn't sleep/weren't able to sleep because it was so hot. We could hear the noise of insects all night.
Saturday
We were able to get water from a stream. We could see some smoke to the south.
Sunday
We couldn't travel/weren't able to travel because it was so wet. We were able to keep dry.
Monday
We were able to walk several miles along the bank of a river. We couldn't cross/weren't able to cross the river because it was so wide.
Tuesday
We were able to kill and eat a monkey. We could hear a plane somewhere above us.
Wednesday
We couldn't walk/weren't able to walk because we were so ill. We were able to sleep for several hours.

40

1 Psycho-Clinic is wonderful. My problem was that I *couldn't fly/wasn't able to* fly. I was afraid of aeroplanes. As soon as my course was over, I *was able to* take a flight to the Canary Islands! I had a super holiday. Now I *can* fly where I like. Next summer I'*ll be able to* go/I *can* go to the West Indies. (I *won't be able to* do/I *can't* do that every year because I haven't enough money.) I *can't* thank Psycho-Clinic enough.

2 Now at last I *can* stand up in front of a group of people! From now on my life will be different. I'*ll be able to* do my job much better in future. I often have to give talks to sales people at work. I just *can't* avoid it. In the old days I *couldn't* sleep/I *wasn't able to* sleep for a week before a talk. I *could* hardly do my work. But now I *can* give a talk without feeling too nervous. Last week I *was able to* get a good night's sleep before talking to a group of twenty people the next day. It's marvellous!

3 Yesterday someone asked me for my telephone number, and for the first time in my life I *was able to* give the number without looking in my book. Before I went to Psycho-Clinic I always forgot numbers and names. I *couldn't* remember/I *wasn't able to* remember them at all. Now, thanks to Psycho-Clinic, I *can* remember much more. If I see someone in the street tomorrow, I won't need to hide–I'*ll be able to* stop/I *can* stop and say hello to them.

4 I didn't like crowds of people. I *couldn't* go/I *wasn't able to* go to the theatre or the cinema. I love horse racing, and I *couldn't* go/I *wasn't able to* go to the races. But the people at Psycho-Clinic *were able to* stop me feeling afraid. Now I *can* do all those things. Yesterday I *was able to* stand in a crowd at a baseball game. I'*ll be able to* lead/I *can* lead a normal life now. There's an interesting show at the local theatre next week, and I'*ll be able to* see it.

41

In Britain you'*re allowed to* drive a car when you're seventeen. You *have to* get a special two-year driving licence before you can start. When you're learning, someone with a full licence always *has to* be in the car with you because you *aren't allowed to* take the car on the road alone. You *don't have to* go to a driving school–a friend can teach you. The person with you *isn't allowed to* take money for the lesson unless he's got a teacher's licence.

Before you'*re allowed to* have a full licence, you *have to* take a driving test. You can take a test in your own car, but it *has to* be fit for the road. In the test you *have to* drive round for about half an hour and then answer a few questions. If you don't pass the test, you'*re allowed to* take it again a few weeks later if you want to. In 1970 a woman passed her fortieth test after 212 driving lessons! When you've passed your test, you *don't have to* take it again, and you'*re allowed*

to go on driving as long as you like, provided you are fit. Britain's oldest driver was a Norfolk man who drove in 1974 at the age of 100.

Before 1904 everyone *was allowed to* drive, even children. Then from 1904 motorists *had to* have a licence. But they *didn't have to* take a test until 1935. In the early days of motoring, before 1878, cars *weren't allowed to* go faster than four miles an hour, and someone *had to* walk in front of the car with a red flag.

42

1 We aren't allowed to light fires.
2 We aren't allowed to play ball games.
3 We have to leave before ten o'clock in the morning.
4 We don't have to worry about food.
5 We weren't allowed to light fires.
6 We weren't allowed to play ball games.
7 We had to leave before ten o'clock in the morning.
8 We didn't have to worry about food.
9 We won't be allowed to light fires.
10 We won't be allowed to play ball games.
11 We'll have to leave before ten o'clock in the morning.
12 We won't have to worry about food.

43

1 You must turn right.
2 You mustn't smoke.
3 You must stop.
4 You must go straight on.
5 You mustn't turn round.
6 You mustn't take photos.
7 You must turn left.
8 You mustn't go faster than fifty miles/kilometres an hour.
9 You mustn't overtake.

44

Well, I'm going to give you some medicine. You *must* take it four times a day before meals. And go on taking it even if you feel better. You *mustn't* stop taking it until you've finished the bottle. You *must* drink all of it. Now, you *must* stay in bed today. It's the best place for you at the moment. You can get up tomorrow if you like. You *needn't* stay in bed all the time when you start to feel better. But you *mustn't* go outside this week. It's too cold. And you really *mustn't* do any work at all. You need absolute rest. You *must* just relax for a few days. You can eat a little if you like, but you *needn't* if you don't want to. But don't forget to keep drinking. You *must* drink as much water as you can. You'll probably be all right again next week, so you *needn't* call me again unless you feel worse. But I'm sure the worst is over.

45

1 The pills ought to be in a safe place. The baby might eat them.
2 There oughtn't to be a hole in the rug. Someone might fall over.
3 The towel oughtn't to be over the cooker. It might catch fire.
4 The drawer ought to be shut. It might fall out.
5 There oughtn't to be (any) broken glass on the floor. Someone might step on it.
6 There ought to be a plug on the kettle. Someone might get an electric shock.

46

1 She would walk. She wouldn't swim.
2 She would keep it. She wouldn't take it to the police.
3 She would listen. She wouldn't move to another seat.
4 She would choose the well paid job. She wouldn't choose the interesting job.
5 She would say no. She wouldn't say yes.
6 She would drive on. She wouldn't stop.

47

1 Four across. Past tense of 'be'.
  It could be 'was' or 'were'.
  It can't be 'were'. It must be 'was'.
2 Six across. It carries things by road.
  It could be 'van' or 'lorry'.
  It can't be 'van'. It must be 'lorry'.
3 One down. Person learning something.
  It could be 'student' or 'pupil'.
  It can't be 'student'. It must be 'pupil'.
4 Two down. Opposite of 'old'.
  It could be 'new' or 'young'.
  It can't be 'young'. It must be 'new'.
5 Three down. You pay to ride through the streets in it.
  It could be 'bus' or 'taxi'.
  It can't be 'taxi'. It must be 'bus'.
6 Five down. Planes travel in it.
  It could be 'sky' or 'air'.
  It can't be 'sky'. It must be 'air'.

48

What's the matter? Why have you stopped?
There's something wrong. It isn't going properly.
Let's have a look.
We *could be*/*might* be out of petrol, I suppose.
We *can't* be out of petrol. We only got some half an hour ago.
Well, if there is something wrong, *can* you/*could* you put it right, do you think?
Give me a chance. I don't know what the trouble is yet.
Look at this steam. The engine *must* be too hot.
Don't take the cap off the radiator. You *mustn't*/ You *shouldn't*/You *oughtn't to* do that. You *might*/You *could*/ You'll get boiling water all over you.
If it's too hot, we'll have to wait until it cools down.
And how long *will* that take?
We *ought to*/We *should* wait about half an hour before we go on.
I suppose there *might be*/*could* be something else wrong with it.
We passed a garage about a mile back. I suppose they'll come/they *might* come and have a look at it if we ask them.
The car *should be*/*ought to* be all right. Our local garage has just serviced it. I paid £30 for a full service.
You *needn't* worry. I'm sure it's just got too hot. Let's wait a bit.
We'll be/We *shall* be late now, I expect.
There's some coffee in the back of the car. *Shall* we have some while we're waiting? There are some sandwiches, too.
I'm starving. I *must* have/I'll have something to eat.
Would you like a sandwich, Lisa?
No, thanks. I *mustn't*/ I *can't* eat bread. I'm on a diet.
We *must* phone/*ought to* phone/*should* phone Matthew if we're going to be late.
We *won't* be very late, I don't think.
You *ought to* buy/*should* buy a new car, Adam.
Well, it *would* be nice if I had the money. But I'm afraid we'll have to/we *shall* have to put up with this old thing for a little longer.

49

Hello, Sadie. Aren't you doing any work? You *ought to be revising* for the exams.
I *would be reading*/I *might be reading* my notes if I had them, but I've lost them.
Good Lord! How awful! Do you want to look at mine?
No, thanks. It's OK. Don't worry, Emma. Exams aren't important.
Not important! You *must be joking*! I'*d be looking* everywhere if my notes were lost.
Well, I'll probably find them before tomorrow.
Have you seen Lisa? She's got a book of mine.
She was in here not long ago. Perhaps she's outside. She *might be sitting* in the garden.

I'll go and have a look. Then I *must be going*/I *ought to be going*. I have to get to the library before it closes.
What are you doing tonight, Emma?
Revising, of course. Aren't you?
I *might be playing* tennis with Rebecca. If the weather stays fine, that is. It'll be too late for revision tonight.

50

1 She shouldn't have touched it.
2 The murderer must have been one of the five people in the house.
3 He shouldn't have told anyone about it.
4 The murderer might have taken it.
5 She couldn't have walked to the study.
6 She might have killed him.
7 He couldn't have taken it.
8 He must have been in London.

51

I'll be sad to leave here. But I *have to* leave at the end of my course.
I still don't know if I can stay longer or not. I *haven't been able to* make any plans during the last two years.
My problem was getting in here. I *had to* get a visa before I left home. I wanted to come here a year earlier, but I *wasn't allowed to*.
Money is a problem, too. I *haven't been allowed to* work since I came here.
Ever since I came here, I've *had to* report to the police every week.

52

Where's Harry, then? I *can't* see him.
Yes, we said seventeen hours. He *should* be/He *ought to* be here by now.
He might not *be able to* find the place. He *might*/He *may*/He *could* have crossed the border in the wrong place.
Impossible! Harry *couldn't have*/*can't* have made a mistake. You know Harry.
Well, I hope he comes soon.
It's the most important job he's ever done for us. He absolutely *must* get the information.
I've often wondered about Harry. You don't think he *might be*/*could* be working for the other side?
No, I don't. Harry is one of us.
Well, I just think this job has been easy for him so far. Too easy. Perhaps the Omaguans know all about Harry.
Someone *might have*/*may have*/*could* have told them about the job. They *might*/They *may*/They *could* have a man in our organization.
I don't believe it. They're not clever enough. But Harry is clever.
But you *can't* be sure. What if it was true?
It *would* be the end for us, of course. But it isn't true.
Harry takes a lot of risks. He does dangerous things. The boss lets him do what he wants. Harry shouldn't *be allowed to* put other people in danger. I told the boss, but he didn't listen. He *should* have/He *ought to* have listened to me.
Shut up, will you? Harry is a good man. Only Harry *could* do/*can* do this job.
It's seventeen oh two. We're late.
You're right. We *must* go/*ought to* go/*should* go at once.
We *mustn't*/We *can't*/We *oughtn't to*/We *shouldn't* stay here any longer.
We've waited and he hasn't come. We *needn't* have driven here at all.
We had to be here. Harry *might* have/*could* have come. He *would* have done if he'd been able to.
Just a minute. There's someone behind that tree. Two men, I think. They *must* be watching us. Why else *would* they/*could* they be here?
Right. Have your gun ready. We may *have to* shoot our way out.
OK, I'm ready.
Let's go then. Come on!

The car *won't* start! Oh, my God! Where's my gun? Give me my gun!
Put your hands up. Get out of the car! Lie down!
It was you, Oskar! You told the Omaguans about Harry, didn't you? You *must* be mad. Oh, my God!

53

Betty Root would be a good Prime Minister. People should vote for her.
They *shouldn't vote* for her, you mean. She'd be no good. George Wright's party is the best.
It *isn't the best*, you know. Betty Root's party is the best. Her people have got the right ideas.
They haven't got the right ideas at all. Remember what happened when Root was Prime Minister? She made mistakes.
She didn't make mistakes. She did well. She took the right decisions.
I'm afraid *she didn't take the right decisions.*
Things were OK in Betty Root's time.
They weren't OK (in Betty Root's time), you know. They were terrible.
Betty understands our problems.
She doesn't understand our problems. But George Wright does. He's been a good Prime Minister.
He hasn't been a good Prime Minister. He's been awful.
George is popular. People like him.
They don't like him, I tell you. They're tired of him.
George Wright will win.
He won't win. Betty Root will. I'm sure of that.

54

Think back to half past six this evening, Lennie. *Where were you?*
Where was I? I don't know. I was walking somewhere. Yes, I went for a walk.
Do you often go for walks?
No, not often, but I did tonight.
Did you go to Dixie's wine bar?
No, I didn't go to Dixie's wine bar.
Have you got a car?
Yes, of course I've got a car. It's a Mavis Corona.
What colour is it?
Blue. Look, *why are you asking me all these questions?*
I'm asking you all these questions because there's been a robbery. Now, the number of the car. *Do you know it?*
No, I don't know it. I can't remember numbers.
Well, I can help you. I think it's BDX 25S. *Am I right?*
Well, you *may* be right. I'm not sure.
Did you steal the car?
No, I didn't. I never steal.
I'm very interested in your car, Lennie. *Where is it?*
I don't know. I've no idea where it is. Someone's borrowed it.
Well, *who's borrowed it?*
A man I know.
Can you remember his name?
No, I can't. I can never remember names.
You forget names too, do you? Well, let's talk about your walk. *Where did you go?*
I went to the park.
Did anyone see you?
No, no one saw me. Well, I don't *think* anyone saw me.
Did you see anyone you know?
No, I didn't see anyone I know.
Are you going to tell me the truth, Lennie?
What do you mean — am I going to tell you the truth? I'm telling it *now*.
You went out for a walk! No one saw you!
Well, *someone* saw me. I've just remembered.
Who was it?
It was a policeman. He's called Phil Grady. He spoke to me in the park. I know him well — he's arrested me twice.
What time was this?
Oh, about half past six, I think.
Just a minute. I'm going to make a phone call.

55

1 Why aren't Puffco/Puffco's tankers serviced until they break down?
2 Why had the driver been on the road for nine hours?
3 Why wasn't the warning sign put up again?
4 Why are lorries allowed to go as fast as they like?
5 Why haven't the police taken any notice of the villagers?
6 Why hasn't a by-pass been built?
7 Why do Puffco/Puffco's drivers still use the route?
8 Why haven't we learned any lessons from past accidents?

56

Hello. You're Wendy, *aren't you?*
Yes. I remember you, too. You're Roger Cowley.
That's right. We were in the same class, *weren't we?* But it's easy to forget people, *isn't it?*
I think I remember most of the people here. Jessica Squires is over there. She reads the news on Television North-West, *doesn't she?*
Yes, she's on television quite often. She's done well, *hasn't she?*
We had a lot of fun at school, *didn't we?*
Er, yes. Don't turn round, but Malone's looking this way.
Mike Malone?
Yes, you can remember him, *can't you?*
Oh, yes.
I hated him. Oh, no! He's coming over here.
Well, it is a reunion. We ought to be friendly, *oughtn't we?*
Hello, Roger. Nice to see you again.
Nice to see you too, Mike.
This reunion was a good idea, *wasn't it?*
Yes, I'm enjoying it. Mike, do you remember Wendy?
Yes. She's my wife.
Oh!

57

Did you see Holland and Mexico on television last night?
Yes, it was a great game, *wasn't it?* Holland were marvellous.
They won't find it so easy against Poland, *will they?*
No, they won't. Poland have got a good team, *haven't they?*
Lobak looks good, *doesn't he?* The Austrians couldn't stop him, *could they?*
It'll be an interesting game, *won't it?*
England haven't been very good, *have they?*
Luck hasn't been on our side, *has it?*
But why is Bodger playing? He isn't very good, *is he?*
He didn't play very well against Peru, *did he?*
He doesn't play as well now as he used to, *does he?*
Well, we should beat Nigeria, *shouldn't we?*
I don't know. Anything could happen, *couldn't it?*
The West Germans are good, *aren't they?* They don't take any risks, *do they?*
They're playing Hungary tonight. You'll be watching, *won't you?*
Yes, of course.

58

1 The Prince and the Delta don't look good, but the Swift does.
2 The Prince and the Delta can't do 150 kilometres an hour, but the Swift can.
3 The Prince and the Swift don't use less than 10 litres of petrol per 100 kilometres, but the Delta does.
4 The Prince and the Delta are cheap to repair, but the Swift isn't.
5 The Prince and the Swift have got four doors, but the Delta hasn't.
6 The Prince hasn't got much room/a lot of room inside, but the Delta and the Swift have.
7 The Prince won a 'Road' magazine prize last year, but the Delta and the Swift didn't.
8 The Prince is good value, but the Delta and the Swift aren't.
9 The Prince doesn't look (very) good, and neither does the Delta.

10 The Prince can't do 150 kilometres an hour, and neither can the Delta.
11 The Prince doesn't use less than 10 litres of petrol per 100 kilometres, and neither does the Swift.
12 The Prince is cheap to repair, and so is the Delta.
13 The Prince has got four doors, and so has the Swift.
14 The Delta has got a lot of room inside, and so has the Swift.
15 The Delta didn't win a 'Road' magazine prize last year, and neither did the Swift.
16 The Delta isn't very good value, and neither is the Swift.

59

I hope this party's good.
I hope so, too. I don't know how we're going to get there.
Is the car still out of action?
I'm afraid so.
What's the matter with it?
I'm not sure, but I think it's something electrical.
Haven't you taken it to the garage yet?
I'm afraid not. I haven't had time.
Well, Martin will be going, won't he? We can ask him for a lift.
Yes, *I suppose so.* I don't imagine there's a bus.
I don't expect so. Not in the evening.
OK, I'll ring Martin. He might be taking Richard, of course.
Oh, *I hope not.* That man talks about horse racing the whole time. He's so boring.
Yes, *I know.*
Do we have to take a bottle to this party?
No, *I don't think so.* Tony didn't say.
We'd better take some wine. There's a bottle in the cupboard.

60

1 Polinski won the long jump and McCall the high jump.
2 Ivor Ketapov won't be running in the 100 metres, but/and no one knows why (he won't).
3 He holds the 200 metres world record but not the 100 metres (world record).
4 British runners have broken records, but British swimmers haven't/but not British swimmers.
5 A Frenchman is leading in the marathon and a Swede in the cycle race.
6 There were big crowds on Tuesday but not on Wednesday.

61

It's the English exam in two weeks. Have you done any work for it?
No, I'm afraid not/I'm afraid I haven't. I haven't had much time lately.
Neither have I./Nor have I./I haven't either. I've been very busy.
I've been to all the classes, though. And I've done the homework.
I haven't. I always have so many other things to do in the evenings.
There's an oral exam, isn't there?
Yes, I think so/I think there is. Mrs Moss mentioned it last week in one of our lessons.
I can do written work all right *but not oral work.*
Oh, nonsense. Your spoken English is very good. You can hold conversations in English, can't you?
Yes, I suppose so./I suppose I can. Perhaps I'll do all right.
Are we allowed to use dictionaries in the exam, do you know?
I don't think so/I don't think we are. Why don't you ask Mrs Moss?
Yes, I will. She'll know, won't she?
I expect so./I expect she will.
I really must pass the exam.
Will you need English in your job?
I'll need it to get a good job.
So will I./I will, too. But don't worry, Ahmed. Your English is fine. You're going to pass.

Well, I hope so./I hope I'm going to. I know *you will.*
I wish I could be so sure. I'm certainly not looking forward to it.
Neither am I./Nor am I./I'm not either. I'll be glad when it's over, in fact.
So will I./I will, too.

62

1 The post box is emptied.
2 The stamps are postmarked at the post office.
3 The letters are sorted into the different towns.
4 The mail is loaded into the train.
5 The mail bags are unloaded after their journey.
6 The bags are taken to the post office.
7 The letters are sorted into the different streets.
8 The letters are delivered.

63

The warship Mary Rose *was built* in the years 1509–10. In 1544 England *started* a war against France, and in 1545 French ships *were sent* across the Channel towards England. Some English ships *went* out from Portsmouth to meet them. One of these ships was the Mary Rose. It was carrying 91 guns and 700 men — twice as many as normal. It *sank* quickly to the bottom of the sea even before it *was attacked* by the French. About 650 men *died.* This terrible accident *was seen* by the king of England himself.

The next month an attempt *was made* to raise the Mary Rose, but it *failed.* The ship *was forgotten* for hundreds of years.

In the 1970s new plans *were made* to raise the ship. Thousands of objects *were brought* up from the ship by divers. Then, on 1st October 1982, the Mary Rose *was lifted* out of the sea. Many people *saw* the raising of the ship on television. Finally the Mary Rose *was taken* into Portsmouth dock 437 years after she had sunk.

64

1 It was won by Italy.
2 They were written by Georges Simenon.
3 He was killed by James Earl Ray.
4 It was invented by John Logie Baird.
5 They were built by the Egyptians.
6 It was directed by Attenborough.
7 They were spoken by Hamlet.
8 He was played by Sean Connery.

65

1 A man has been killed in a motorway accident.
2 The Olympic Games have begun.
3 Some children have been injured in a gas explosion.
4 A picture has been stolen from a museum.
5 Charles and Diana have arrived in India.
6 Some secret papers have been lost.
7 A famous house has been sold to an American.
8 Ray Jenks has won an important race.
9 A dead body has been found in a park.
10 Fifty 'Style' shops have been bought by the Wilson-McArthur group.

66

1 Costs have to be reduced.
2 The factory must be kept open.
3 Action must be taken.
4 The staff should be warned.
5 Things ought to be made clear to them.
6 No more new staff will be employed.
7 The situation cannot/can't be allowed to continue.
8 The next meeting will be held on May 8th.

67

The world's first electronic computer *was built* at the University of Pennsylvania in 1946, although computer-like machines *had been built/were built* in the 19th century. Computers *were sold* commercially for the first time in the 1950s, and a lot of progress *has been made* since then. Computers are now much smaller and more powerful, and they *can be bought* much more cheaply.

Computers *are used/have been used* in many fields — in business, science, medicine and education, for example. They *can be used* to forecast the weather or to control robots which make cars. The computer's memory is the place where information *is kept* and calculations *are done.*

A computer cannot think for itself — it *must be told* exactly what to do. A lot of difficult calculations *can be done* very quickly on a computer.

And computers don't make mistakes. Stories *are heard/have been heard* sometimes about computers paying people too much money or sending them bills for things they didn't buy. These mistakes *are made* by the programmers — the people who give the computer its instructions. Some years ago, a computer-controlled rocket belonging to the USA went out of control and *had to be destroyed.* The accident *was caused/ had been caused* by a small mistake in one line of the programme. This mistake cost the USA $18 million.

Criminals have found out that 'computer crimes' are often a lot easier than robbing banks. Hundreds of millions of dollars *are stolen* from American businesses every year by people changing the information in computers.

Large numbers of home computers *have been sold* recently, especially in the USA and Britain. People know more about computers than they used to, and computers are playing a bigger part in our lives. Progress *is being made* all the time. Many people believe we can look forward to the day when even our household jobs like cleaning *are done/will be done* by computer-controlled robots.

68

1 The tennis player Kathy Duprey was given £50,000 for winning a competition.
2 £40,000 has been paid to the skier Anne Stolberg to advertise ski trousers.
3 The ice hockey team Phoenix Flyers was given/were given $20,000 each to play in front of the cameras.
4 £250 is paid to (the) footballer Wayne Simmonds for every goal he scores.
5 The cyclist Luigi Delgado was offered £25,000 to advertise a soft drink.
6 The boxer Howard Duke will be paid $3 million for his next fight.
7 A holiday in the West Indies has been promised to the London Wonders basketball team if they win the league.

69

They'll need to have the garage wall re-built.
They can replace the broken glass themselves.
They'll need to have a new floor laid in the dining-room.
They'll need to have the bedroom ceiling repaired.
They'll need to have a new kitchen window put in.
They can paint the outside of the house themselves.
They can decorate all the rooms themselves.
They'll need to have the electrical wiring checked.

70

1 If you choose a Sunspot holiday, you'll have a great time.
2 You'll sleep a lot better if you sleep in a Dreamway bed.
3 People will notice you if you wear Rodeo jeans.
4 If you shop at Kwikbuy, you'll save money.
5 If you use Luxidor Paint, your house will look beautiful.
6 You'll know what's happening if you read the Daily Talk.
7 If you wash with Whizz, your clothes will be cleaner.
8 If you drive a Delta, you won't want to drive any other car.

71

1 If the pay was good, I could afford a nicer flat.
2 If my boss didn't give me so much work, I wouldn't have to stay late.
3 If his writing wasn't so awful, I could read it.
4 If he listened to me, I wouldn't have to tell him everything twice.
5 If the offices weren't such a long way from here, I wouldn't spend so much time on the bus.
6 If there were some cafés nearby, I wouldn't have to take sandwiches.

72

Miss Lester, what is the situation in Omagua?
Well, it's very bad. Thousands of people have died, and thousands more *will die* soon if they *don't get* help. The people have very little food or water. And if we *don't do* something soon, things *will get* much worse. There will simply be nothing left to eat.
Is the British government doing anything to help? If they *sent* food, that *would help* to save lives, wouldn't it? After all, Omagua was once a British colony.
Yes, indeed. And the country is very poor, of course. But our government refuses to do anything quickly. They say they need time to find out about the problem. But we haven't got any time. It *will be* too late if they *don't do* something soon.
Well, it doesn't look as if Omagua is going to get any help for the moment. So what next? What *will happen* if the country *doesn't get* enough food or enough money to buy food?
Well, if our government *isn't* willing to help, we'*ll have to* ask people to send us money. In fact, we're asking them now.
How much are you asking people to give?
We're asking them just to send what they can. Even small amounts will be welcome. We'*ll be*/We'*d be* very grateful if people *send/sent* what they can afford. After all, if everyone in the country *gave* just 10p, we'*d have* a lot of money, wouldn't we? I'm sure if people *knew* exactly what things were like in Omagua, they'*d want* to help.
And are you hopeful that people will send money?
Oh, yes. If people *hear* about the problem, as they're doing now, then they'*ll help*, I'm sure. They always have done before.
Is there still time to get food and money to the people who need it, Miss Lester?
Oh, yes. We'll put the money to good use immediately. If people *post* money to us tomorrow, the food *will be* in Omagua by the end of the week.
Well, it's certainly a good thing that you're able to help the Omaguans. If your organization *didn't exist*, things *would be* much less hopeful. Now, can you tell us the address where people should send money? . . .

73

Gary and Emma wouldn't have got wet if they had had their anoraks.
If they hadn't forgotten to bring a map, they wouldn't have lost the way.
They wouldn't have been late if they had gone the right way.
They would have been able to eat at the café if it hadn't been closed.
If they had had some food with them, they wouldn't have been hungry.
If Alison hadn't fallen and hurt her leg, they wouldn't have had to go more slowly.
They wouldn't have missed their bus home if they hadn't got to Raveley so late.
If Adam hadn't been at home, he wouldn't have been able to come and fetch them in his car.

74

I think a new road is a good idea. It'*ll keep* the traffic out of the town if they build a by-pass. The traffic in the High Street is terrible. If they'd had any sense, they'*d have built* a by-pass years ago.

But what about the shopkeepers? If there was a by-pass, then people *wouldn't stop* here. And there'll be fewer customers in the shops if there's less traffic in the town.
I don't agree. I think more people *will want* to shop here if it's quieter and pleasanter.
Tourists *won't come* into the town if there's a by-pass.
If the High Street *was* less busy, it would be a lot easier to cross the road.
There'*d be* less noise if there were fewer heavy lorries.
And the traffic doesn't do the buildings any good. Everything shakes when a heavy lorry goes past. Do you remember those old houses in West Street? They had to knock them down because of damage by lorries. If there'*d been* a new road ten years ago, they *wouldn't have had to* do that. And cyclists have been knocked off their bikes by lorries. One man was killed. That *wouldn't have happened* if the lorries hadn't had to use the High Street.
Don't forget that if you *improve* the road system, then the traffic may simply increase. Or you'll just move the problem to another town.
But look at the situation now — dozens of lorries moving very slowly through the town. It *would save* a lot of time if they travelled more quickly along a by-pass.
The by-pass would use up good farmland that we can't afford to lose.
The route goes right through Gordon Bentley's farm. It'*ll cut* his farm in two if they build it there. He only bought the farm three years ago.
Well, if that *happened*, they'd pay him for the land.
He told me yesterday he *wouldn't have bought* the farm in the first place if he'*d known*.
But a by-pass is for the whole town.
Well, if I *was* Gordon, I'*d be* angry about it.
I'm angry now about the traffic in the High Street. If they *don't give* us a by-pass, there'll be trouble, I can tell you.

75

If you've got a job to do, it always takes longer than you think.
If you're in an accident, it's the other person's fault.
If you want to buy something, they usually don't make it any more.
If you're absolutely sure about something, you're probably wrong.
If you type your own letters, they're usually short.
If you try to make a difficult situation better, you usually make it worse.

76

1 If it should be foggy at the airport, the plane might not be able to take off.
2 If my luggage should be put on the wrong plane, I might never see it again.
3 If my house should be broken into, I might lose everything.
4 If I should lose my money, I might have to come home early.
5 If I should lose my passport, I might not be able to get home.
6 If I should have an accident, I might have to go into hospital.
7 If it should rain all the time, I might have a terrible holiday.
8 If everything should go well, I might have nothing to worry about.

77

1 It says he will have lots of energy, and he may have to travel.
2 It says she will have problems at work, and she should ask her friends for help.
3 It says he will meet someone interesting, and his life may change suddenly.
4 It says they are feeling rather unhappy, but they will hear some interesting news.
5 It says her life is getting more exciting, but she must control her feelings.
6 It says he is worrying a lot, but his problems aren't very great.

7 It says her life feels empty, but she will find romance.
8 It says her boss or teacher will not be pleased with her, but it won't be her fault.
9 It says he should spend more time with his friends because he is working too hard.
10 It says everything is going well for them, but they must think before they make any decisions.

78

1 News Extra said (that) Arnold Motors had never paid any tax.
2 Newsday Magazine said (that) Arnold spent the company's money at a Las Vegas casino.
3 International News said (that) when he died, he would probably leave more than $500 million.
4 Modern World said (that) Stanley Arnold never spoke to his children.
5 The Daily Free Press said (that) he was planning to leave his money to a dogs' home.
6 World Magazine said (that) Arnold had friends in the Mafia.
7 The Saturday Reporter said (that) the police ought to ask Stanley Arnold some questions.
8 The Daily Talk said (that) no one would be sorry when he'd gone.

79

1 Mel said they'd had a wonderful time.
2 Gale said their fans were great.
3 Benny said he felt really bad about leaving.
4 Zoë said she'd enjoyed herself.
5 Paul said they'd be back.

80

1 They asked me if/whether I had/I've got a car.
2 They asked me if/whether I could drive/I can drive.
3 They asked me where I went/where I'd gone to school.
4 They asked me what exams I took/I'd taken.
5 They asked me what I knew/I know about animals.
6 They asked me if/whether I liked/I like animals.
7 They asked me why I wanted/I want the job.
8 They asked me if/whether I was/I'm willing to work on Saturdays.

81

She asked me why I shopped/I shop there, and I told her I shopped/I shop there because it was/it's cheap.
She asked me if/whether I could/I can get everything I wanted/I want at Brisco, and I told her I couldn't/I can't get good bread.
She asked me how far away my home was/is, and I told her it was/it's one mile away.
She asked me if/whether I had come/gone there by car, and I told her I had.
She asked me how much I had just spent, and I told her I'd (just) spent about £15.
She asked me if/whether I'd come/go to Brisco again, and I told her I would.

82

They asked us not to park in the centre of Milchester.
They told us to show our tickets.
They told us to wear our numbers on our shirts.
They asked us to wear running shoes.
They told us not to carry any bags or bottles during the run.
They told us to follow the correct route.
They asked us to run on the left.
They asked us not to leave litter.

83

1 Mr Crane said that lots of people used/use the buses.
2 Mrs Manston asked how they could/can get to town.

3 Mr Budge replied that most people in the village had a car/ have (got) a car.
4 The chairman told everyone to keep quiet and listen.
5 Mrs Davies asked what was going to/what's going to happen to the school bus.
6 Mr Budge answered that it would/will continue to run.
7 Mr Rice said that the village needed/needs a bus service.
8 Mr Budge wondered if/whether the villagers could/can start their own service.
9 Mr Hepplestone asked everyone to protest to the government.

84

1 The Silonians have refused to give away Bingozi.
2 The Magundians have promised to give full rights to Silonians in Bingozi.
3 The Silonians have advised the Magundians to think again.
4 The Magundians have suggested meeting for discussions.
5 The Silonians have warned the Magundians to expect trouble.
6 The Magundians have invited the Silonians (to come/to go) to Magundi to discuss the problem.
7 The Silonians have threatened to start a war (if the Magundians do not leave Bingozi).
8 The Magundians insist on looking after their people in Bingozi.

85

He wishes he could find work.
He wishes he hadn't left school when he was twelve.
He wishes he'd had a real job.
He wishes his health was good/better.
He wishes he had (some) friends.
He wishes people liked him.
He wishes the children weren't afraid of him.
He wishes he hadn't got into trouble with the police.
He wishes he'd known his parents.
He wishes he hadn't had (such) a bad start in life.

86

It's time we *found* Givens, isn't it? And we've still no idea where he is. The way things are going, it'll be Christmas before we *catch* him.
I wish Maxley Prison *had looked* after him a bit better last week.
If they*'d discovered* the escape more quickly, we'd have had a better chance of getting him.
And now we haven't got enough men. If we *had* more men, we'd probably find him.
We don't even know where his girl-friend is.
If only we *knew* where she lives now. I bet he's with her. We'll get him in the end.
I wish they *hadn't let* him escape in the first place.
When we finally *find* him, he'll probably have a gun.
Of course. So we'll just have to be careful. He won't have a chance if he *tries* to shoot his way out.

87

1 Have you got a lawn to mow? It's easier to mow it with a *Swish* machine.
2 Have you got some shoes to clean? It's best to clean them with *Gleem*.
3 Have you got a dirty job to do? It's sensible to do it in *Atkinson's* work clothes.
4 Have you got some luggage to take? It's easier to take it in an *Alton Sahara*.
5 Have you got a dog to feed? It's better to feed him *Chomp*.
6 Have you got some sums to do? It's quicker to do them with a *Numerex* calculator.

88

1 Bill makes them work very hard.
2 He forces them to take the game seriously.

3 Bill wants the players to feel proud of the club.
4 Bill teaches them to play well together.
5 He makes them watch films of other teams.
6 Bill lets them relax after a game.
7 The club expects the players to behave.
8 Bill doesn't allow them to go to night-clubs.
9 The fans want the team to do well.
10 The fans would like the club to win everything.
11 Bill invites schoolboys to visit the club.
12 The chairman has persuaded local companies to give money to the club.

89

1 The group were forced to go with the guerrillas.
2 They were made to walk fifty miles to the guerrilla camp.
3 Miss Lester wasn't allowed to send a message to anyone.
4 She was made to carry a heavy bag.
5 The group were expected to look after injured guerrillas.
6 They were allowed to move around the camp.
7 They were allowed to talk to each other.
8 Miss Lester was warned not to try to escape.

90

It's been impossible for her to feel at home here.
Will it take long for the boss to give us a definite decision?
I've arranged for the psychologist to see Kelly on Friday.
We'll have to wait for her to write her report.
There isn't any reason for us to keep her here any longer.
It's quite usual for children to be in here for months.
It would be a mistake for everything to happen in a big hurry.
It's important for the children here to know about our plans for them.

91

1 They didn't know how to get the spaceship back.
2 They couldn't think where to look.
3 They weren't sure whether to wait in the street.
4 They had no idea where to go.
5 They didn't know whether to hide.
6 They had no idea how to contact Chupron.
7 They weren't sure whether to go to the police.
8 They didn't know what to think.

92

Are you still working for Electrobrit, Nigel?
No, I'm not. I'm afraid I lost my job there. And Polly's lost her job too. We're having rather a difficult time at the moment.
Oh, dear. I'm sorry *to hear* that.
I've been out of work for six months now. I expected *to find* a new job fairly quickly, but it isn't so easy, I've discovered. Jobs are hard *to find* these days.
With Polly not working we've very little money *to spend*. After I lost my job I managed *to make* my bank manager *lend* us some money, but he won't let us *borrow* any more now. And there are lots of bills *to pay*. I really don't know what *to do*.
Do you think you might *find* a job if you moved somewhere else?
Well, perhaps. We've talked about it of course. We've even wondered whether *to go* abroad. We could always *make* a fresh start in a different country. Polly wants me *to look* for a job in America. And I've written to Australia House, although I'm still waiting for them *to answer*.
Do you like the idea of living abroad?
I don't know really. I think on the whole I'd rather *stay* here if I had a job. But the situation has made us *think* carefully about our future. We decided we ought *to find* out what opportunities there are. I've agreed *to think* about all the possibilities.
Well, I hope you find something soon.
I simply must *find* a job soon, or I don't know what we shall *do*.
Well, let me *know* what happens, won't you? Look, here's my new address and phone number. Give me a ring some time.

OK, David. I'd better *go* now. I've got a bus *to catch.*
I hope *to see* you again soon.
'Bye, David.

93

Racing driver Chuck Loder, who had a bad accident in last year's Grand Prix, is likely *to be coming* out of hospital soon. He agreed *to be interviewed* by our sports reporter, although he has refused *to be photographed*, as his face still shows the marks of the accident.

Chuck was very cheerful when he spoke to us. His health now seems *to be improving* slowly. He expects *to be sitting* at the wheel once again before very long.

Many people think that last year's race at Bruckheim ought never *to have taken* place. It was the last race on the old track, which is going *to be re-built* soon. The owners of the track expect *to have completed* the work in time for next season.

Chuck hopes *to be driving* in next year's Grand Prix. We wish him luck. Read his personal story of the Bruckheim accident in next week's Daily Talk.

94

2 (horse) riding
3 fishing
4 camping
5 skiing
6 sailing
7 climbing
8 (ice) skating

95

She left the Polytechnic without taking any exams.
Elaine decided to see the world before making her home in Britain.
She thought about her career while filling shelves in a supermarket.
On returning to Britain, Ms Archer bought a small food store.
She made her stores a success by pleasing the customers.
She has risen to be head of the company in spite of being a woman in a man's world.

96

Mike's not much good around the house. Do you get any help from Paul?
Yes, he doesn't mind *helping* usually.
Mike sometimes does *the shopping*, but that's all, really.
I have to do all *the cleaning* of course.
Paul does *the ironing* quite often — that's a great help because I hate *ironing*. And he's a very good cook. He usually does *the cooking* at weekends. We both enjoy *cooking*, in fact.
I like cooking too, but Mike's no good at it. I do *the cooking* in our house. And I do all *the washing*. Mike doesn't even know how to use the washing-machine!

97

1 They insist on going on strike.
2 He thinks it's wrong to risk starting a world war.
3 They're tired of working for low wages.
4 She doesn't agree with cutting down trees.
5 He wants the government to stop helping the Magundians.
6 They believe in talking about peace, not war.
7 She's keen on banning nuclear bombs.
8 He doesn't like being out of work.

98

He's stopped us having coffee breaks.
He's always telling us to work hard.
He doesn't agree with people working at their own speed.
He quite often wants me to work late.
I wouldn't mind him/his asking me occasionally.
He seems to expect me to spend my life at the office.

I don't like him watching me all the time.
He hates people being friendly with him.

99

1 Let her talk to the press. She likes/enjoys/loves talking to the press.
2 You'd better let them photograph her. Melinda likes/enjoys/loves being photographed.
3 Don't laugh at her. She doesn't like/She hates being laughed at.
4 Try to arrange things so that she doesn't have to wait around. Melinda doesn't like/Melinda hates waiting around/having to wait around.
5 You'll have to look after her. She likes/enjoys/loves being looked after.
6 She won't get up early. Melinda doesn't like/Melinda hates getting up early.
7 It doesn't matter if people stare at her. She likes/enjoys/loves being stared at.
8 Never ignore her. She doesn't like/She hates being ignored.

100

Milchester Council has decided *to let* 82-year-old Mrs Nellie Battle go on *living* at her home at 29 Croft Street. The Council had wanted *to knock* down all the old houses in the street because they were planning *to build* a new car park there. The future of this plan is now uncertain.

The story began five years ago when the people of Croft Street agreed *to move* to new homes. Unfortunately the Council forgot *to ask* Mrs Battle. When they finally remembered her, everyone else had already gone. But the Council failed *to persuade* Nellie to do the same. 'My grandson's just finished *decorating* the sitting-room for me,' she said at the time. 'I can't imagine *leaving* now.'

The Council offered *to pay* Mrs Battle £500 and promised *to give* her a new house, but she still refused *to move*. 'I can't help *liking* it here,' she told our reporter. 'I miss *seeing* the neighbours of course. I enjoyed *talking* to them.' Croft Street has stood almost empty for the last five years. There seemed *to be* no way anyone could move Nellie from number 29.

Now comes the Council's new decision. Mrs Battle is very pleased. 'I kept *telling* them I wouldn't move,' she said today. 'I don't mind *being* on my own any more. And I expect *to live* till I'm a hundred. I hope *to be* here a long time yet.'

We have also heard this week that the Council cannot now afford *to build* the car park. One or two of the people who used *to live* in Croft Street have suggested *repairing* the old houses so that they can move back into them. They dislike *living* in the new houses they moved into five years ago.

101

Have we done all the shopping now?
Yes, I think so. I must remember *to post* this letter.
I remember *passing* a postbox somewhere.
Just a minute, where's my purse? It isn't in my handbag. Did you forget *to bring* it?
No, I had it not long ago. And my credit card is in there. Oh, my God, what are we going to do?
Just stop *worrying* and think. You must have put it down somewhere and forgotten *to pick* it up. Try *to remember* when you had it last.
I remember *having* it in the shoe shop.
Then you stopped *to buy* a newspaper . . .
Oh, it's all right. It's here in the shopping bag. Sorry. I can't remember *putting* it there.
You could try *chaining* it to your hand next time.

102

1 He heard a/the telephone ringing. It went on for a long time.
2 He saw a plane crash into the sea.
3 He saw a bird flying in the sky.

4   He heard a woman screaming. He thought she would never stop.
5   He saw a man jump out of a car as it was moving.
6   He saw a tree burning.

103

There was an earthquake in the Kitamo region at ten o'clock yesterday morning. It lasted about a minute. Many buildings collapsed. *Frightened* people ran into the streets. Many were injured by *falling* bricks and stones. After the earthquake, buildings in many parts of the city caught fire. The heat was so great that firemen could not get near many of the *burning* buildings. Hundreds of people have died. The hospital is still standing, but there aren't enough beds for all the *injured* people. Things look very bad in Kitamo now. There are hundreds of badly *damaged* houses, and those that caught fire are now just *smoking* ruins. The streets are covered with *broken* glass, and *fallen* trees block the way. Everywhere there is the sound of *crying* children.

104

1   Hurrying along the street, he suddenly stopped outside a travel agency./He hurried along the street, suddenly stopping outside a travel agency.
2   Standing outside, he looked twice at his watch./He stood outside, looking twice at his watch.
3   Having waited five minutes, he continued along Oxford Street to Hyde Park.
4   He ate a sandwich sitting on a seat.
5   Having looked again at the paper, he put it in a litter bin.
6   Leaving the park,/Having left the park, he stood at the side of the road.
7   Running into the road, he stopped a taxi.

105

1   Warned by air traffic control, the airport fire service prepared to fight a fire.
2   Believing the aircraft was going to crash, some of the passengers shouted in panic.
3   Having brought the plane down safely, the pilot felt very relieved.
4   Worried by the risk of fire, everyone hurried to get out.
5   Using chemicals, the firemen soon put out the fire.
6   Having had enough excitement for one day, most of the passengers put off their journey.

106

13-year-old Annabel Waites of Mudford has won first prize in a national art competition. Her *winning* picture is a painting of Mudford Hill.

I talked to Annabel at her home in Embury Road. At the moment she has a *broken* arm, which she got *playing* netball. Fortunately it's her left arm, so she can still paint. Annabel usually listens to music while *painting*. And she always paints *standing* up because she feels more comfortable that way. 'I often feel very tired after *finishing* a picture', she told me. 'It takes a lot out of me.'

Annabel was working on a half-*finished* picture of horses in a field. And on the wall was a beautifully *drawn* portrait of her dog Beezer. *Being* an animal lover, Annabel often paints pictures of animals. On another wall I noticed a picture of a lawn *covered* with *fallen* leaves.

Encouraged by her success, Annabel hopes to make painting her career, although she knows it will not be easy. But *helped* by her art teacher, Mrs Emma Goodenough of Portway School, she has developed an individual style.

Annabel has many other hobbies, and she often goes *skating* with her friends.

107

This small country is mostly farmland. The *animals* seen most often are *cows* and *sheep*. Most *farms* have a few *geese*, too. There are *donkeys*, but not many *horses*. There's a lot of wheat and *potatoes*, and there are *tomatoes* on the south side of the hills. In summer the *men*, *women* and *children* work together in the *fields* seven *days* a week. The *people* work hard all their *lives*.

The only two *factories* in the country are in the capital. One makes *toys* and *games*, and the other makes *knives* and *forks*. All these *things* are for export.

The east of the country is thick forest, the home of wild *ponies*, *deer* and *wolves*.

Photos of the *cliffs* along the coast show how beautiful the country is. But not many *tourists* visit it because the airport is too small for most *aircraft*.

108

1   She's going to give Alan a football.
2   She's bought Shaun a watch.
3   She's going to give a camera to Emma.
4   She's bought Nick a book.
5   She's bought some hankies for Angela.
6   She's going to give Matthew a game.
7   She's bought some perfume for Gillian.
8   She's going to give a scarf to Laura.

109

1   The farmer's dog
2   The roofs of the houses
3   The directors' room
4   The children's supper
5   The edge of the lake
6   The walker's rest
7   The side of the hill

110

two jars of marmalade, some eggs, a pineapple, five pounds of potatoes, some sugar, a packet of cornflakes, a loaf (of bread), some bananas, three tins of beans, some washing powder

111

Hello, Geoffrey. How are you?
OK, thanks, but I'm fed up with this rain.
Yes, let's hope we got *some* better weather soon.
And how are you?
I'm fine thanks. You're at college now aren't you?
Yes, I'm doing *a* course on farming. I'm just going to the library, actually. We've got *some* homework, *an* essay on farm management, and I have to do *some* research.
And how is the course going?
Oh, fine. I made a rather bad start, but my tutor gave me *some* good advice. I think I'm making *some* progress now.
Good.
And where are you going?
To the travel agent's. I need *some* information about flights to Malrovia. My brother's out there at the moment.
How is he getting on?
Very nicely. I had *a* letter from him yesterday with *some* news. He's got *a* job drilling for oil.
That sounds *an* exciting job.
Well, I must go. I've got lots to do. I've just moved into *a* new flat. It's very nice, but I need *some* new furniture — I haven't even got *a* table.
Well, good luck.

112

The Clayton Clothing Company is going to build a new factory in Milchester. *This news was* announced by company chairman Mr David Clayton yesterday. Mr Clayton spent the morning in Milchester before returning to the Clayton *headquarters* at Granby.

The Clayton company *has* been in existence for 130 years and *is* famous for its 'Polymode' *goods*. The slogans 'You're never alone with a pair of Polymode *trousers*' and 'Polymode *jeans are* the *ones* for you' are well known. The company's profit last year of £2 million *was* the highest in the clothing business.

Mr Clayton will not say how *many* new *jobs* there will be, but my *information is* that there will be about 500. The *news is* very welcome because *work is* hard to find at the moment, and 2,000 unemployed people *is* a high figure for a small town.

113

'You know old Ben, who sits outside the bus station every day and begs for money? Well, he must be a rich man. His clothes *are* old and dirty, his hair *is* never washed, and his glasses *are* broken, but his earnings *are* more than enough to buy new clothes. Someone told me he takes £10 a day in summer. People *are* generous, aren't they? Now £10 *is* not much to live on, but he never spends any of it, you see. His savings *are* hidden away somewhere. He's been begging there in the same place for twenty years, which *is* a very long time. And it's against the law, you know. But obviously the police *are* quite happy about it.'

114

Cleopatra was an Egyptian queen.
Confucius was a Chinese philosopher.
Nehru was an Indian politician.
Newton was an English scientist.
Raphael was an Italian painter.
Rockefeller was an American industrialist.
Tolstoy was a Russian writer.
Wagner was a German composer.

115

Push *a metal rod* through *a cork* and then put two pins into *the cork*, as in Picture 1. Take two more corks and push *some nails* into them. Put *the pins* on two glasses and move *the cork* to *the right place* so that it balances, as in Picture 2. Then you need *a candle* and *some matches*. Stand *the candle* on *a saucer* under one side of *the rod* and light it. *The heat* that comes from *the candle* will make *the metal* expand (= grow bigger). This extra length will make *the rod* fall, as in Picture 3. *The experiment* shows that *heat* makes *metal* expand.

116

Thomas French was one of the greatest explorers in *history*. He travelled to *South America, Greenland* and many other parts of *the world*. He was born in *1886*, on *Christmas Day*. His family lived near *Regent's Park*. They were rich, and *money* was never a problem. Thomas left *school* because he wanted to go to *sea*. He sailed across *the Atlantic Ocean* with some friends. At twenty he joined an expedition to *Africa*. Later he led expeditions to *the Andes*, to both Poles and even to parts of *the USSR*. He also climbed *Mount Everest* twice. *The history* of all these journeys is in his diaries, which show us *the life* of an explorer in the 1920's. *Breakfast* was French's favourite meal, and he always ate well. He went to *bed* early but often got up in *the night* to write his diary. He also took hundreds of photos, which are now on show at *the National Gallery*.

117

Graham Mackay is *an* engineer. He works on *an* oil rig in *the* North Sea. He works on *the* rig for two weeks and then has two weeks *at home* in Glasgow. *The* rig is 100 miles off *the* coast of Scotland. *The* oil company's helicopter flies him to and *from Aberdeen Airport*. He does *an* important job, and he's paid over £350 *a* week.

Graham works twelve hours *a* day during his two weeks on *the* rig. His shift finishes *at midnight*, when he goes *to bed*. Although *the* work is important, it's rather *a* boring job. He shares *a* cabin with three other men. One of them is *a* friend of his, *an* American called Lee Driver, who comes *from New Mexico*.

The men aren't allowed to *drink alcohol*, so Graham *has milk or tea* with his meals. Most of the men *smoke cigarettes*. *The* weather can be pretty bad. Sometimes *there are storms*. Everyone's always glad to get back to *the* mainland.

118

Trevor says we're giving a party on Saturday.
We're thinking of giving *one*. *It* was Alison who first thought of the idea.
Gary won't be here. *He*'s going to London.
Gary won't mind if we go ahead without *him*.
Are we going to have food?
It would be expensive to buy food for all the guests. Let's just ask *them* to bring something to drink.
Have we got any glasses?
There are *some* in the kitchen cupboard. *They*'ll be all right. We can use *them*.
There won't be enough, but we can borrow *some*.
We can't use my record player. There's something wrong with *it*.
What about a cassette recorder? Hasn't Daniel got *one*?
He had *one*, but he's sold *it*.
Who are we going to invite?
Who was that girl who came here on Friday?
Rosemary.
Well, don't invite *her*. *She* wasn't very nice. I don't like *her* at all.
We all went to Margaret and Angela's party, so we ought to invite *them*. But let's talk about it tomorrow. I'm too tired tonight. *It*'s getting late.

119

1   This is Adam's ruler. It must be *his* because it's got *his* name on it.
I'll give it to *him*.
2   Are these gloves *yours*, Rebecca?
Yes, they are. Thanks. They haven't got *my* name in them, but they belong to *me*.
3   I think these notes belong to Lisa and Melanie. These pages are part of a project of *theirs*.
I can't see *their* names on it, but I'll ask *them* about it.
4   Adam and I have been looking for these magazines. Someone took them from *our* room. They belong to *us*. We're using the pictures for a project of *ours*.
5   Isn't this pen Emma's?
I don't think it's one of *hers*. I know she's lost *her* calculator, but I haven't heard *her* say she's lost a pen.
6   Is that book *mine*?
Yes, it's got *your* name in it, so it must belong to *you*. Here you are.
Thanks, Gary.

120

Lots of people have already bought Bill Hawk's super new book. They've saved *themselves* a lot of money by doing jobs *themselves*. Here are a few examples.

Mr Purlin of Hamleigh repaired the roof of his house *himself*.
'We decorated the whole house *ourselves*. This book made it easy,' say the Cleat family of Huxton.
The Spriggs of Granby put in central heating *themselves*. 'I asked *myself*: why not?' said Mr Sprigg. 'With Bill Hawk's help it wasn't very difficult.'
'I put in a new bath *myself*,' says Mr Hunter of Milchester.
Mrs Flashing of Wayford says 'We wanted a garage. A friend said 'Why don't you build it *yourselves*?' He showed us the book. So we did it *ourselves*. Now we feel really pleased with *ourselves*.'

Mrs Stiles of Backworth fitted a new front door all by *herself*. 'I couldn't imagine *myself* doing anything like that until I read this book.'

121

I go to Weight Losers now, you know. I'm trying to lose weight. I have to force *myself* to eat the right food. My husband doesn't think I'm fat. 'You'll make *yourself* ill,' he tells me. But it's doing me good. Lots of people go to the club. They're all trying to lose weight or keep *themselves* slim. We all weigh *ourselves* on the scales and write down our weight. Then the members all tell *each other* their weight. Yesterday one man was one kilo heavier than the week before. He said he couldn't stop *himself* eating cakes. The teacher says 'You must control *yourselves*, all of you!' Helen goes too, you know. She's losing weight. She's very pleased with *herself*. The Johnsons were there yesterday too. They're always arguing with *each other*. They've lost a lot of weight, so they must be really starving *themselves*.

122

I need a new umbrella. I really must buy *one* soon.
I saw *some nice ones* in Bymore's when I was here last month.
I don't know the stores here very well. *Which one* is Bymore's?
It's *the new one*, *the one* opposite Harridge's.
Oh, yes, I know. Actually, Diane, I think your umbrella is *a very nice one*. Where did you get it?
Oh, I've had *this one* for a long time. I don't think you'll find *one* like this now.
They must have umbrellas in this store. I wonder which floor they're on.
I think it's *this one*. Oh, yes, here they are.
I don't like *these brown ones*.
This one here is nice.
Well, I prefer *that one* next to it, *the red one*. But it's rather big. I like *the ones* that fold up very small.
There's *one* here like that.
Yes, but I don't want *one* that colour.
Which one do you like best?
I think *the ones* in Bymore's were better. Shall we go there?
Yes, OK. Which way is the escalator?
I think there's *one* over there.

123

There aren't any beds.
There are some electric cookers.
There aren't any tables.
There are some sofas.

There aren't any shelves.
There are some mirrors.
There's some wallpaper.
There isn't any paint.

124

Dear Polly,
It hasn't been easy to start this letter because I've been very busy with the course. We don't get *any* time to ourselves. The course is well organized. There are fifteen of us in three separate groups. *Each* group has its own tutor. *Each* of us also has our own individual timetable for part of the week. It's very hard work, but at least I've lost *some* weight.
The worst thing is that we have to get up at six o'clock *every/each* morning. I can't say I'm loving *every* minute of it!
There simply isn't enough food. Lunch is different *every/each* day, but yesterday it was a carrot and today a lettuce. Of course I was allowed *some* water with it.
I've become friendly with *some* other people on the course. We're getting to know *each* other quite well.
I must stop now. My next training period begins at *any* minute.
Love, Teresa

125

All the luggage goes in the back. Put *everything* in the back of the bus. And *each* piece of luggage must have the owner's name on it.

I've got *something* to eat here, look.
Yes, you can keep that with you.
Is it true we'll have to do written work *every/each* evening?
Yes, it is.
I can't find a seat. There's *nowhere* for me to sit.
Well, *each* seat has a number. Yours is ten.
Neil is sitting there. He says we can have *any* seat we like.
Well, he's wrong. He'll have to sit *somewhere* else.
I think we're ready now. There's *nothing* else to do before we go.
There's *someone/somebody* missing. Nick isn't here. We've looked *everywhere* for him, but we can't find him *anywhere*. Has *anyone/anybody* seen Nick?
I've asked the others, but *no one/nobody* knows *anything* about him.
Oh, it's all right. Here he is.
I hope *everyone/everybody* has been to the toilet. We don't want to stop *every* five minutes, do we?

126

They haven't sold many machines.
They've sold a lot of steel.
They haven't sold much coal.
They haven't sold many electrical goods.
They've sold a lot of clothes.
They haven't sold much food.

They've sold fewer/less machines.
They've sold more steel.
They've sold less coal.
They've sold more electrical goods.
They've sold fewer/less clothes.
They've sold less food.

127

George Wright and his party have made far *too many* mistakes during their time as the government. Mr Wright doesn't really spend *enough* time at his job, I'm afraid. Our Prime Minister spends *too much* time playing golf. While he's doing that, our industry is dying. A lot of factories have closed in the last few years — *too many* factories, in my opinion. And we've just learnt that *some more* factories are going to close soon, thanks to George Wright again. The Progressives simply don't spend *enough* money on the really important things, like helping industry. And of course they spend *too much* on things that no one needs. We don't want *another* Progressive government after this one. Mr Wright would like to give us *some more* of the same medicine. But the medicine is killing our country. You gave the Progressives a chance to put the country right, and you've seen the result. Don't give them *another* chance.

128

I borrowed several chairs, but we still haven't got *enough* for everyone.
There are lots of children here. How *many* were invited?
There's lots of room in here. Well, quite *a lot*, anyway.
There's food over here, children. Would you like *some*?
Wayne wants a drink of milk, but I can't find *any*.
You've only had a biscuit, Natalie. You haven't eaten *much*.
There aren't many clean plates. There are just *a few* in the cupboard.
You've finished your milk, Wayne. Let me pour you *some more*.
No, there's only one kettle here. I can't find *another*.
And I can't find any clean cups. There are *none* in here.
There weren't many cups. There were *fewer* than I thought.
The children have drunk nearly all the orange juice. There's only *a little* left.

129

1　One of them is an island.
2　Neither of them is/are in Spain.
3　Three of them are in South America.
4　Both of them are oceans.

5 Two of them are in London.
6 All of them are in the USA.
7 None of them is/are in Europe.
8 Both of them are in Australia.

130

1 (And) who loves Princess Flora? ~ Mike Perry.
2 (And) who does Princess Flora love? ~ Lord Midwinter.
3 (And) who does Peter Kane love? ~ Sophie Salinsky.
4 (And) who does Lord Midwinter love? ~ Sophie Salinsky.
5 (And) who loves Lord Midwinter? ~ Princess Flora.
6 (And) who loves Sophie Salinsky? ~ Lord Midwinter and Peter Kane.
7 (And) who does Sophie Salinsky love? ~ Mike Perry.
8 (And) who does Jackie Logan love? ~ Mike Perry.

131

1 *What* goes up but never comes down?
2 *Who* is paid money for taking something away from you?
3 *What* can go through a closed door?
4 *Which* of these words is longer: 'laughs' or 'smiles'?
5 *What* has fingers but no arms?
6 *Which* sheep eat more grass, black ones or white ones?
7 *Who* invented the first pen?
8 *Which* has more tails, one cat or no cat?
9 *What* is the difference between an African elephant and an Indian elephant?
10 *Which* king of England wore the biggest shoes?

132

1 *What's* your name?
2 *Where* do you live?
3 And *whose* is the bicycle? *Who* owns it?
4 *When* was it stolen?
5 *Where* did you leave it?
6 *What time* was this?
7 *What kind* of bicycle is it?
8 *What colour* is it?
9 *How old* is it?
10 *How much* did it cost?

133

I was waiting for someone.
Who were you waiting for?
I don't know. I was afraid of something.
What were you afraid of?
I'm not sure. Somebody ran towards me.
Who ran towards you?
A man I didn't know. Then I shouted at someone.
Who did you shout at?
I think it was my brother. But then I fell over something.
What did you fall over?
Something lying in the road. Somebody was pointing at me.
Who was pointing at you?
My father. He was talking to someone.
Who was he talking to?
I don't know. I woke up then.

134

1 'The Mind Machine' is about a computer which controls people's thoughts.
2 'Eureka!' is about a scientist who discovers the secret of the universe.
3 'Spaceville' is about some people who build a city in space.
4 'Zero' is about an accident which starts a nuclear war.
5 'The President' is about a dictator who rules the world.
6 'Danger Hour' is about a cloud of gas which pollutes the earth.
7 'Starfight' is about a war which breaks out in space.
8 'Wait for Death' is about a man who lives for a thousand years.

135

1 Those are the friends I went with.
2 That's the pool we swam in.
3 That's the dress I bought.
4 Those are the people/some people we met.
5 That's the boat we went for a sail in.
6 That's the castle we visited.
7 That's the beach we liked.
8 That's the lake we walked round.

136

1 Socks are things (that/which) you wear on your feet.
2 A briefcase is something (that/which) you carry papers in.
3 A greengrocer is someone who sells fruit and vegetables.
4 A present is something (that/which) you give to someone.
5 A kettle is something (that/which) heats water.
6 Soap is something (that/which) you wash with.
7 A target is something (that/which) you try to hit.
8 An artist is someone who paints pictures.
9 A seat is something (that/which) you sit on.
10 An umbrella is something (that/which) keeps the rain off you.
11 Oars are things (that/which) you use to row a boat.
12 A mirror is something (that/which) you can see yourself in.

137

I saw Roger Cowley on Saturday.
Roger Cowley?
Yes, he's the man *who works at Electrobrit.*
It's Roger Cowley *whose wife owns the Top Shop.*
What's the Top Shop?
It's the shop *that/which sells dresses.* It's the one (*that/which*) *I went in yesterday.*
Oh, I know. It was Roger Cowley *whose car was stolen from outside his house.*
That's right. It was the car (*that/which*) *he bought from Richard Hunter.*
And who's Richard Hunter?
I don't think you've met him. He's the man (*who*) *I invited to our party.* He didn't come, though.
Is he the man *whose sister was on a TV quiz show*?
No, that's Bob. Richard is the man (*who*) *David plays golf with.*
Yes, but I was talking about Roger Cowley.

138

1 Food bought at Brisco costs you less.
2 Someone listening to a Meditone radio hears every word.
3 Cakes made with Bakewell flour taste wonderful.
4 Hed-Cure is the only thing to make your headache really better.
5 A person sitting in a Super-Plush chair is sitting comfortably.
6 The most exciting toy to give your child is a Playworld toy.
7 Everyone notices the man wearing a Windsor shirt.
8 A floor covered with a Wonderlay carpet looks ten times better.

139

1 Len, who has finally found a new job, is giving a big party.
2 Craig, who/whom Len has invited, is hoping that Donna will be at the party.
3 Craig also wants to borrow some money from Gordon, whose cycle repair business is doing very well.
4 The new club in Jubilee Road, which everyone is talking about, is very popular with young people.
5 A disco, which took place at the club last weekend, kept people awake half the night.
6 The new manager at the plastics factory, who/whom no one likes, wants Donna to work late.
7 He has arranged a staff meeting, which starts at ten o'clock tomorrow.
8 Donna is staying at number 33 with Teresa, who has given her the spare room.

9   The woman at number 35, who Donna spoke to yesterday,/
to whom Donna spoke yesterday, is behaving rather
strangely.
10   Meanwhile Robin, whose wife has left him, is explaining his
problems to Harriet.

140

I think we should go. You'll get a *higher* salary with Multitech
than you do now, and we'll have a *better* standard of living.
Don't forget London is the *most expensive* place we could
possibly go to. For example, house prices are the *highest* in
the country. A house will be *more difficult* to find there than in
Milchester.
But it's probably the *biggest* chance you'll ever get. That's
the *most important* thing. And it'll be *easier* for me to find a
good job than it was here.
London is a *bigger* place than Milchester. Life won't be so
quiet.
Well, I'd like a *more exciting* life. It is a bit boring here
sometimes. And it'll be much *more convenient* for shops and
theatres, living in London. You've never really liked your job
here. And things have got *worse* recently.
Yes, they have. And Multitech is certainly one of the *best*
companies in the business. But I don't want to go unless you
really want to.

141

1   The Superior is just as comfortable as the Libretto.
2   The Swift is more spacious than the Sahara.
3   The Delta is cheaper than the Prince.
4   The Sahara is just as reliable as the Libretto.
5   The Prince is less comfortable than the Swift./The Prince
isn't as comfortable as the Swift.
6   The Delta is faster than the Sahara.
7   The Superior is less economical than the Delta./The Superior
isn't as economical as the Delta.
8   The Swift is easier to drive than the Superior.
9   The Sahara is better-looking than the Prince.
10   The Swift is more comfortable than the Libretto.
11   The Prince is the most reliable.
12   The Swift is the easiest to drive.
13   The Swift is the most comfortable.
14   The Libretto is the most spacious.
15   The Superior is the fastest.
16   The Superior is the best-looking.

142

1   Food is getting more and more expensive. The more
expensive it becomes, the hungrier/the more hungry people
are.
2   Industry is getting weaker and weaker. The weaker it
becomes, the greater our problems are.
3   Things are getting worse and worse. The worse they
become, the more important it is to do something.
4   People are getting poorer and poorer. The poorer they
become, the smaller our chances of success are.
5   The situation is getting more and more hopeless. The more
hopeless it becomes, the more difficult it is to put (it) right.
6   People are getting more and more desperate. The more
desperate they become, the more necessary it is to act.

143

Dear Helen,

Thank you for your letter. Is it *really* four months since I last
wrote? I'm sorry, but I've been very busy *lately*.

I'm *already* working for my exams./I'm working for my exams
already. I've planned my revision *carefully*./I've *carefully*
planned my revision. I *usually* work/*Usually* I work until about
ten o'clock in the evening./I work until about ten o'clock in
the evening *usually*. I've *just* finished for today.

Of course I don't *always* keep to my plan./I don't *always*
keep to my plan *of course*. I saw a marvellous film
yesterday./*Yesterday* I saw a marvellous film. It was called
'The Secret Game'. Have you seen it?
Actually I don't *often* go out./I don't go out *often, actually*.
Suzanne comes *here* about once a week. We talk *a lot*.

I hope to visit England again *next year*./*Next year* I hope to
visit England again. I had a lovely time *there* last year. It
would be great to see you *again*. I'm trying *hard* to save
some money.

How are you? Is your new flat all right? Please write *soon*.

Love,

Maria

144

She doesn't often argue with people.
She often worries.
She never takes risks.
She's always late for work.
She doesn't often tell jokes.
She usually laughs at comedy shows.
She often wishes things were different.
She isn't often sad.

145

1   The service at the Grand is fairly good. It's a bit less good
than at the Castle. The service at the Castle is very good.
2   The food at the Grand isn't very good. It's a lot less good
than at the Castle. The food at the Castle is very good.
3   The Grand is very clean. It's a lot cleaner than the Castle.
The Castle isn't very clean.
4   The Grand is fairly quiet. It's a bit less quiet than the Castle.
The Castle is very quiet.
5   The Grand is very convenient. It's a bit more convenient than
the Castle. The Castle is fairly convenient.
6   The prices at the Grand aren't very reasonable. They're a lot
less reasonable than at the Castle. The prices at the Castle
are very reasonable.

146

1   Stella is progressing satisfactorily. She does her homework
well.
2   Emil speaks English fluently. He reads widely.
3   Milena works hard. She learns fast.
4   Victor speaks slowly. He pronounces some common words
incorrectly.

147

Well, the party is going very *nicely*, isn't it? Have one of
these sausages. They taste *good*.
No, thanks.
You don't sound very *happy*, Angela. And you look *pale*. Are
you all right?
I feel rather *tired*. And I'm *hot*.
It is getting a bit *warm* in here, isn't it? Well, I can *easily* open
this window.
Thanks. Actually, my head aches quite *badly* too. I think it's
slowly getting worse.
I'm *sure* the music isn't helping. It seems rather *loud*, doesn't
it? Look, would you like me to take you home?
No, it's all right, thanks. But if I could sit *quietly* somewhere
for a few minutes, I might be OK.
I'll ask Lynn if there's somewhere you can go.

148

1   You have to speak really clearly. Can you speak *more
clearly*, please, Helen?
2   You didn't wait long enough, Lynn. Can you stay a little
longer in the doorway?
3   You haven't learnt your words very well, Peter. I hope you
know them *better* next time.

4 You aren't angry enough, Sarah. Can you shout rather *more angrily*?
5 Angela, that isn't far enough. Walk *further/farther* to the left.
6 And you're supposed to be nervous. Can you look round a bit *more nervously*?
7 I want you to hit the table hard. You can hit it *harder* than that, Bob.
8 Be careful when you lay the table, Sue. Try to do it *more carefully* next time.

149

Street scene. There are three shops. *In* the middle there is a baker's, which is *between* an antique shop and a toy shop. The toy shop is *on* the right. There is a phone box *on* the left *at/on* the corner of the street. A car is coming *round* the corner. There is a man on a bike *behind* the car. There is also a car parked *opposite* the baker's. This car has a suitcase *on* its roof. A woman is just stepping *off* the pavement to walk *across* the road. She has come *from* the baker's/*out of* the baker's. Two girls are standing *outside/by/ near* the baker's. A window cleaner is climbing *up* a ladder *to/towards* the window *above* the toy shop. He has got a bucket *in* his hand. A woman is looking *out of* the window/ *through* the window. A boy is walking *along/on* the pavement *under* the ladder *towards* the street corner. There is a man *in/inside* the antique shop looking *through* an old telescope. There is a young man *in/inside* the phone box, and three people are standing *on* the pavement waiting — a woman, a man and a boy. The boy is *at* the back of the queue.

150

Stan Crowe hopes to run against James Boto of Kenya in a 1500 metres race in Paris *on* June 16th. Both men will want to break Cliff Holding's world record. Holding ran the 1500 metres *in* 3 minutes 28 seconds last year. Holding will also be running in Seattle *on* June 14th, two days *before* the Paris meeting.

British fans have been hoping *for* several months to see Crowe win back his record. He last ran against Boto *in* April, when he fell and hurt himself *during* the race. He was just behind Boto *at* the time. The two men had not met *since* the last Olympic games in Peking. Crowe has had to rest *after/ since* his accident, but he was back in action *at* seven o'clock *on* Saturday evening when he won a rather slow race in Edinburgh. He hopes to be fully fit *by* the end of this month at the latest. If he is not fit for Paris, he will have to wait *until/till* the Commonwealth Games. These games take place in Ottawa *from* August 14th *to/until/till* the 20th.

151

On a Thursday evening *in* October, 1931, *at* about eight o'clock, the ship 'Voyager' sank. The ship had been sailing *since* the end of September, when she left London, and was on her way *from* England *to* Australia. The only survivor was an Englishman called Wilfred Batty, who saved himself *by* swimming two miles. He spent three years *on* an island *in* the middle of the Indian Ocean.

The island was quite small, and he could walk *round* the whole of it *in* an hour. He climbed *up* the one hill and put a flag *on* it *as* a signal. *At* night Batty slept *in* a cave, where he felt quite *at* home. *During/In* the day, he often fished *with* a home-made net. He cooked the fish *over/on* a wood fire.

Batty stayed *on* the island *for* almost three years, *until/till* August 1934. A ship was sailing *past/near* the island, and the captain saw Batty's signal. The sailors found a man *in* a long blue coat *with* dark hair and a beard, looking rather *like* a gorilla. Batty was soon home, and a few years later he finally arrived in Australia *by* air.

152

1 Prices will rise. The question is, how <u>much</u> will they go up?
2 Someone calculated these figures, but the government won't say <u>who</u> worked them out.
3 The Prime Minister says he's going to raise the question in Brussels, but <u>when</u> is he going to bring it up?
4 We know the petrol tank exploded. <u>Why</u> did it blow up?
5 So the government are going to increase taxes. Well, how <u>much</u> are they going to put them up?
6 The Council say they're going to demolish the building, but <u>why</u> are they going to knock it down?
7 The government say they discovered the mistake, but <u>when</u> did they find it out?
8 The plan succeeded. <u>Why</u> did it come off?

153

1 We didn't close them down.
2 We didn't put it up.
3 But we listened to them.
4 We didn't let it down.
5 But we didn't have to look for them/look for any.
6 We dealt with it.
7 We kept it down.
8 But we care about them.

154

1 It is important to act quickly. *As soon as* you see a customer behaving suspiciously, inform the control team by radio.
2 Follow the customer *as* he moves around the store.
3 Do not speak to the customer inside the store. Wait *until* he has left the store.
4 *After* you have informed the control team, a second detective will join you to help with the arrest.
5 Arrest the customer outside and bring him to the control room for questioning. Do not question him *before* you get to the control room.
6 Remember that the control team have been filming the customer *since* you first informed them about him.

155

1 I've no idea what my name is.
2 I don't know where I live.
3 I've got a feeling (that) I'm a long way from home.
4 I'm not sure why I think so.
5 I know (that) something strange has happened to me.
6 I can't understand how it happened.
7 I've heard (that) I just walked into the hospital.
8 I can't remember when I came here.

156

1 Even though we brought out two new models, sales didn't increase.
2 Even though we made a big effort we failed to sell enough bikes.
3 Although they're good bikes, they're expensive.
4 Although people want quality, they don't want to pay for it.
5 While sales are going down, costs are increasing.
6 In spite of reducing our work-force, we've still got a high wages bill.
7 Even though we bought some new equipment, we've still had production problems.
8 Whereas other companies are moving ahead, we're standing still.

157

1 Ingrid is learning it because she likes learning languages.
2 Anita is learning it so that she can help her daughter with her homework.
3 Martin is learning it because he might need it some time.
4 Claudia is learning it (because she wants) to get a better job.
5 Gaston is learning it so that he'll be able to understand/so that he can understand American films better.

6   Andrea is learning it because she has to do it at school.
7   Sven is learning it so that he'll be able to read/so that he can read engineering textbooks in English.
8   Jan is learning it (because he wants) to impress his girl-friend.

158

1   There was fog, so their flight was delayed.
2   The plane was so late (that) they got to bed at three in the morning.
3   It was such a long way to the beach (that) it took an hour from the hotel.
4   It was such a crowded beach (that) there was hardly room to sit down.
5   The hotel was so noisy (that) they couldn't sleep.
6   Their room had such an unpleasant view (that) it made them feel quite miserable.
7   They weren't enjoying themselves, so they went home.
8   The holiday was so disappointing (that) they decided to ask for their money back.

159

Driving a car can be expensive. The bicycle, *on the other hand*, is a cheap form of transport. A bicycle *not only* costs very little *but also* lasts much longer than a car. It is *also* very cheap to use *because* of course it doesn't need any fuel. In fact, it costs practically nothing *after* you've bought it. It *also* helps keep you fit *because* you get exercise *when* you ride it. Another good thing about a bicycle is *that* it doesn't pollute the air. *If* everyone rode bicycles instead of driving cars, we wouldn't be using up the world's oil so quickly.

Although the bicycle has these advantages, it has some disadvantages too. It is convenient only for relatively short journeys, *whereas* by car you can travel quite a long way in comfort. Another problem is *that* the cyclist is not protected from the weather and gets wet *when/if* it rains. Cycling isn't very nice in heavy traffic *either*. In Britain there are very few cycle paths, *so* bicycles have to share the road with cars and lorries. The best place for a bike ride is a quiet country lane. Main roads and city streets are often *so* busy *that* it needs some courage to take a bike on them. The cyclist has no protection, and *so* he is more likely than a motorist to be seriously hurt *or* killed *if* he does have an accident. Cycling keeps you healthy, *but* the cars may kill you!

160

The car doesn't feel safe.
It *does* feel safe. There's nothing wrong with it.
The lights don't work.
They *do* work. We mended them.
You didn't replace the front tyres.
We *did* replace them. I remember doing it.
The back doors won't open.
They *will* open, you know.
And the heater doesn't work.
It *does* work. We checked it.
But you didn't check the battery.
Yes, we *did* check it. The battery is OK.
Anyway, the bill isn't correct.
It *is* correct. I wrote it myself.
You don't know what you're talking about.
We *do* know/I *do* know what we're/I'm talking about.
Repairing cars is our business.

161

1   It was Bozo who shot the policeman in Marseilles.
2   It was in Monaco that he went into hiding.
3   It was Ross who bought the guns.
4   It's the Standard Bank that they're planning to rob next.
5   It's Gregory who finds out all the inside information.
6   It's on Long Island that they're going to meet next week.
7   It's Morocco that Grabski intends to go to afterwards.
8   It's the Mafia that/who he's afraid of.

162

1   It was the Atlas that/which won the 'Road' magazine prize.
2   It did win the Monte Carlo rally last year.
3   What the Atlas gives you is reliability.
4   You do have lots of room in an Atlas.
5   It's the expert design that/which makes you feel so comfortable.
6   What you'll never believe is how much luggage it holds.
7   It's the low price that/which will really surprise you.
8   The Atlas does cost less than £7,000.
9   What you'll never want to do is let anyone else drive your Atlas.
10 What you ought to be driving now is an Atlas.

163

1   What this country needs is a sense of purpose.
2   What people want is strong government.
3   What I think is that we too often take the easy way out.
4   What you don't realize is how bad things are.
5   What I say is (that) we're going downhill.
6   What I'd like to see is some action.
7   What I believe is that our problems can be solved.
8   What I'm looking for is some positive thinking.
9   What you don't understand is how much things have changed.
10 What we're all hoping for is a better world.